Kenneth Gardnier was born on the Caribbean island of Dominica, a former French and English colony but now an independent state. His father was a successful hotelier and Kenneth learned much from hotel chefs, after being taught to cook by his mother at the age of eight. He has worked in England as an actor for over fifteen years, as a member of the Royal Shakespeare Company, in television and with the Northumberland Theatre Company. He played a major role in two London restaurants, *Borshtch 'n' Tears* and the Creole Caribbean restaurant *Le Caraïbe*, which was voted restaurant of the year in 1981. He has contributed to several food magazines and to the *Sunday Times Colour Supplement*. He continues to work as an actor.

To Vikki
with thoughts of times
Past — Times remembered
and all that is yet to
come
with love
Kenneth

KENNETH GARDNIER

Creole Caribbean Cookery

Illustrations by Helen Clark and Andrew Leppard
Photographs by Jon Rowe and Stuart Thorpe

GRAFTON BOOKS
A Division of the Collins Publishing Group

LONDON GLASGOW
TORONTO SYDNEY AUCKLAND

Grafton Books
A Division of the Collins Publishing Group
8 Grafton Street, London W1X 3LA

A Grafton Paperback Original 1986

Copyright © Kenneth Gardnier 1986

ISBN 0-586-06911-9

Printed and bound in Great Britain by
Collins, Glasgow

Set in Plantin

All rights reserved. No part of this publication may be reproduced, stored in a retrieval system, or transmitted, in any form, or by any means, electronic, mechanical, photocopying, recording or otherwise, without the prior permission of the publishers.

This book is sold subject to the condition that it shall not, by way of trade or otherwise, be lent, re-sold, hired out or otherwise circulated without the publisher's prior consent in any form of binding or cover other than that in which it is published and without a similar condition including this condition being imposed on the subsequent purchaser.

To my mother, Lister.
Who taught me, from a very early age,
how to cook, sew, wash and iron.
Thank you always.

'A word may be added about the word "creole", which is often believed by those who have not visited the West Indies to apply only to people of coloured descent. This is incorrect. A creole is anyone actually born in the West Indies. Thus, a child born of white parents in those islands is a creole. The term is even applied to animals and produce, and it is not unusual to hear a creole cow, a creole dog, or creole corn spoken of.'

SIR ALGERNON ASPINALL
The Pocket Guide to the West Indies
(Sifton, Praed; 1935)

Contents

Acknowledgments

Gratitude is due to the following people, whose help has been indispensable:

Dawn Arnall, Jane Ayshford, Michael and Fane Baynham, Nico Beck, Gary Bogard, John Brookesmith, Bill Carter, Helen Clark, Jane Conway-Gordon, Dylyn and Chris Dalton, John Gallagher, Diane Harkness, Tamara and Alexander Jacob, Sandra Knight, Lister Lancelot, Andrew Leppard, Andrée Molyneux, C. J. Newnes & Partners, Yannis and Charlotte Petsopoulous, Errol Romilly, Jon and Mary Rowe, Stuart Thorpe, Normalyn Zarbransky and the editorial staff of Grafton Books.

PART ONE

Ingredients and Methods

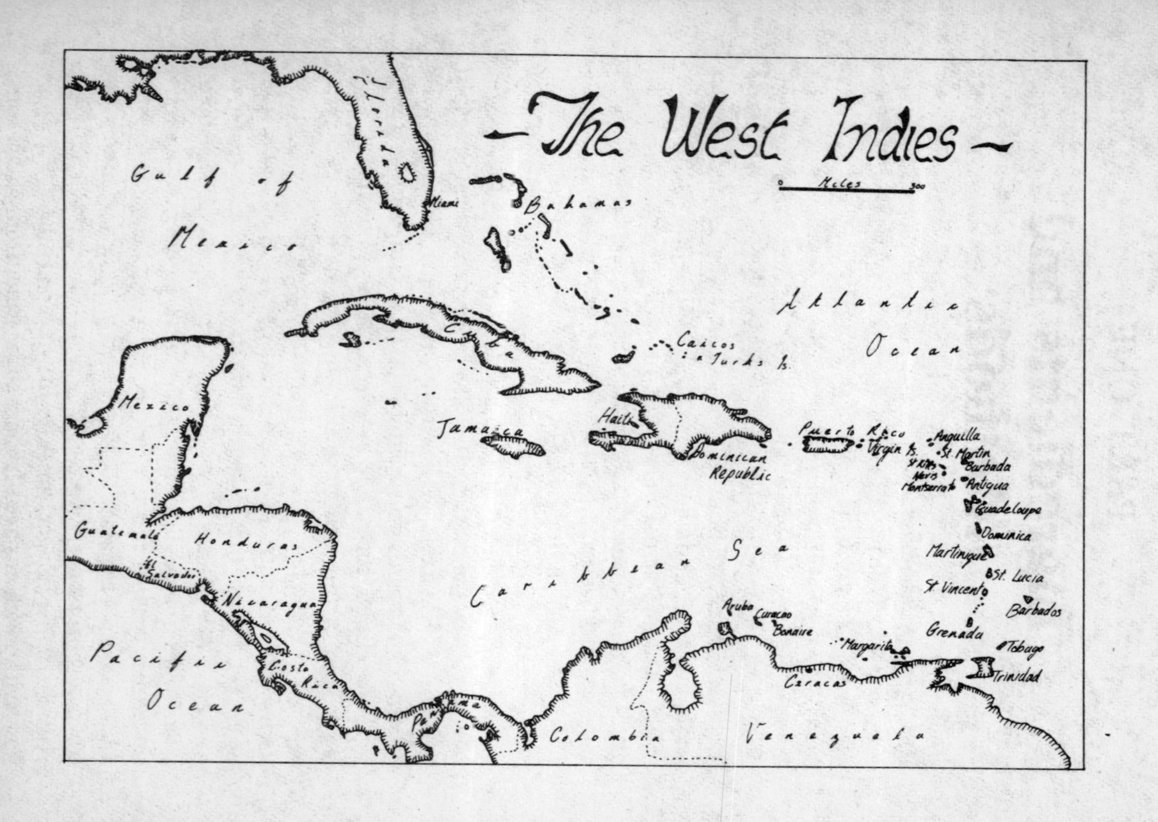

- The West Indies -
0 Miles 300
Gulf of
Mexico
Florida
Miami
Bahamas
Atlantic
Ocean
Cuba
Caicos
Turks Is.
Mexico
Jamaica
Haiti
Dominican
Republic
Puerto Rico
Virgin Is.
Anguilla
St. Martin
Barbada
St. Kitts
Nevis
Montserrat
Antigua
Guadeloupe
Dominica
Martinique
St. Lucia
St. Vincent
Barbados
Grenada
Tobago
Trinidad
Guatemala
Honduras
El
Salvador
Nicaragua
Caribbean Sea
Aruba
Curacao
Bonaire
Margarita
Caracas
Pacific
Ocean
Costa
Rica
Panama
Colombia
Venezuela

Introduction

Creole Caribbean cooking, like the people of the Caribbean, was created out of the traditions and motives, customs and culture, of many races – Spain and England, France and Portugal, Holland and Africa. First came the explorers and the adventurers; the buccaneers and the privateers; the pirates and the priests. Then came the plantation owners and the slaves; the traders, the merchants; the Oriental indentured labour from China and India.

From the time of Christopher Columbus's encounter with the 'New World' in 1492, when the indigenous inhabitants were the Arawaks and the Caribs, the Colonial powers fought for an Empire. They were fighting for that 'Emerald Necklace' around the neck of the Caribbean sea: from Cuba to Puerto Rico, round to Antigua and Martinique, through the Windward Islands as far as Trinidad and across to tropical America – Colombia, Venezuela, and the Guianas. Among these territories were some of the most precious jewels, fit for any crown that could possess and hold them. And in the waters of the blue Caribbean sea some of the greatest naval battles were fought. It was in these waters, off the coast of Dominica, on 12 April 1782, that Admiral Rodney won in one day the most decisive and greatest naval battle against the Comte de Grasse of France, thus saving the Empire for Britain. The rewards were many: gold, silver and precious stones, spices and fruits, cotton and indigo, tobacco and cochineal.

But over the preceding centuries much, much more had been introduced – the famous ackee from Africa, oranges and lemons from Spain, breadfruit from the South Seas (which had caused Captain Bligh of the *Bounty* much difficulty), ginger, cloves, turmeric and nutmeg from Asia. The soil of the Caribbean Islands, being inexhaustibly fertile, produced in abundance, and sometimes without much effort, cocoa and coconuts, avocadoes and eddoes, plantains, bananas and yams, pineapples and pawpaw; soursops, sweetsops, guavas, mangoes and sweet potatoes; coffee, ginger, limes, grapefruits and other citrus fruits; and, with much enslaved labour, sugar cane, from which comes that elixir among drinks, rum. Sugar cane has played an important part in the fortunes and misfortunes of the Caribbean, in its history and in its wealth. Sugar cane was introduced into the islands by Christopher Columbus on his second voyage in 1493, and it was with the introduction of sugar cane that the slave trade between Africa and the West Indies began, a trade which continued to flourish as the demand for cheap labour increased on the sugar plantations.

As with the vegetation there was also a profusion of wild life: wild geese, parrots and other birds; agoutis, and wild pigs; iguanas, turtles and edible frogs. The rivers teemed with mullets and a variety of crayfish, some as large as a young girl's hands. The seas gave as much: lobsters and prawns, tuna and flying fish, groupers and red snappers to name but a few. Also there were land crabs, sea crabs and freshwater crabs. Later on other foods were also imported, to feed the slaves, who could not survive on sweet potatoes, yams and cassava alone. So in came salted cod and smoked herrings, pigs' snout, pigs' tails and mackerel in brine. Rice was also one of the crops introduced from the Old World and was later found to grow most successfully in the Guianas. Today, Guyana, as the northernmost of the three is now called, is the region's largest grower of rice – it is still cultivated, as it has been for well over a century, by farmers of indentured East Indian descent. So many Caribbean Creole meals are eaten with rice – rice and peas, fowl-down-in-rice, and as many pelau dishes as are imaginable. In fact Creole rice dishes could fill an entire cookery book in themselves.

Beef, lamb and poultry are mostly imported from the richer nations of the world, England and New Zealand being two of the major suppliers, and, of course, the countries of the River Plate. Pork remains a favourite meat; there is hardly a family, rich or poor, that has not had at one time or another a pig or two running loose in the yard. It is not uncommon to see pigs roaming the land as if they owned it, foraging for whatever food they can find, be it on the beach or the 'savannah' of any main town. The word savannah means, in the Islands, a park or greensward, such as is called in Britain a common, a green or even a heath. As a geographical term, savannah refers to a region of sub-tropical Africa.

Smallholdings and the preparation of home-grown food have

always been vital features of the Caribbean way of life, even in urban areas. There is the same overlap between subsistence farming and the small cash crop as elsewhere in those latitudes. The tradition of cooking one's own food has some spontaneity about it. Wherever people happen to find themselves, they will have to cook – in the home, by a river bank, on coalpots in the street or in a hunter's *ajupa* or camp in the rain forest, beneath lush towering trees.

Even in the largest towns or the smallest villages, one seldom has to go far to get the best of fresh ingredients, since many of them grow wild or are farmed to excess, such as spices, ground provisions, herbs, fruit and staple vegetables. And through poverty and sometimes the lack of plenty, we have also learned to make the best use of the precious little we have or the plenty we have not.

Until about the mid-1950s, electricity was a rare luxury very few of the poorer classes could afford – it was costly to carry cables through forests and over mountainsides to remote villages. Therefore most cooking was done out in the open, away from the main dwellings: on charcoal pots or wood fires set between three to four stones; in small bamboo or log cabins roofed with palm leaves or sheets of 'galvanize'; in communal wooden sheds with burners set up two or three feet above the ground, over which would be suspended hooks and wooden cross-beams for the slow curing and smoking of 'boucan' meat and fish. No braff (broth) after midnight mass at Christmas would be a worthy dish without pork, salted and smoked over a fire of wood, green banana skins and dry coconut shells. Even the word buccaneer comes from 'boucan', a word and technique attributed to the Caribs. It is said that the same term was used by them for the curing of cashew nuts, which are also roasted to remove the poisonous shell and give the nut its delicate and unique flavour.

The wealthy land-owners and merchants of the villages and main towns also had their kitchens set away from the main house, usually with a shingled or galvanized covered passageway leading from house to kitchen. Many a servant or common-law wife has trudged between cooking shed or kitchen to the main dwelling, several times a day, even in the height of the rainy season, to poke the coal or wood fire on which a stew, sancoche or pepperpot is gently simmering. In most cases, especially among the peasantry, everything would go into one pot – fish, chicken, a piece of smoked pork, pig's tail or snout, yellow freshwater crabs, dark land crabs, coconut milk, yams, bananas, eddoes. Everything is used, nothing wasted, not even the chicken's feet – spiced and nicely seasoned up, never was there a worthier ingredient in a pepperpot kept going for months on end.

Today the cooking is still done out in the open air, the drifting smells of charcoal and wood fires, the scent of freshly roasted coffee and cassava bread, mingling with the fragrant tropical air. There is nothing like it as one wakes up in the morning in a fishing village by the sea, or in some hill or mountain hamlet as the sun climbs and filters through lush green foliage, with the dew remaining wet on the ground. On a hot English summer's day many of the dishes in this book can be prepared in the open and cooked on a charcoal barbecue, giving them some of the characteristic flavour of many a Caribbean dish.

Many islands claim a certain speciality as their own – in Jamaica there is ackee and saltfish; in Martinique, colombo; in Curaçao, Keshy Yena; in Dominica, crab backs and mountain chicken; in Cuba, gipsy's arm (*biazo jitano*). Each island at one time or another has claimed Sancoche, Callaloo and Pepperpot. Caribbean creole cooking has a distinct and unique flavour, with an astonishing variety of dishes: think of curried goat and curried mutton; crabs and lobsters; red beans and pigeon peas; meat or fish cooked in coconut cream; black pudding and souse; stuffed avocadoes or Christophene au gratin; pineapples stuffed with shellfish, chicken, rum and spices; macaroni pie; Edam cheese stuffed with meats or shellfish.

But in the end it is still true Creole cookery, combining the flavours and ingredients of many races – the French, the Spanish, the Dutch, the Portuguese, the English, the Africans, the Indians, the Chinese and the Caribs: we have all contributed our own culinary skills. The Caribbean is indeed the 'melting pot of all nations', and out of many came one pot – Creole Caribbean Cooking.

Glossary

Accra, Accras, Akkra Originally a West African fritter made with black-eyed peas, it is very popular throughout the islands, especially the French and Dutch speaking ones. Today accra is also made from a heavy batter with other ingredients, the most common being flaked saltfish. Vegetable accra is also very good. In Dominica accra is made with 'ti-ti-oui's a tiny fish caught in the rivers as it swims up from the sea: ti-ti-oui is about a third of the size of a small whitebait!

Achee, Ackee, Akee The fruit of an evergreen tree originating from West Africa and introduced by Captain Bligh of the *Bounty* into the West Indies. It has a scarlet pod and shiny black seeds. The edible flesh twixt pod and seeds is pale cream in colour and has a texture and flavour similar to scrambled eggs. It can be used in curries, casseroles and cheese dishes; but it is best known as one of Jamaica's national dishes: Ackee and Saltfish. It is available canned in a few Asian and West Indian shops and most open markets dealing in tropical produce.

Allspice, Pimento The brown berries from an evergreen tree native to the West Indies and Latin America. The berries are very similar to peppercorns, but have the scent and flavour of cloves, nutmegs and cinnamon combined. Hence 'allspice'.

Annatto, Anato, Achote The prickly pod or seed of a tropical American tree, also cultivated throughout the islands. The deep orange pulp surrounding the seed is basically used as a colouring agent, especially in cooking oils and lard; but the crushed seeds can be used as a spice. It has a delicate flavour. The colouring from this seed, achote, is available in some Oriental shops.

Arrowroot Starch obtained from the root of the cassava plant, which is popular as a thickening agent. It leaves no taste. Arrowroot must always be added to your sauces at the last minute; if cooked for too long, it thins down again. The best arrowroot comes from St Vincent and is easily obtainable in Britain. In the country districts a less refined product of arrowroot is used as a feed for babies, children and invalids. It is boiled with water and sugar, with a consistency and texture, when cooked, of a thick jelly. I find it very pleasant and it reminds me of relatives and of childhood. Arrowroot is also used for thickening stews and the fillings of pies and turnovers. In the past we used it in the Antilles for stiffening the garments of our national costumes (*wob dwiyet* and *la robe creole*).

Bakes A dumpling, made with baking powder and flour, fried in oil. Popular in most of the islands; especially Trinidad and Grenada. A good substitute if you run out of bread, since it is the earliest form of staple and is very quick and easy to make. Various recipes for bakes are dealt with in the section on Breads.

Banana, Bluggoe, Cocoy, Fig, Plantain (the *musa* family) Known as *figue* or *fig* on the French and Patois speaking islands. This is a very large family (*musa*), which includes the plantain and the bluggoe or cocoy, a rather stumpy, short and fat first cousin which is green or purplish-red in colour even when unripe, or green turning to yellow when ripe. Both the banana and plantain are green until ripened. With the exception of the banana and other members of the family close to it, the plantain and the cocoy are eaten only when cooked. All edible *musas* are largely used as a starchy vegetable when still green and often as appetizers and in desserts when ripe. Ripe plantains are fried, stuffed or boiled. The same goes for cocoy. All, when green, must be soaked briefly or well washed in cold water and, when peeled, thoroughly rubbed with lime or lemon before being cooked. It is also advisable to squeeze a little lime or lemon juice into the cold water in which they are to be boiled. This helps retain the natural colour. Green bananas, particularly, tend to cook to a sticky and unattractive grey if not treated in this way. The milk or enzyme secreted from all three when green can stain badly. Avoid bringing the fruit into contact with any cloth or clothing. Have a good look at your hands after peeling a green banana.

Bay This is a tall evergreen West African tree, now widely cultivated in the West Indies, primarily for the oil extracted from its berries and leaves; the end result is bay rum, used for medicinal purposes and in scented toiletries. The berries from the bay rum tree are also used in cooking and are similar to melegueta peppercorns, which are very rare and much sought after.

Beans, Peas, Pulses In the islands the terms *beans* or *peas* are used interchangeably. The beans or peas most commonly used are red kidney beans, black beans, black-eyed peas, pigeon peas (gungo beans) and green peas. They are used either fresh or dried. Lentils are also popular (*see* Techniques).

Breadfruit Originally a native plant of the South Pacific. A large green fruit from 5–8 inches across, it can only be eaten when cooked. Breadfruit can either be boiled, stuffed or roasted on charcoal. Creamed breadfruit is excellent with many dishes, especially coconut and saltfish-based dishes. It was in order to supply the West Indian Islands with the plant that Captain William 'Breadfruit' Bligh made his historical voyage in HMS *Bounty* to the South Seas in 1787. It is well known that his crew mutinied and set him adrift with eighteen of his officers. Captain Bligh and his officers survived and made a second voyage, on the *Providence* in 1793, with the breadfruit plants from the island of Otahiti in the Pacific to St Vincent in the Caribbean. Breadfruits are available in some Asian and West Indian shops and markets from May until December. When buying them, you should make certain they are not soft – for then they are too ripe. Breadfruit is also available canned all the year round, but then it can only be used as a boiled vegetable. The gummy milk (similar to that of the rubber plant) excreted from the trunk is used by children in the Caribbean to trap birds (*see* Techniques).

Calabaza A West Indian green pumpkin of various shapes and sizes. The flesh is of a cream-yellowish colour and has a very delicate flavour. Ideal as a vegetable or in soups. Available in most West Indian shops or markets selling tropical provisions.

Callaloo, Callilu, Calaloo The best known and most famous of all Caribbean soups. The callaloo itself is the young leaf of the dasheen or taro plant. Available fresh from some Asian and West Indian shops or markets dealing in Caribbean provisions. Can also be bought canned. The best substitute is spinach. Though dissimilar in size, the flavour and texture is more or less the same. Callaloo leaves must not be eaten unless cooked, otherwise they will cause irritation in the mouth.

Cane Syrup Juice of the sugar cane. Very popular in the French speaking islands in rum punches. Can be purchased freshly squeezed from vendors in markets and on street corners especially in Martinique and Guadeloupe. Sold in cans in West Indian and Asian shops in Britain.

Cashew Nuts An evergreen tree and native to many parts of the tropics. At one time widely cultivated but not so much nowadays, it having been replaced by other crops. A few trees are still to be found on many of the islands. The red fruit is edible, but the dark green shell to the pendant nut below is poisonous, and contains substances that can burn the skin.

Cassareep Juice of the grated cassava root. When strained and boiled down with spices such as cloves and cinnamon with brown sugar added, it is used as a flavouring, preservative and thickening agent in Pepperpot (*see* Techniques).

Cassava, Manioc, Yucca Root of a tropical plant 2–3 inches in diameter and about 10 inches long, with a rough bark-like dark skin not unlike a yam, with a hard white flesh. It formed part of the staple diet of the Arawaks and Carib Indians. There is a bitter cassava which is poisonous until the juice is extracted and the meal cooked. It is unobtainable in this country, but sweet cassava can be obtained from Asian and West Indian shops or markets dealing in tropical provisions. It can be eaten as a vegetable or made into a rough or fine flour for breads and cakes. It is also the base for tapioca (*see* Farine, p. 13; also *see* Techniques).

Chillies *See* Peppers.

Chives, Cive A member of the onion family. West Indian chives are much stronger flavoured and similar in size to a spring onion (*see* Herbs and Spices).

Chorizo, Chaurice A pork sausage seasoned with garlic and hot peppers, then smoked. Used mainly in the Spanish speaking islands. Available from many delicatessens, where you will be able to choose from several different kinds.

Christophene, Chayote, Cho-cho A tropical pear-shaped squash, often with a prickly skin, pale green to whitish cream in colour. Widely used as a vegetable in Caribbean cooking. Like garlic, pineapple and the green paw-paw, it is also used as a meat tenderizer. Available fresh, canned or pickled from shops and markets dealing in Caribbean produce.

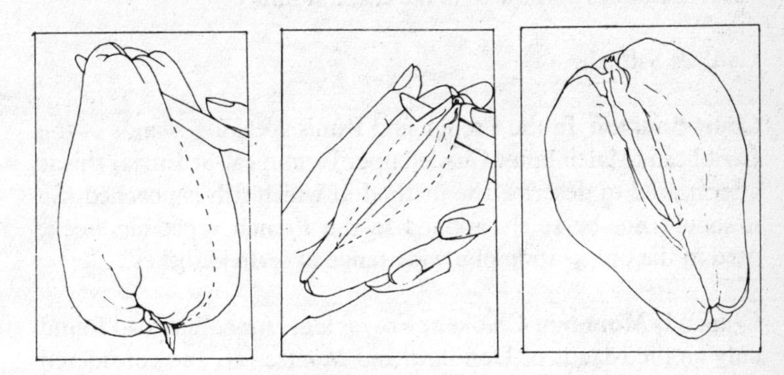

How to core a christophene

Cinnamon, Canel, Canela One of the oldest known spices. Cultivated in India, Madagascar, the Seychelles and most of the Caribbean. The tree is evergreen and is one of the Laurels, and can reach a height of 30 feet or more. When the trees are matured and of a reasonable size, the thicker branches are cut off; the outer skin of the bark is scraped then peeled off with a sharp knife or similar implement and left to dry in the sun. The most pliable pieces curl into 'sticks' when dried.

Cloves, Clous de Girofle A native not only of the West Indies but also of Tanzania, India and Madagascar; a large evergreen tree which grows to 30 feet or more. The clove itself is the unopened flower bud. The buds, before they are picked and dried, are a deep burgundy red and grow in clusters. The heady scent of the opened flowers can hang in the air over an entire valley.

Coconut The fruit of the coco palm. When the outer skin is still green or yellow, the water can be taken from the kernel as a refreshing drink or mixed with rum or gin. The white flesh is soft and almost jelly-like. It is referred to at that stage as a 'jelly nut' and is very sweet and delicious to eat. When the coconut is hard and dried, the outer skin turns brown as does the hard inside shell. Then the meat is firm and when liquidized or grated, the milk extracted is used in sauces, drinks and sweets. (*see* Techniques on how to make coconut milk).

Cod *see* Saltfish.

Court Bouillon In the French and Patois speaking islands of the Caribbean (Martinique, Guadeloupe, Dominica, St Lucia) this is a term used to describe the method in which fish is poached. So it should not be solely applied to the French vegetable stock, used in the preparation of a wide range of seafood dishes.

Crapaud, Mountain Chicken, Frogs' legs An edible toad found only on the islands of Dominica and Montserrat, and considered a great delicacy. In other countries, other edible species of *bufo* or *rana* are used. The legs are coated in flour then fried. The body is sometimes used in stews and soups. Available frozen from the better delicatessens and some fishmongers.

Crayfish, Écrevisse, Booke, Bouque Recipes in this book refer to the freshwater crayfish found in the streams and rivers of the islands. In the rivers the crayfish makes its home under rocks and can grow up to the size of a lobster. Pacific prawns or any large prawn can be used as a substitute. Bookes are very dark, almost black in colour but much smaller and are found among the floating weeds in slow-running streams. Substitute any shrimp.

Curacao (Curaçāo) A liqueur made from bitter oranges on the Dutch island of that same Portuguese name.

Dasheen A member of the Taro group of root vegetables (eddoe, tannia, malanga, yantía). It has a dark brown rough skin and the sizes vary from the size of an avocado to a large pineapple. It is from this member of the arum family that the best callaloo leaves come. The flesh of the dasheen can be white, very pale yellow or pale grey. Peeled before being cooked, it is boiled in salted water and then can either be creamed, roasted or fried with bacon for breakfast (*see* Techniques).

Escovitch, Escabeche A method used for the pickling of fish, other seafood, poultry and game before it is cooked, then marinaded in oil and vinegar.

Farine A rough coarse meal made from cassava. Used for a flat bread, often called 'bammie', baked in the oven or prepared over charcoal. Also used with avocado pulp in a saltfish dish, or served with smoked herrings. Sometimes a spicy fish sauce is poured over the mixture. Farine is used in breads and cakes as well.

Floats Flat baked or fried bread, either proven with yeast or otherwise unleavened.

Frijoles Black beans, related to the red kidney bean. Native of the Americas and available in health food shops, delicatessens and supermarkets.

Funchi, Fungee A pudding made from cornmeal or cornflour, related to coo-coo, from Dutch speaking countries.

Ginger A native not only of Asia but of the Caribbean, this is a light brown root, with a very strong, pungent flavour. It is in fact a rhizome and belongs to the same family as turmeric (*see* Herbs and Spices).

Guava Heavily scented fruit of an evergreen tree, with a green or yellow soft skin. The tree can grow up to 12 feet or more and is found wild on some islands. The flesh of the fruit is a rich pink or pale yellow. Eaten as a fruit, or made into jams, jellies, ice-creams and also used in rum punches. Stewed guava is delicious. Available fresh or tinned.

Gunga, Gungo Peas *see* Pigeon Peas.

Keshy Yena Stuffed Edam cheese, baked with various mixtures such as poultry, meat, seafood or fish. A speciality of the Dutch islands. The name is given in a Spanish-based creole language called Papiamento or Papamiento. In Spanish the dish would be called *yueso relleno*.

Mace The outer blade surrounding the hard brown shell of the nutmeg. Deep bright red in colour, it turns to pale yellow when dried. (*see* Nutmeg)

Mango Fruit of a large evergreen tree which may reach a height of about 20 feet with as wide a spread. A native of India, it was introduced into the West Indies over 200 years ago and has by now developed several strains. There are many varieties of fruit and they come in all shapes and sizes. From green they turn into all shades of yellow, pink, rose-coloured and red. Some mangoes have a strong exotic aroma. Some mangoes are stringy and fibrous and others have the texture of a nice ripe peach and are very sweet. It is a pity that the majority of the mangoes imported into Europe are so tasteless. And it surprises me greatly that the marketing boards of the various countries from which they come should allow them to leave their shores in the first place. In their country of origin quite a few of those mangoes would be feed for animals or just left to rot on the trees or the ground. The locals would hardly give them a second glance, much less a bite. Two of the best buys possible are either the Julie (grafted mango), from the Caribbean, or the Alphonse, from India. Mangoes can be eaten by themselves or used in chutneys, jams, ice-creams, mousses, relishes, fruit salads, pies, flans, and drinks. Available fresh or tinned from many shops and markets. But take care when buying fresh and choose well.

Mountain Chicken *see* Crapaud.

Nutmeg, Muscade, Moscada An evergreen tree, native to the East Indian islands. Introduced to the Caribbean in the late 16th and early 18th centuries, and now extensively cultivated on most of the islands, especially Grenada. It also produces mace. The mace is a tough peel that covers the outer hard shell of the nut itself. The outermost softer fleshy skin or pericarp of the nutmeg is yellow in colour and resembles an apricot – when ripened, this splits into two perfect halves, revealing the mace which is then a very rich red and is beginning to split into a beautiful Art Nouveau pattern. The mace is peeled off and the hard black shell cracked, to expose the nut. Both are used in meat, poultry, vegetable dishes, drinks and desserts.

Okra, Okroes, Bindhi, Ladies' Fingers, Gumbo Introduced into the West Indies from Africa – also cultivated in India and beyond. Mainly used as a vegetable and in stews and soups, it is one of the ingredients in callaloo soup. But it is, first and foremost, mixed with cornmeal to make coo-coo, principally in Barbados, for which there is a recipe. You can buy it in Asian and West Indian shops, many greengrocers and supermarkets. Always buy this product fresh.

Otaheiti Apple, Pomerac Red pear-shaped fruit of an evergreen tree, originating in Tahiti. Eaten by itself or used in pies, puddings and jams. It can be found only occasionally in shops and markets specializing in Caribbean and Far Eastern produce.

Pawpaw, Papaya A medium-sized tree native to the West Indies and tropical America, which is soft-wooded and dangerous to climb. When unripe the skin of the fruit is green, the flesh a creamy green colour. But both skin and flesh change to yellow or orange when ripe. It can weigh anything from half a pound to ten pounds. The unripened fruit is served cooked as a vegetable or stuffed with meat or cheese. Green pawpaw is also used in chutneys and relishes or boiled with spices in a sugar syrup to make desserts. The green fruit and the ace-of-clubs leaves are made use of as tenderizers for meat and poultry. But, more than that, many believe that the green pawpaw, used as a medicinal agent, will cure the most difficult sores, and there are instances where this has proved to be not such an old wives' tale either.

When ripe, pawpaw is eaten by itself or used in fruit salads. Fresh pawpaw has become very popular and can now be found in many small greengrocers and supermarkets. It is available canned as well. The white milk excreted from the green pawpaw can cause skin irritation. Avoid contact with the eyes.

Peppers, Chilli The same family as the sweet or bell pepper. Widely grown in Mexico, the West Indies, Africa and India. The seeds are the hottest part and should not be used unless so stated, though the majority of West Indians who love hot peppers will not agree with that. West Indian peppers vary in size and shape considerably; from half the size of a matchstick (in Patois, *pima zozio*; in English, bird pepper) to a small lime (*Bom de Ma Jacques* in Patois; in English, Mrs Jake's Bottom or Scots Bonnet). Colours range from green to many shades of yellow, scarlet and maroon. These peppers have a subtle taste and aroma of their own, despite their strength, regardless of colour or ripeness. For strength and flavour the best buy is the Scots Bonnet. Pepper Sauce is also available in most shops. Red ones from Jamaica and Trinidad are radiant and slightly sour. From Barbados comes a rich yellow one that has a definite fragrance. Sauces from the USA or Brazil should obviously not be a first choice in Caribbean cooking.

Pigeon peas, Gunga peas These are the size of small garden peas or petit pois but they are interestingly shaped and variegated in colour. The trees can grow to a height of about 9 feet, with pods of about 2 to 3 inches. The pods are slightly furry and flat between the peas. It is strange to open pods from the same tree to find that the peas are either green, cream, light brown, a soft red or a deep purple; but they all dry, alas, to the same brown colour. Pigeon peas, imported fresh from the Caribbean, can be bought from November until about the beginning of March. You can also buy them fresh or frozen from other parts of the world. Other tropical countries yield crops at different times, so now in England pigeon peas are available almost all the year round. They can be purchased from Asian and West Indian shops or in markets selling Caribbean produce. Green pigeon peas from Jamaica can be acquired in cans from many shops, but they must be well drained before use. To keep an emptied pod in the wallet after the shelling is judged to be lucky.

Pimento *see* Allspice.

Plantain (musa) *see* Banana.

Saffron Stamens of a member of the Crocus family, grown in Asia and Southern Europe. Once extensively cultivated in Saffron Walden. Use very sparingly, crushed in a mortar with a pestle.

Salted Cod, Saltfish Very popular in all the islands. Also known as *Morue* (*Lamowee*) on the French and Patois speaking islands. At one time salted cod was considered fit eating only for slaves and the poorer classes but today it graces many a table – rich or poor. When purchasing, insist on cod: thus buy from Spanish, Portuguese, Italian and Greek shops, asking for *Bacalhau* (*see* Techniques).

Sorrel, Rosella A member of the Hibiscus family; it is grown for its red sepals to make drinks, jams or jelly. It is most popular as a Christmas drink, the time of year when it is harvested. It is available dried in some markets and health food shops. And, during the month of December, fresh in markets selling West Indian produce.

Soursop Fruit of a tropical American tree with a prickly skin which remains green even when ripe. The pulp is almost pure white, scented and has a delicate flavour. It is eaten as a fruit and used in drinks, sherbets and ice-creams. The juice, when extracted through a strainer or muslin, has the consistency of thick cream. Available fresh from open markets and specialist shops. The juice is also sold in cans.

Sugar cane In appearance, sugar cane resembles bamboo and the colours range from green to yellow, light red to a deep purple. The sweet flesh is creamy white and extremely sweet but cannot be swallowed – it must be chewed and then spat out since it is full of fibre. As already mentioned, sugar cane was introduced into the Caribbean by Christopher Columbus on his second voyage in 1493. The plants came from Gomera in the Canaries. From sugar cane come several products including molasses and rum. From the late 15th until the middle of the 16th century, the produce of sugar cane was treated in Europe as a kind of honey and recognized as an expectorant with medicinal properties. Today the cultivation of sugar has fallen well below what it was in earlier centuries, beet sugar having infiltrated much of the market. Fresh sugar cane can be bought from most markets, some supermarkets and better greengrocers. Avoid buying cane that is shrivelled. Pieces of cut cane and the extracted juice can be found in cans in Asian and West Indian shops.

Sweet potato, Patate, Boniato Native to tropical America, the West Indies and the Pacific. The plant itself is a vine which grows along the ground. The skin of the potato can be pink, pale cream or yellow, white or reddish brown. The flesh is white, pink, yellow or bright orange. Some tubers are sweeter than others and softer in texture when cooked. It is served as a vegetable, boiled, fried or baked; also used in cakes, sweets and breads. Thinly sliced and glazed in butter, brown sugar, cinnamon and grated nutmeg, the sweet potato makes a delicious pudding or dessert. You can find sweet potatoes in quite a few supermarkets, greengrocers, Asian and West Indian shops and markets (*see* Techniques).

Tamarind The pod of a large tropical tree found in India, East Africa and the Caribbean. The name is Persian and means 'the fruit of India'. The trees can grow to a height of 20 feet or more. They line the sea coasts of many a Caribbean island, but will grow anywhere it is moderately dry – in the Islands a coastal region is dry because of the constant passage of wind from the sea. The bittersweet leaves are chewed by young children in the Islands. But adults might not admit to their need for a digestif, for vitamins and chlorophyll. The seed pods have brittle shells and grow to about 8 inches. They ripen from pale green to brown. The edible flesh is bound together by a few strong fibres and surrounds the seeds. There are several seeds in each pod. Whole tamarind pods and the packeted pulp are available from Asian and West Indian shops.

Tannia, Eddo, Taro, Nautía A member of the arum family, with a similar skin to the dasheen, but on the whole smaller in size and drier in texture. The colour of the flesh is either white, pale yellow, cream or pale violet. The young leaves are also used, for callaloo. Can be bought in Asian, West Indian shops and markets dealing in Caribbean produce (*see* Dasheen under Techniques).

Taro *see* Dasheen and Tannia.

Vanilla A native of the Caribbean and the Pacific, also grown in the Indian Ocean. It is the pod of a perennial climbing vine and a member of the orchid family. The flowers are pollinated by hand or insect. The green pods are picked when fully matured and about 6 to 9 inches long, just when they turn to yellow. They are then sweated in the hot sun and dried. Then they turn almost a black brown in colour and become shiny.

Yams These are the edible tubers of a large family of vine plants. They can weigh anything from 225g (½ lb) to 50kg (110 lb) or more. The skin is brown and the flesh can be white, yellow or pale cream. The yellow one, called ladies' yam in Dominica, has a nutty texture when cooked. Yam is a starchy vegetable and should be treated in the same way as dasheen (*see* Techniques). True yams are in no way like the Louisiana yam; which is indeed a sweet potato, though softer and brighter in colour than most potatoes from the Indies. Yams can be boiled, creamed, stuffed, baked or roasted. They are available in shops and markets specializing in tropical produce.

How to Choose Produce

Choosing produce is not as daunting as it may seem. While a few things, such as vegetables and fruits, are not labelled in stores and markets, most suppliers, shopkeepers and stallholders will name and describe a fruit or vegetable and maybe even be happy to give you hints on how best to use it, albeit garrulously. Many shopkeepers and stallholders would be happy to ensure further that a customer does not go away with anything but the best. I have had many such experiences in the markets of Brixton and Shepherds Bush. Some market stallholders will even tell you to come back on the following day or when new stock is coming in. So be guided and remember what you learn. Even if you come from the West Indies, there may well be many things produced and eaten in the Caribbean that you have not yet discovered, or you may know them by different names. Do not be surprised if you are corrected: our culture is being corrupted.

It is a pity we can't all buy direct from New Covent Garden Market, in Nine Elms Lane. There you can see all the varieties of fruits and vegetables in all their exotic splendour; some you would hardly believe it possible to find in Europe.

In the glossary, I have tried to give as much information as possible. The following is a more comprehensive list of herbs and spices most commonly used in Caribbean cooking, some of which would be useful to keep in store. When buying herbs and spices, it is best to buy whole or fresh whenever you can. But never buy more than a small quantity at a time; fresh, whole or ground. You should always try to grind your own spices just when needed. All you require is a mortar and pestle or an electric coffee grinder; equipment that you have chosen carefully, as an extension of your own hands.

There is a very wide variety of herbs and spices grown in the Caribbean, indigenous or introduced. Today in Europe it is possible to purchase them either fresh, whole, dried or ground in the larger supermarkets, health food shops, Asian and West Indian shops. Ask for help if in doubt; furthermore, consult within the Caribbean community, particularly among the older people; for, as the Jamaican women's theatre company called Sistren said at the end of their famous performance in London two years ago, 'they hold the secrets of the past'.

Herbs, Spices and Other Condiments

Allspice, Jamaica Pepper, Pimento These dark brown berries are sold under any of the given names. They are best bought whole, since, like peppercorns and melegueta, they will stand out in any recipe and create an experience when encountered in the eating. They can also produce an exquisite flavour in a meat, fish or vegetable dish if they are lightly crushed in a mortar with a pestle. If, however, the berries are finely ground, then the flavour will clearly be stronger; as a result the taste of other ingredients could be cancelled.

Anise, Nannee Similar in appearance to fennel seeds but slightly larger and milder. Delicious in meat and vegetable dishes. On some of the islands sprigs of fresh anise seeds are put into white rum to give a liquorice flavour. The rum so treated turns a pale green colour after a few days. It makes a drink not unlike the French liqueur, Anisette, which turns white when ice or water is added to it. Obtainable dried from most shops where spices are sold. Can be grown in Europe in a sunny position, in a sandy rich soil. Star aniseed is a different variety of product and is not referred to in any of the recipes in this book.

Annatto If you take annatto seeds and pestle them in a mortar with oil or fat added, you will preserve their delicate flavour. The perfumed and coloured oil will keep a long time. If the crushed seeds are mixed with water or stock, the flavour may vanish unless rushed to the pot. Bottled annatto liquid, marketed as *achote*, will impart brilliant colour to your food, but barely any flavour is to be noticed.

Bay The leaves of the West Indian bay are much stronger and much more oily than the ordinary bay tree of Europe. The leaves give turtle and pork dishes a wonderful flavour, and the dried berries can be used instead of melegueta peppercorns which are the berries of a similar West African tree. West Indian bay leaves may not be available here, but any home-grown bay leaf will be equally useful.

Chives Caribbean chives are much thicker and stronger in flavour than British plants. They look more like spring onions, though the leaves are sometimes longer. Use home-grown chives or any spring onions that are commercially available. But distinguish between the two when advancing into the field of shallots and onions. Chives can be grown in a heavy, well-watered soil in a shaded position. If you are growing them for immediate eating during the season, do not allow them to flower. Avoid dried or frozen chives.

Cinnamon Both the peeled bark and leaves are used in Caribbean cooking. The leaves may not be possible to come by. Use in pork, game and poultry dishes (excellent when preparing baked hams). Its sweet aromatic flavour goes well in most sauces, apple pies, cakes, sweets and drinks. It is best to grind your own for sweet dishes, though powdered cinnamon will give a fairly good result. Cinnamon sticks, boiled for a few minutes in a little water, then with milk added and sweetened, is a good drink to try. Cinnamon is believed to have medicinal properties, for relieving flatulence, for instance, and it also forms part of the cure in medicines for the treatment of internal haemorrhages. In many of the islands it is boiled together with ginger for the cure of colds, and the relief of fevers and stomach aches. Many Caribbean people start the day with a tisane made of ginger, cinnamon and fresh mint.

Cloves Used in meat, poultry, fish and even more so in pork and ham dishes. Ground cloves, used sparingly, are excellent in cakes and puddings. Whole cloves are basic to mulled wine. Cloves are also recommended for all sorts of ailments and are most effective to the relief of toothache.

Coriander The seeds are widely available and are used mostly in curries and pork dishes. The leaves which look like a very large parsley are available from Mediterranean and Asian shops. Coriander leaves are delicious in many soups and sauces and can be used in certain instances in the same way as English parsley.

But a distinction has to be drawn between English and Continental parsley which is sold with no root and resembles coriander. Coriander leaves, stored in a plastic bag, unwashed and with roots intact, will keep in a refrigerator for a few weeks. When choosing between coriander and Continental parsley (known as Salsa) ask the shop assistant which is which. Coriander can be grown from seeds in England.

Cumin, Geera Best bought whole. There is a very dark cumin seed which can be bought from most Asian shops. But the better known lighter-coloured seed will do just as well. Used mainly in curries and in breads, but is also delicious in meat, lamb, chicken and cheese dishes. Cumin can be grown for its seeds in a well sheltered but sunny position in any rich well-drained soil.

Fennel Similar to anise seed in taste and appearance. Very good in certain meat and vegetable dishes especially cabbage. Can be bought in packets from most shops. Can be grown in Britain.

Garlic Use fresh whole cloves, either crushed flat with a knife or spoon, if used whole, or very finely chopped with a sharp knife. A garlic press is a useful tool to have. I personally avoid using powdered garlic. Garlic can be successfully grown in any small garden as one would cultivate onions or spring onions.

Ginger Fresh ginger can be bought from almost any large supermarket, occasionally from greengrocers and always from Asian and West Indian shops. Use in sauces, curries, cakes and drinks. The light brown skin should be peeled away before the root is either grated or chopped, then mostly fried in the early stages of any cooking. Fresh ginger will keep best if planted in some sandy soil and watered about once a week. Place the pot in which it has been planted on a window ledge and within a short time it should sprout leaves. You can then dig the ginger up whenever needed, cut off what you need and replant. Do not buy ginger that is too wrinkled, choose a firm, fat piece. Powdered ginger is sold in most shops but is best used only in cakes and bread.

Lemon Peel *See* Orange peel for the modern version of a classic preparation. But an infusion of lemon peel (originally the Portuguese *chá de limão*) is still enjoyed in Guyana, Surinam and Cayenne.

Lime leaves These can be used as a garnish, infused as a tisane or introduced into a marinade in the same way as a bay leaf.

Lime peel Peeled in the same manner as the orange. Use in hot spiced drinks such as mulled wines, or ground for cakes and certain boiled sweets (*see* Orange).

Mace Buy whole blades from supermarkets, Asian and West Indian shops. Use with meats, poultry, fish, cakes and sweets (*see* Glossary).

Nutmeg Used in drinks, cakes and meat dishes. Buy whole and grate when needed (*see* Glossary).

Orange Peel The skin of the orange is carefully peeled, without the white inner flesh, in one long strip with a sharp knife. It is then hung up to dry anywhere in the kitchen. Pieces are then broken off and used in cakes, sweets and hot drinks. Sweetened hot orange peel tea is a delicious refreshing drink.

Parsley Keeps best with the stems in water or stored in the refrigerator, in a plastic bag. Can be grown in a heavy well-watered soil; but the plant does not like too much sun.

Peppercorns Black and white. Best bought whole. Black pepper should be coarsely ground. White pepper responds to fine milling.

Saffron Can either be bought in threads or powdered from supermarkets, Asian and West Indian shops. Used as a colouring in foods and has a delicate flavour. It is sometimes best to soak the threads in a little hot water before adding to whatever dish. It is very expensive, and though some people may disapprove, turmeric can be used as a substitute, mainly to provide the distinctive orange colour; but the particular taste of saffron is to be preferred.

Salt Most Caribbean cooks prefer to use sea salt; which is indeed best. The amount of salt you will use will of course be according to taste. Though again a greater amount of salt is made use of in some Caribbean cooking. The acquired taste for salt, I suppose, in the Caribbean, results from long and extensive use of salted meats and fish. Furthermore, there is the need to replace the loss of salt from the body through perspiring so much under the hot sun. However, Rastafarians and some other communities reject salt for religious or dietary reasons. Their example could merit consideration in the long term.

Tamarind The leaves are used in salads. When the seeds are removed, the black sticky pulp which has a very sharp, sour but slightly sweet taste is used in sauces, curries, chutneys, drinks, sweets and relishes. The pulp, rolled into small balls and coated with sugar, is very popular. When removing the seeds, check that there are no bits remaining from the brown brittle shell.

Thyme I know of at least four varieties cultivated in the Caribbean for culinary use. The best choice in Europe is either the French or Spanish thyme. Grows well in England in a sunny position in a light well-manured soil. Can be purchased in dried form from most shops; but again is best bought fresh from your greengrocer whenever available. Use to flavour any meat dishes, fish or poultry. Fresh thyme is delicious with tomatoes and salads. Excellent in egg and vegetable dishes and as a herb in salad dressing.

Turmeric Used mainly for colouring, since the flavour is so mild. It is bright yellow and will cause stains – so be careful how you use it. Ground turmeric is available under the Indian name, *haldi*, but the whole root can also be found. The root is to be pounded or grated; it can also be lightly crushed, put into the cooking and later discarded. Turmeric is a useful substitute for saffron.

Vanilla Use in cakes, puddings, ice-cream and drinks. A vanilla pod can be used more than once. Vanilla is also used to flavour perfumes and tobacco. Unfortunately today the vanilla essence or flavouring, as it is now called, is synthetic, made from coal tar, waste paper pulp and chemicals. So, make your own vanilla sugar (*see* Techniques). The pods are available in some health food shops, supermarkets, Asian and West Indian shops.

Other condiments used in Caribbean cooking are: olives, capers, soya sauce, coconut oil, tomato ketchup, Angostura bitters, mushrooms, honey, and nuts (pecans, walnuts, cashews and almonds). Herbs include oregano, marjoram and rosemary. Worcestershire sauce is also widely used, as are various wines, liqueurs, sherry and brandy. Of the kinds of sugar you would find in a Caribbean kitchen, raw cane and Demerara are the most useful. Many of the islands make great use of cream and milk, especially tinned milks like sweet condensed milk and evaporated milk.

Equipment

I have assumed that any kitchen where a fair amount of everyday cooking takes place will have the necessary gadgets, tools and utensils for the preparation and cooking of any of the recipes in this book – a range of the sharpest knives, a kitchen saw and a cleaver, kitchen needles, heavy pots and pans, casseroles, kitchen scales, a blender, measuring cups, wooden spoons, spatulas and whisks.

Caribbean cooks insist on having to hand one or two large heavy pots with lids for the preparation of stews and substantial one-pot dishes for parties; e.g. Rice and Peas, Pelaus, Callaloo, Braffs (broths), Bean and Dumpling soups, Black puddings, etc. Also needed are two large frying or sauté pans. A large roasting pan or baking dish is needed if you are to attempt a suckling pig, and a fair-sized oval casserole or fish kettle for whole fish. You will also need glass or enamel bowls for marinading – though some heavy glazed plastics will do just as well. It is essential to possess a good sharp grater for the grating of coconuts, cassava roots and such like – and if you own a blender or food processor all the better. A mortar and pestle is a must; and if you are fortunate to have a large wooden one, brought back from the Caribbean or India, then you can make the delicious 'tonton' – a method of pounding into a fine creamy paste boiled vegetables such as yams, dasheen and breadfruit. There is a recipe for 'tonton' in the vegetable section. The same method, applied to plantain is called 'foo-foo'.

It would be a wonderful thing to have in your possession a West Indian coalpot; but then again, in the summer you will be able to make use of a European barbecue – several types are available in most hardware stores and garden centres. For Rum Punches and other home made drinks you will need at least one large glass or enamel bowl, spirit measures, a fine strainer, a cocktail shaker, a jug or two, a long stirring rod or spoon, a wooden swizzle stick, a small fine grater for nutmeg, and a good strong strainer or blender to purée fruits such as guavas, ripe pawpaws, mangoes, ripe bananas, pineapples or any other soft tropical fruits. A juice extractor or citrus squeezer is also needed.

Techniques

BANANAS
To peel a green banana or plantain, first cut off both ends with a sharp knife. Then make two or three slits lengthways in the skin down to the flesh. But do not cut in too deep. Lift the skin with the back of the knife, then with your thumb peel the skin by gradually lifting sideways away from the flesh. Scrape off with a sharp knife any green fibres that may still cling to the flesh. *See* Glossary for further notes on choosing and cooking.

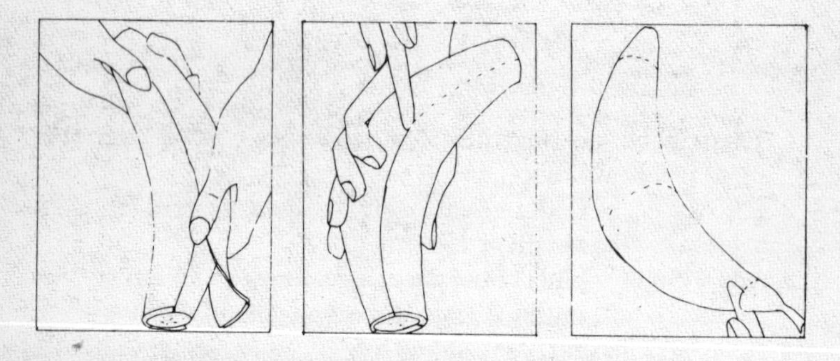

How to peel a green banana or plantain

BREADFRUIT
Can be peeled and cored before cooking or cut into convenient pieces, washed thoroughly and rubbed with lime or lemon then boiled in salted water with skin and core intact, and peeled when cool.

CARAMEL *colouring or browning*
Caribbean cooks prefer to use their own colouring, mixing sugar with the meat as it is being fried, or adding already prepared caramel colouring.

225g (1 lb) brown sugar
Water

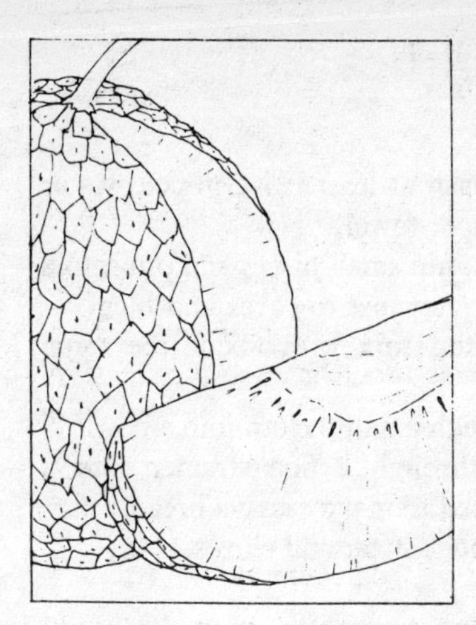

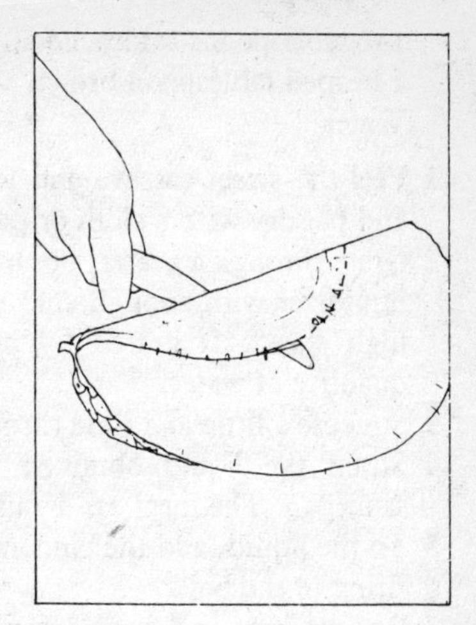

How to core breadfruit

1 Thoroughly mix together 2–3 tablespoons water and the sugar in a heavy saucepan.
2 Cook over a medium heat until a dark brown, stirring constantly. Do not allow to burn.
3 Add 425ml (¾ pint) of hot water, continue to boil and stir on a medium heat until the caramel becomes slightly syrupy.
4 Remove from heat, cool and bottle.

The caramel must definitely not be allowed to burn, as it will taste bitter; but if it is too little cooked, it will still be sweet. Never, never pour cold water into caramel, since the temperature is very high and severe eruptions would result, causing burns, to say the least. When adding your hot water, pour in a little at a time stirring continuously. Caramel should keep for months, and does not even need to be refrigerated.

HOW TO MAKE CASSAREEP
(*used in Pepperpot Stew*)

1.5kg (3 lb) sweet cassava root (available from Indian and West Indian shops)
1 stick cinnamon, freshly ground
4 cloves, freshly ground

1–2 tablespoons caramel colouring
1 heaped tablespoon brown sugar
Water

1 Peel the sweet cassava and wash at least twice in cold water and pat dry with a cloth or paper towel.
2 Grate through a grater, or cut into small pieces and put into a liquidizer with enough cold water just to cover and blend at high speed. If grated by hand mix with about the same quantity of water.
3 Squeeze a little at a time through a damp cloth into a bowl.
4 Strain the liquid obtained through a fine strainer into a saucepan. The meal can be used to make cassava bread.
5 To the liquid, add the cinnamon, sugar and cloves.
6 Bring to the boil.
7 Reduce heat and cook, stirring constantly, until the liquid thickens to a starchy consistency. Do not allow to burn.
8 Add the caramel colouring.
9 Simmer, stirring, for another 3 minutes.
10 Remove from heat and cool.
11 Will keep for weeks if refrigerated. Use as needed.

COCONUT MILK

A dry coconut must contain its liquid, otherwise it may prove rancid, so before buying be certain to shake it and check for the sound of the water by holding it close to your ears. The coconut water, if not too sour, can be used in rum punches, sweets and sauces. To retain the water pierce two of the three eyes with a sharp instrument such as an ice pick, skewer or sharp screw-driver. One of the eyes, from where the seedling would eventually germinate, will be much easier to pierce than the other two. Next you must strain the liquid into a jug. To break the coconut tap the brown shell with a hammer or similar implement a few times, then place it on a hard surface and give a final sharp blow; it should be broken into pieces. Remove the flesh from the shell by levering off with a small dull knife. I have found an ordinary table knife much safer for this purpose. Using a sharp knife, cut the flesh into pieces about 2½–4 cm^2 (1 to 1½ square inches). Place these into a blender with the coconut water and about 450 ml (¾ pint) of warm water and blend at high speed until the coconut turns into a purée. From time to time switch off the machine and scrape any bits that cling to the sides back into the mixture jar with a wooden spoon or rubber spatula. Strain through a clean tea cloth, muslin or cheese cloth into a bowl. To get as much of the milk as possible, the ends of the cloth must be brought together and wrung tight by twisting. Discard the pulp.

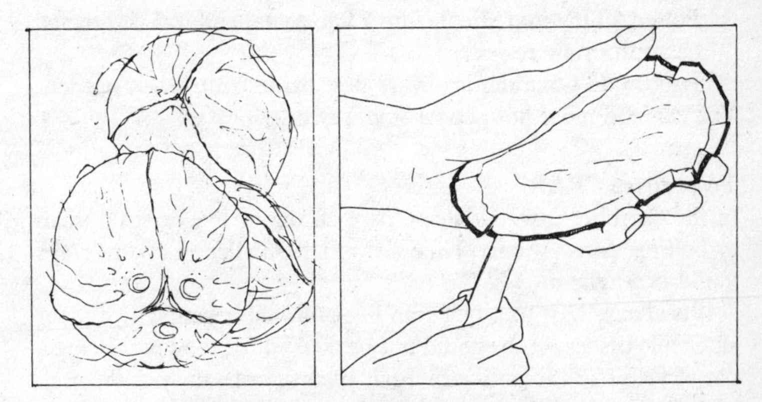

Removing the flesh from a coconut

For the making of coconut cakes, sweets, jams and praline, the coconut should be grated by hand after first having peeled off the brown skin with a sharp knife. Grating by hand can be a tedious chore but that is how it is still done in the islands, after centuries, even for making coconut milk.

For a rich thick coconut cream, simply follow the basic instructions as for coconut milk; but set the liquid aside in a glass bowl and allow the cream to rise to the top. Skim off the cream into another bowl and retain the lighter liquid remaining, to be added to the cream, if necessary, to obtain the consistency you need.

Coconut milk is also available canned (some brands of which I have found preferable to the solidified cream in packets).

Poudre de COLOMBO
This is a well known creole curry powder from the islands of Martinique and Guadeloupe, and is ideal for chicken, fish or vegetable curries where a lighter taste is called for.

½ teaspoon turmeric (I have used the freshly grated root, but it is not always easily available)
1 teaspoon coriander seeds, freshly ground
1 teaspoon mustard seeds, freshly ground
3 cloves garlic, pressed or pounded
Pinch ground ginger
½ hot pepper, seeded and chopped (*see* p. 37)

Pound all the ingredients into a fine paste, and use as directed in the appropriate recipe.

Poudre de Colombo is always best made fresh when needed. You can add more hot pepper if you wish.

To prepare CRAB

In the Caribbean, we either prepare our crabs live or scald them in boiling salted water. They are much smaller than the crabs found in England.

It is always best to buy a crab live and boil it yourself. But for all Creole dishes, crab should not be cooked for too long. Bring a pot of water to the boil with a fair quantity of salt, put the crab in, bring back to the boil, lower the heat and simmer for about 20 minutes. Remove from the pot and allow to cool. To clean it, lay the crab on its back. Break the claws by bending back and twisting them off. Twist off the legs by turning and snapping them at the joint closest to the body. Remove the flap from the underside and discard. Take the crab in both hands with the back of the hard shell turned towards your body and resting in the heel of the palms, eyes downward. The protruding end of the underpart to which the legs were attached should face upwards. Now using both thumbs push the crab's undercarriage away from the hard shell. Having done this, remove and discard the thin membrane covering the edible brown meat of the shell. Using a small spoon extract all this from the shell. Remove and discard the small sac located behind the crab's mouth.

From the undercarriage pull off the soft gills (dead man's claws) which are situated along the edges. On no account must there be any bits of 'dead man's claws' left with any part of the meat.

If serving the undercarriage, for instance in callaloo soups and stews, split it down the middle, in halves.

To extract the meat from the claws and legs, crack with a wooden hammer or similar implement, and either pull away the shell or use a skewer or sharp-pointed instrument to extract the meat; the same with the undercarriage.

CURRY POWDER

There are many different recipes for curry powder in the islands, especially in Trinidad and Guyana, where the largest communities from the sub-continent of India are to be found.

15g (½ oz) cloves
15g (½ oz) poppy seeds
25g (1 oz) coriander seeds
15g (½ oz) mustard seeds
50g (2 oz) cumin seed
1 dried hot pepper
25g (1 oz) ground cinnamon
15g (½ oz) peppercorns
65g (2½ oz) ground turmeric
25g (1 oz) ground ginger

1 Roast the cloves, together with the poppy, coriander, mustard and cumin seeds in a dry pan until the mustard begins to pop and hop.
2 Allow to cool slightly.
3 Put all the ingredients into a mortar and grind into a powder with a pestle.
4 Store in a tightly closed jar and use as needed.

DASHEEN, YAM, *and* TANIA

Using a sharp knife peel down to the skin the same way you would any vegetable, then cut into appropriate pieces for cooking. Do not forget to wash all vegetables with lime or lemon in cold water, and to squeeze a little citrus juice into the water in which they are to be boiled. Do not leave any cooked vegetables to sit in the water for too long after you have turned off the heat. Remember also that cooked vegetables left covered in a pot even after the water has been drained will continue to cook, so shift the lid to the side.

How to scale and clean a large FISH

Lay the fish on its side on a wooden chopping board. Using a very sharp knife or a pair of kitchen scissors, cut away the pelvic and anal fins at the belly and the dorsal ones at the back. Now do the same with other fins. To scale the fish, grasp the tail and, using a blunter knife, scale upwards towards the head. With most large fishes like red snappers it is best to do this with the fish submerged in cold water in the sink. That prevents the scales from flying all over the kitchen. To gut the fish cut down the belly from the head to the vent, and extract the viscera by holding on to the gills and pulling them downwards towards the tail. Always wash the fish thoroughly both inside and out, removing all traces of blood and scales. Any stubborn clots of blood clinging to the inside of the fish should be scraped out with a knife.

TO BONE A RED SNAPPER, GROUPER OR ANY SIMILAR SIZE FISH

Having scaled, removed all fins and gutted the fish, use your very sharp knife to open the belly of the fish as far down to the tail as possible, to expose the backbone and ribs. Now carefully lift each rib bone embedded in the flesh with the point of a small sharp knife, without cutting away too much of the flesh. Nip off each rib at the joint of the spine with the knife or twist it off with the thumb and forefinger. Flatten the fish, to open it as widely as you can, and run the knife down each side of the backbone as close as possible, but without cutting through the skin at the back. Break the spine off at the head with thumb and forefinger or use a pair of kitchen scissors. Carefully pull the backbone out downwards towards the tail, then twist or cut it off.

Use the spine in a stock.

BONING A FLYING FISH OR SIMILAR ROUND FISH

Scale, then cut away all fins except the dorsal fin. Now place the fish on its belly. Using a very sharp knife cut down from the head on each side of the dorsal fin, hugging as close to the bone as possible, to separate the fillets from the spine. Avoid cutting away too much of the flesh. Now sever the spine bone at the head and tail and carefully pull off. Remove the gills and extract the viscera, or what is left of it, having pulled out the spine. Use as directed in the recipe.

FRUIT

To ripen mangoes, avocadoes, pawpaws, plantains, bananas and soursops, especially in the winter, wrap them in newspapers, towels, an old jumper or any thick cloth or clothing and place in the airing cupboard. Thus, you can buy your fruit, when still green and hard, a few days in advance.

Do not put any unripened fruit together with, or close to limes, lemons, grapefruits or oranges. The citrus fruits most certainly retard and prevent other fruits from ripening properly.

Never freeze ripe mangoes and ripe avocadoes. Mangoes, if frozen and then defrosted, will go very soft and the skins will turn almost a dark grey. Friends from England, freezing mangoes to take back with them, have fallen into this trap.

HOT PEPPERS

These *must* be used fresh. Do not buy too many as they tend to lose their flavour and strength even when stored unwrapped in a cool place. Use sparingly, or to taste; *always* remove the seeds, unless cooking whole, and avoid contact with the more sensitive parts of the body. If your fingers have been in contact with chopped chillies, rub your hands with lime or lemon juice and wash them once in soap and water.

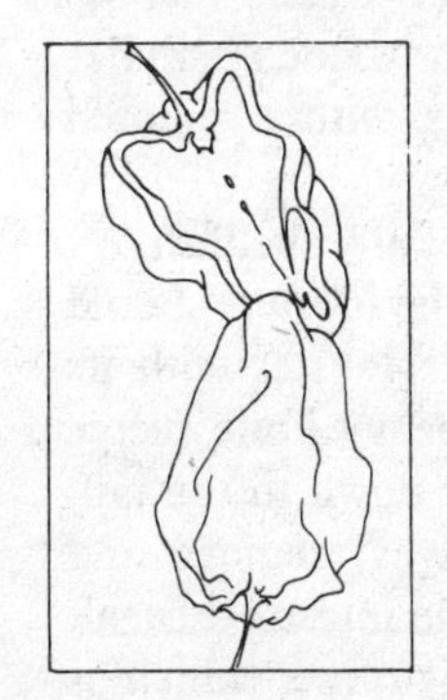
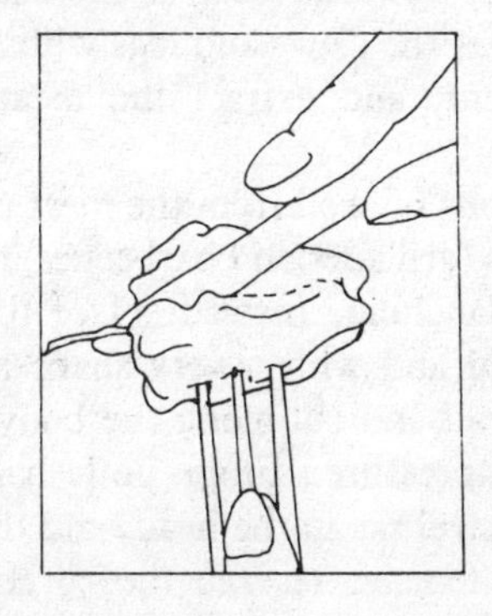
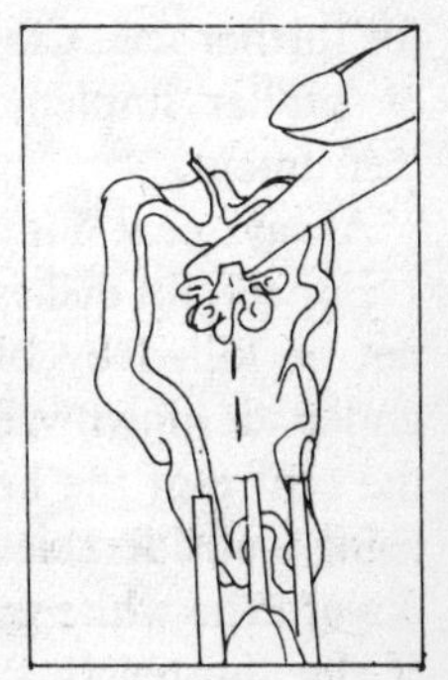

How to handle a hot pepper

Of the varieties of peppers available in Britain, you will find long fruits in most well-stocked greengrocers: of these there are two kinds – the smaller tend to be the stronger and the larger and fleshier ones have a touch of sweetness which can be most agreeable in dishes with bitter ingredients, such as aubergine. Then there is the famed *Bom de Ma Jacques* or Scots Bonnet, so named because it resembles a large Tam o' Shanter.

To prepare a LOBSTER

Always buy your lobsters live whenever you can.

Kill a lobster by immersing it in boiling salted water with or without other seasoning similar to a court-bouillon. The lid must be tightly held down for the first few minutes. Lower the heat and simmer. Allow an average of 12 minutes for each pound. Set the lobster aside to cool before cutting it up and extracting the meat.

To clean a lobster, lay it on its back and twist off the claws and legs. Set aside.

With the lobster still on its back use a sharp knife and cut lengthways down each side close to the shell of the underside. Tear away the bony covering, working from the tail towards the head. Lifting from the tail prise the flesh free. The meat should all come out in one piece, leaving the shell whole for stuffing.

If it is a female lobster, she may contain a pink roe. Reserve this for further use. You absolutely must discard the gravel sac which is between the eyes. Scoop out the palish-green liver, which is in the shell, upwards towards the head. Retain this too for further use. Crack the claws and legs with a wooden hammer or similar implement, and extract the meats with a pointed instrument.

Always pick out bits of shell from the meat of any shellfish.

For certain dishes (grillades and barbecues) the lobsters should not be killed by blanching. Instead, place the lobster with its underside downward and with a very sharp heavy knife pierce the centre of the head and cut along the body down to the tail, using considerable pressure. From both halves, remove and discard the white gravel sac in the head, and the intestinal canal. If the lobster is a female, reserve the coral or roe, which is blackish in colour and can be added to a stew or sauce. Lightly crack the claws, but keep them whole.

Now rinse the lobster under cold running water and use as directed in the recipes.

For recipes requiring lobster meat, you will obviously have to extract the flesh and cut into suitable pieces.

MARINADES

Marinating plays a very important part in Creole Caribbean cooking, and all of the islands have their own methods. It is not only the best way to 'season up' meats and fishes but it also helps to break down the fibres and tenderizes many a tough piece of meat. The citric acid of lime or lemon almost pre-cooks fish, tender meat or young poultry. Chopped fish or whole prawns and crayfish can be marinated in lime or lemon with herbs and spices, left overnight or for about 24 hours, and then served and eaten without any further need of cooking.

If possible, use only fresh herbs. The list is endless as you will see from reading the list of herbs and spices (*see* p. 22).

Rums, wines and liqueurs also form part of some marinades, as do sherry, soya sauce, oil, vinegar, Worcestershire sauce and tomato sauce and sofrito. If ever, in desperation, you must use dried herbs, tie them in a piece of cheesecloth – even then you will not get the same result as from the same method with a classic bouquet garni. Sometimes the use of dried herbs can't be helped, especially in Britain. That is why I suggest you grow your own; in a flower pot or a window box.

I cannot give here all the various marinades used on the different islands, but this is a basic one (other marinades are given in the recipe section according to the dish).

Juice 1 lime or lemon
1 tablespoon malt vinegar
1 tablespoon light rum (always use rums from the Islands)
1 tablespoon salt
1 onion, sliced finely in half rings
1 sprig parsley
1 sprig thyme, fresh
1 sprig celery leaves, or a short celery stalk crushed with a meat chopper or rolling pin
1 whole chilli pepper, cut in half, need not be seeded
150ml (¼ pint) water

1 Mix all the ingredients in a bowl large enough to contain the meats or fish to be marinated.

2 Add the meat or fish to the marinade – rub in well.
3 Set aside, and leave for at least 4 hours or as directed in the recipe.

The amount given is sufficient for 1.5–1.8kg (3–4 lb) of fish, meat or poultry.

PIGS' TAILS

These can be bought fresh, on occasion or to order, otherwise they are obtainable fresh or preserved in cochineal (an extract from the dried body of a tropical American insect, used in dyeing material and conserving food). If you are using fresh meat, singe off the hairs, blanch the tails in boiling water and remove any excess blood or fat from the severed end. Skimming off any such scum may also be necessary during cooking. Salted pigs' tails should be soaked for a few hours – they should be already properly prepared prior to curing, so they can then be used at once. Dyed pigs' tails will be sold to you direct from the bucket in a market or specialist shop. Rush them home, since they will be wet and very red, and place them in a bowl under running water for an hour or so, until the proper colour of pork meat is restored. You may have to scrape off some hairs but you will not be able to singe them.

In order to remove all of the dye, you can further parboil the tails in a few changes of water, although this may not always be necessary.

PULSES

Red kidney beans, Black beans, Black-eyed beans, Pigeon peas (gunga beans), Lentils, Cannellini or Fasoul beans. It is not really necessary to soak the beans overnight; but they will take a much longer time to cook if not soaked. Always wash beans thoroughly and check for any foreign pieces, such as small chips of broken stone. All of the kidney bean family, especially red kidney beans, must be boiled at a very high temperature for at least 10 to 15 minutes to remove the poisons contained. Caribbean cooks are absolutely right to believe that salt should not be added to the beans until they are fairly tender since salt arrests the cooking.

All beans can be purchased dried or canned from most shops,

but fresh pigeon peas are available from Asian, West Indian shops and markets dealing in Caribbean and other tropical produce most times of the year. But best is from November to June. When soaked and cooked all pulses will swell up to about two or three times the uncooked volume. So always use less than called for in the recipes where the fresh product is stipulated.

PUMPKINS

Are best boiled in the shell unless being used in soups or stews. But always remove the seeds and fibrous parts.

RICE

This invaluable staple comes in two conditions: raw and parboiled (or pre-fluffed – this is the modern American term). Raw rice is white, pre-fluffed slightly yellow in colour. The second is preferable for various reasons – it does not require so much washing, a good deal of the starch is already removed, whilst the steaming process (which is designed to improve the food yield of the product) concentrates the goodness of the husk into the kernel before the rice is milled. All cooked rice is white. Of the varieties of rice available, the long-grained Patna and Basmati are considered superior. Of the shorter grains, Italian Arborio rice is slightly glutinous and creates the kind of fluffy dish with less separated rice than the Indian kinds would make – but this risotto rice is not in the least cumbersome to eat. Chinese rice is often glutinous and is usually labelled as such, being used in some dishes from countries with strong Chinese and Malay communities, such as Trinidad. A similar glutinous rice, but with a different taste, is sometimes called Carolina and is best not used with entrée dishes. All raw rice must be sorted and cleaned, grain by grain, before the first wash or soak.

SALTFISH

Only use cod. It can be bought in packets from Asian and West Indian shops and markets – but it is best to buy fresh from Spanish, Portuguese, Greek and Italian delicatessens or from open markets, which carry whole salted cod. You can then choose what you are buying both in quality and freshness. If the saltfish is too thin or dehydrated, do not buy it. Also if it is sold in a packet, you must ensure you are not being sold Saithe, Ling or any other salted fish. Dried cod is best soaked overnight or for at least 6 to 8 hours, with as many water changes as possible. The soaking of the fish not only removes most of the salt but also replaces any of the moisture that has been lost through the salting and drying process. When not properly soaked, the product tends to be rather chewy even after it is boiled. When boiled the slimy skin of the saltfish is best peeled off with a knife. When choosing saltfish avoid too much of the fin and tail parts – too many bones and not enough flesh – they tend to be on the tough side. When using some recipes for grilled, roast or baked saltfish, it is best to cook the fish with the skin on. It is also a good idea to oil the trivet to prevent the fish from sticking.

Thickening SAUCES

I have found that a butter and flour roux changes the flavour and character of most Creole cooking; a flour and water paste is best or better still, Arrowroot. But always add the Arrowroot at the very last minute – for if it is cooked too long it simply disperses in the liquor, which then becomes thin once more.

STOCKS

Make your own whenever possible. But to save time any good bouillon cube will do. Always choose a light coloured stock cube. The darker stocks contain too much artificial colouring and their flavour is not at all consistent with Creole cooking.

SWEET POTATOES

Treat as most other root vegetables. But they can also be cooked unpeeled, having been cut into suitable pieces to shorten the cooking time, but be careful not to overcook. Test with a fork or skewer. Cooking breadfruits and sweet potatoes with the skin on helps prevent them from absorbing too much water and also cooking into a mushy mess. When cutting or peeling rub with lemon or lime. The Louisiana Yam, which is a variety of sweet potato, needs less cooking time and is best cooked in its jacket.

VANILLA SUGAR

900g (2 lbs) caster sugar
2–3 vanilla pods

1 Make a slit lengthways down each pod – then put together with the sugar into an airtight jar.
2 After about a week you can use the sugar when needed.
3 Top up each time with fresh sugar, shaking well to mix old with new. The pods should retain their flavour for at least 3 months.

One of the great secrets of making life easy in the kitchen and making Creole cooking a joy rather than hard work, is to have all ingredients at hand. Have whatever is to be chopped, peeled, ground or seeded ready at the outset. Timing is of the utmost importance. If you are prepared you will be able to face any frustrations, trials and tribulations.

PART TWO
Recipes

Hors d'Oeuvres, Soups and Breakfast Dishes

Appetizers can be served at any time of day as a snack. They may be part or the whole of a first course and may even be served with the main course. Sometimes they form part of a buffet lunch, supper or party, and they are very much in evidence at breakfast time, especially at a large Sunday breakfast or brunch. As for the soups, they are exotic and very filling. You will find on many of the Islands that soups are served as a main meal or at a party with bread and even vegetables.

Island cooks make extensive use of various fresh vegetables, fish and beans, highly seasoned and spiced.

The following are just a few of the many hors d'oeuvres and soups.

WUGAY DE CWEBICHE

ROUGAIL DE CREVETTES (ECREVISSE)

CRAYFISH MOUSSE

(Martinique)

675g (1½ lb) shelled crayfish (or prawns)
1½ tablespoons lime or lemon juice
1 clove garlic, chopped
⅓ hot pepper, seeded and chopped (*see* Techniques)
1 tablespoon vegetable oil
Black pepper, freshly ground
Salt to taste
Lime or lemon wedges for garnish.

1 Put all the ingredients into a mortar, except of course the citrus wedges, and pound into a smooth well blended paste.
2 Taste for seasoning.
3 Oil a mould of your choice, press the mixture firmly into it and turn out at once and carefully arrange on a dish and serve garnished with the citrus wedges.
4 You may also garnish with lettuce leaves or watercress if you so wish.

Serves 4 to 6

CRAB BACKS

Dominica

Though this is the recipe I am most used to, Crab Backs are also very popular in Martinique and Guadeloupe. You will need eight small crab or scallop shells.

On the Islands, about ten live land crabs would be used for this dish, after being purged. If using live European crabs, *see* Techniques.

It is also possible to buy very small crabs already dressed from some of the better fishmongers and suppliers, but you may have to order in advance. If using these (you should try to find them whenever possible), extract the meat and reserve the shells, and follow the recipe as directed. If preparing a large number of Crab Backs for a party, simply trust yourself and adjust the recipe by using your discretion.

Crab and scallop shells can be re-used several times if properly washed and dried each time and then stored in a dry place.

900g (2 lb) cooked crab meat, both brown and white parts
2 tablespoons butter
1 tablespoon oil
1 small onion, very finely chopped
2 cloves garlic, pressed or finely chopped
2 tablespoons chives, finely chopped
6 allspice berries, freshly ground (or substitute 4 cloves and a pinch of nutmeg)
½ hot pepper, seeded and finely chopped (*see* Techniques)
2 teaspoons thyme
1½ tablespoons Worcestershire sauce
2 tablespoons dark rum (*from the Islands*)
1 tablespoon fresh lime juice
110g (4 oz) fresh breadcrumbs
Black pepper, freshly ground
Salt to taste

1. Flake the crab meat very finely with your fingers.
2. Heat the oil and butter in a heavy but shallow frying pan and fry the onion until lightly brown.
3. Add the garlic and stir in for about half a minute.
4. Now add all the other ingredients including 50g (2 oz) of the breadcrumbs but not the crab meat.
5. Lower the heat and sauté for about 2 minutes, then taste for seasoning, especially salt.
6. Blend in the crab meat thoroughly.
7. Fill the crab or scallop shells with equal amounts of the mixture and sprinkle the remaining breadcrumbs over each one.
8. Bake in a pre-heated oven 190°C (375°F/Gas 5) for 30 minutes or until golden brown.
9. The Crab Backs can be served immediately while still hot, or they may be eaten later, when cold.

Serves 8

CRABE AU FROMAGE

CRAB BAKED WITH CHEESE

Guadeloupe

675–900g (1½–2 lb) cooked white crab meat (fresh or frozen)
75–110g (3–4 oz) fresh breadcrumbs
½ teaspoon hot peppers, seeded and chopped fine (*see* Techniques)
1½ tablespoons dark rum (preferably *Vieux* from Guadeloupe or Martinique)
2 teaspoons lime juice
4 tablespoons double cream
1 teaspoon Worcestershire sauce (optional)
Black pepper, freshly ground
Salt to taste
4 tablespoons freshly grated cheese (I use Gruyère)
Lime wedges

1. Pre-heat the oven to 190°C (375°F/Gas 5).
2. In a large bowl, thoroughly blend all the ingredients except the cheese and lime wedges.
3. Place an equal amount of the mixture in 6–8 small crab shells, scallop shells or small individual oven-proof dishes.
4. Sprinkle over each an equal amount of cheese and bake in the oven for about 10 minutes.
5. Serve hot with a wedge of lime on each.

Makes a delicious hors d'oeuvre.

Serves 6–8

ROUGAIL DE MORUE

FRIED SALTFISH WITH TOMATOES

French Speaking Islands

450g (1 lb) salted cod
3 tablespoons oil
2 medium onions, finely chopped
½ hot pepper, seeded and chopped (*see* Techniques)
1 teaspoon fresh parsley, chopped
2 teaspoons lime or lemon juice
Black pepper

5 tomatoes, sliced
Salt to taste

1. Soak the saltfish overnight or for at least 8 hours – changing the water at least twice.
2. Drain the saltfish, then remove the skin and all the bones.
3. Pat dry, then flake with your fingers.
4. Heat the oil in a shallow pot and fry the shredded fish until lightly brown. Do not allow to stick to the pot.
5. Add the chopped onion, hot pepper, parsley, citrus juice and black pepper.
6. Cover the whole with the slices of tomato, sprinkle a little salt on the tomatoes.
7. Cover completely and simmer until the tomatoes are cooked.
8. Taste for seasoning, without disturbing too much.
9. Continue to cook uncovered until all the liquid has been evaporated and the dish is almost dry.
10. Serve piping hot.

Will serve as a main dish with Riz Creole, Red beans and a green salad.

Serves 4–6

SALTFISH EN CHEMISE

SOUSE OF SALTED COD

Dominica

This dish is often served at breakfast time, and sometimes as a main meal accompanied with sliced avocadoes.

450g–675g (1–1½ lb) salted cod, soaked overnight
2 medium onions, finely sliced
1 sprig parsley, chopped
Small piece of hot pepper, seeded and chopped (*see* Techniques)
1 tablespoon chives
3–4 tablespoons vegetable oil
Juice 1–1½ limes
1 clove garlic, pressed or finely chopped
Black pepper, freshly ground
Salt to taste
225g (½ lb) tomatoes, sliced

2–3 hard boiled eggs, quartered lengthways
Lettuce leaves for garnish

1. Bring a pot of water to the boil.
2. Drop in the saltfish and allow to boil uncovered for about 10 minutes.
3. Drain and allow to cool.
4. Bone and skin the fish.
5. Pat dry and flake with the fingers into fine shreds.
6. Put into a bowl with the onions, parsley, hot pepper and chives.
7. Make a dressing with the oil, lime juice, garlic and black pepper.
8. Pour over the saltcod mixture and toss a few times, then taste for salt.
9. Arrange in an attractive serving dish with the sliced tomatoes and sliced eggs, then garnish with the lettuce leaves.
10. Serve on its own with bread or as part of a breakfast or buffet.

In islands to the south this dish is known as Fishy Bowl, or as Brule Jol, with avocado and/or cucumber included. In Jamaica a richer dish, with more tomato and red spices, is called Escovitch, derived from the Escabeche of the Spanish-speaking islands, where sofrito (a strong red relish) is used.

Serves 4–6

PATE DE MORUE AUX HARENGS SAURS

SALTFISH AND SMOKED HERRING PÂTÉ

French and Patois speaking Islands

225g (½ lb) salted cod, soaked overnight
2 smoked herrings (soaked overnight in milk or water)
50g (2 oz) fine breadcrumbs
2 cloves garlic, pressed or finely chopped
Black pepper, freshly ground
1 tablespoon brandy
4 cloves, ground
4 small bay leaves
Butter

1 Rinse the saltfish in cold water and put into a saucepan with cold water, bring to the boil and simmer covered for 15–20 minutes, then pat thoroughly dry.
2 Meanwhile, dry and grill the smoked herrings for about 3 minutes on each side, then allow to cool.
3 Remove skin and bones; if there are roes, retain with the meat.
4 Put the skins and bones into a saucepan with a little water and bring to the boil, cover and simmer for about 5 minutes, then press through a fine sieve into a bowl.
5 Now skin and bone the saltfish.
6 Moisten the breadcrumbs in the smoked herring liquid.
7 Now pass all the ingredients, except the bay leaves and butter, through a food processor (or Mouli) and taste for seasoning, then mix well with a fork.
8 Grease an ovenware baking dish with some butter and lay the bay leaves on the bottom, then pack the mixture into the dish.
9 Cover with foil and bake in a pre-heated oven 190°C (375°F/ Gas 5) for about 35–40 minutes.
10 Remove from the oven but do not remove the foil until quite cold, then pour some melted butter over the dish and refrigerate before serving.

Serves 4–6

HARENG SAUR AUX TOMATES

SMOKED HERRING AND TOMATO SALAD

French and Patois speaking Islands

3–4 smoked herrings (kippers, bloaters or kippered mackerel can be used)
675g (1½ lb) tomatoes, neatly sliced
1 small hot pepper, seeded and chopped (*see* Techniques)
1 tablespoon parsley, freshly chopped
1 onion, in fine half rings
3 tablespoons olive oil
Juice 1½ limes or lemons
Black pepper
1 clove garlic, crushed
Salt (just a little to taste)

1 Thoroughly dry and grill the herrings for about 4 minutes either side (delicious done over wood or charcoal).
2 Remove the skin and bones.
3 If there are any roes, save for the salad.
4 Shred the herrings and put into a salad bowl with the sliced tomatoes, chopped hot pepper, parsley and onion.
5 Make a dressing with the oil, citrus juice, black pepper, garlic, with salt to taste and pour over the herrings and tomatoes.
6 Toss gently and serve, garnished with tomatoes.

Serves 4–6

If serving as a main meal, accompany with Farinade de Zavoca (an avocado and farine mix), over which a Creole fish sauce is poured.

This is ideal as a weekend or holiday breakfast with hot bread or toast.

ESCOVITCH

SOUSED FISH

Jamaica

This is a development of the classic Spanish dish called Escabeche.

2 sweet peppers – 1 red, 1 green
1 teaspoon hot pepper, seeded and chopped (*see* Techniques)
2 bay leaves
3 onions, sliced in thin half rings
1–1½ tablespoons sea salt
2 cloves garlic, thinly sliced
6 blades chives, tied together
Black pepper, freshly ground
300ml (½ pint) water
150ml (¼ pint) vinegar (preferably white)
75ml (3 fl ozs) olive oil
1.25kg (2½ lb) red snapper, filleted
Juice of 1 lime

1 Put the sweet peppers, hot pepper, bay leaves, onions, salt, garlic, the bunch of chives and a little black pepper into a pot.

2 Pour in the water, vinegar and 3 tablespoons of oil, and bring to the boil.
3 Turn down the heat, cover and simmer gently until the vegetables are tender but still fairly firm.
4 In the meantime, pour the rest of the oil into a heavy frying pan and when hot fry the fish, a fillet or two at a time, until lightly brown on both sides.
5 Place the fried fillets into a large serving dish with some depth and pour the hot vinegar mixture over the fish.
6 Discard the bay leaves and chives and add the lime juice.
7 Serve hot or refrigerate to serve cold.

This is also excellent as a main dish.

Serves 6

SOUSE

English speaking Islands

This dish is indispensable to our cuisine and forms part of a Sunday morning ritual, either for a breakfast or brunch. It is served accompanied by many other wonderfully mouth-watering, spicy and colourful delicacies; black pudding being one of the most important. Followed by stuffed crab backs, saltfish and smoked herrings with tomatoes, cucumber salads, and various other dishes including fried ripe plantain. And a continuous flow of gin and coconut water, rum and coke, and lots of rum punches.

Half a pig's head
4 pigs' trotters
Salt to taste
170ml (6 fl oz) lime juice
2 hot peppers, seeded and chopped (*see* Techniques)
4 tablespoons chives, finely chopped (or 2 medium onions grated)
2 tablespoons fresh parsley, chopped
2 cucumbers, peeled and cut into fine rounds
Watercress for garnish (optional)
1 sweet pepper, seeded and finely sliced

1 Get the butcher to clean and cut up the pig's head, and cut the trotters into 5 cm (2 inch) pieces.

2 Wash the meats a few times in cold water.
3 Place in a large pot with enough cold water to cover, with salt and half the lime juice.
4 Bring to the boil, lower the heat and simmer until the meats are tender. Do not allow to overcook. The meats must remain fairly firm and not fall apart.
5 Continually skim off any scum that forms.
6 When the meats are tender, drain and discard the liquid.
7 Wash the meats immediately under cold running water: this helps get rid of any excess fat and scum.
8 Remove all the meat and skin from the head and cut up into 2.5 cm (1 inch) pieces.
9 Place the meats into a bowl together with the remaining lime juice, salt to taste, ½ of one of the hot peppers and about 5 tablespoons of warm water.
10 Cover and leave in a refrigerator or a very cool place for at least 3 hours. Turn the meat pieces a few times in the bowl.
11 When ready for use drain and discard the liquid.
12 Place the meats into a serving bowl and add the rest of the hot pepper, onions or chives, salt to taste, a little chopped garlic if you wish, parsley and ½ the cucumber.
13 Mix well and taste for seasoning.
14 Allow to stand for a few minutes.
15 Garnish with watercress, the remainder of the cucumber, and the sweet pepper.

Hot buttered bread is excellent with this dish; and obviously the Black Pudding and all else that goes with it.

Souse can be prepared with the trotters only. But try to get trotters with a good deal of meat on them.

Serves 8–10

BOUDAINE

BOUDIN

BLACK PUDDING

English, French and Patois speaking countries

This uniquely Creole fresh sausage is essential at weekends, on feast days and at Carnival time.

450g (1 lb) pig's entrails (chitterlings – i.e. intestine)
225g (½ lb) lard

450g (1 lb) onions, finely chopped
3 cloves garlic, finely chopped
1 or 2 hot peppers (*see* Techniques)
2 heaped teaspoons fresh thyme
2 bunches chives, finely chopped
2 litres (3½ pints) pig's blood
3 tablespoons rum
5 bread rolls, soaked, squeezed dry, then broken down (you may use more)
2½ tablespoons salt

You will also need
A medium sized funnel
Kitchen string
Banana leaves or strong brown paper
A *large* pot, preferably cast aluminium or iron

1 Using the handle of a wooden spoon, carefully turn the chitterlings inside out and wash them very thoroughly under cold running water – then turn them right side out again.
2 In your big pot, melt the lard and quickly sauté the onions, garlic, hot peppers, thyme and chives for no more than 3 minutes, mixing well.
3 Remove from the heat and allow to go completely cold.
4 Now put the contents of the pot into a large bowl with the blood, rum, bread and salt and stir to blend all together very well.
5 Bearing in mind that the chitterling will contract in length when filled with the mixture, cut off a sufficient length of unbroken entrail that will coil in the pot. Tie this at one end.
6 Insert your funnel at the open end of the intestine and pack the mixture in but not too tightly, since the pudding will expand during the cooking. Bursting is a disaster to be avoided.
7 You may make more than one pudding at a time by twisting and tying the chitterling at convenient lengths to make smaller sausages or *boudins*. Allow 2.5 to 5cm (1 to 2 inches) for tying and cutting. Do not make your ties too tight, to avoid the tearing of the chitterling.
8 Line the pot with banana leaf or brown paper. The metal

must be well covered, for should the pudding touch the bare pot during the cooking, it will burst.

9 Fill the pot with cold lightly salted water, being careful not to break or shift the lining, and place over a medium heat.

10 When the water is just warm, carefully introduce the pudding to the pot by sliding it in and coiling it comfortably.

11 Simmer at a very low heat until the pudding becomes sufficiently swollen and is quite firm. Test by lightly pricking with a needle or pin to see if the juices rise in bubbles to the surface.

12 Serve whilst still fairly hot. However, Black Pudding is often eaten cold – but it is unwise to keep it for longer than a day.

So be prepared to entertain or to give several of your batch to friends. This is what happens before Carnival when people are busy making costumes or *working mas'*.

This recipe is derived from one given to me by my friend Errol Romilly, who is an esteemed costume designer, or *mas'man*, for the annual Notting Hill Carnival.

ACCRA 1

Trinidad, Grenada, St Vincent, Dominica

340g (¾ lb) saltfish, soaked overnight or for at least 8 hours
140g (5 oz) plain flour sifted with 1 teaspoon baking powder
1½ tablespoons chives, finely chopped
1 onion, finely chopped
Black pepper
2 teaspoons hot peppers, seeded and chopped (*see* Techniques)
Salt to taste
2 cloves garlic, finely chopped
1 teaspoon curry powder (optional)
85ml (3 fl oz) water
Oil for frying

1 Have ready a large platter lined with paper towels.

2 Bring some water to the boil in a saucepan or pot, drop in the soaked saltfish, turn off the heat and leave to cool.

3 Rinse the fish under cold water; skin, bone and shred it into fine pieces.

4 In a bowl mix the fish with the sifted flour, chives, onion,

pepper, hot pepper, salt, garlic and curry powder; then slowly add water to form a thick paste.

5 Heat the oil in a large frying pan, drop the paste by the tablespoon into the oil and fry until golden brown.
6 As you take each Accra out of the oil, drain separately on the paper towels.

Ideal for snacks at parties, for breakfast or as an hors d'oeuvre, eaten with Floats (see p. 245).

In Grenada Accra is sometimes flattened in the pan with a wooden spatula when turning brown.

An equivalent dish from Jamaica is called Stamp and Go.

Makes about 20

ACCRA 2

This is the original African version of the dish of the same name that has been developed, principally in Trinidad, into one of the classics of Caribbean cuisine.

225g (½ lb) black-eyed peas, soaked overnight
½ hot pepper, seeded and finely chopped (*see* Techniques)
1 egg (optional) well beaten
Salt to taste
Black pepper, freshly ground
1 tablespoon corn flour
Oil for frying

1 Having soaked the peas overnight, drain them and drop into a saucepan of fast-boiling water – leave for about 2 minutes.
2 Drain them again, and when cool, remove and discard the skins, then rinse under cold water.
3 Either pound the peas together with the hot pepper in a mortar and pestle, or pass through a blender or mouli, using a fine blade.
4 Now mix the ground peas, using a wooden fork or spoon, with the egg, salt and black pepper.
5 Sprinkle in the corn flour, a little at a time, and continue to beat until the mixture is fluffy and the quantity has almost doubled.
6 Heat the oil and fry by the tablespoonful until golden brown.
7 Drain off excess oil on paper towels.

8 Best served very hot, neatly arranged on a large dish or banana leaf (*see* Appendix).

Serves 4, about 5 Accra per person

AUBERGINE ACCRA

ACCRA d'AUBERGINE

French and Patois speaking Islands

6 medium sized aubergines, preferably of the Chinese kind
2 eggs
110g (4 oz) plain flour
½ teaspoon baking powder
Salt to taste (fine salt)
2 tablespoons milk or water
1 tablespoon chives, finely chopped, or spring onions
Black pepper
½ teaspoon hot peppers, seeded and chopped (*see* Techniques)
1 clove garlic, chopped
Oil for frying

1. Peel and wash the aubergines, rubbing them with lemon or lime to prevent discolouring. Cut into pieces.
2. Bring a saucepan of water to the boil, drop in the aubergine pieces and simmer for 8–10 minutes.
3. Drain thoroughly, then pass the aubergines through a fine sieve into a mixing bowl.
4. Beat the eggs and blend them with the aubergine purée.
5. Sift the flour, baking powder and salt, and pour into the aubergine mixture, a little at a time, mixing well.
6. Add the milk or water in the same manner.
7. Mix in all the other ingredients.
8. Taste for seasoning.
9. Heat the oil in a heavy frying pan. Cook the mixture by dropping into the oil by the tablespoonful and frying until golden brown on all sides.
10. Drain on kitchen paper.

Serves 4, about 5 Accra per person

AVOCADO DIABLO

One of my own recipes, created for the restaurant called Le Caraïbe

275g (10 oz) saltfish, soaked for at least 8 hours
1 tablespoon oil
1 tablespoon butter
2 small onions, neatly chopped
3 cloves garlic, crushed
1 tablespoon tomato purée
½ teaspoon sugar
Black pepper
3 tablespoons coriander leaves, chopped (if unavailable use parsley but do try to find coriander)
Salt to taste
½ red hot pepper, seeded and chopped (*see* Techniques)
110g (4 oz) peeled prawns (optional)
1 green sweet pepper, evenly chopped
2 tomatoes, peeled and evenly chopped
2 tablespoons lime juice
4 ripe avocadoes
Lettuce leaves
Parsley to garnish
Lime wedges

1. Boil the saltfish for 20 minutes, then remove any skin and bones, and cut into small cubes and set aside.
2. Heat the oil and butter in a shallow pan and sauté the onions for about 2–3 minutes.
3. Add the garlic, tomato purée, sugar, black pepper, coriander leaves, a little salt and the hot pepper and simmer slightly uncovered for 3–4 minutes.
4. Now add the saltfish, prawns, sweet pepper, tomatoes and lime juice; mix in well but avoid breaking up the saltfish and vegetables.
5. Simmer uncovered until any liquid has reduced by half.
6. Arrange the lettuce leaves on individual dishes and cut the avocadoes in half lengthways, removing the stones.
7. Taste the mixture for seasoning, season if necessary but do not cook too long – 2 minutes more at the most.
8. Fill the avocado halves with the mixture, hot from the pan, place on the lettuce leaves, garnish with parsley and serve immediately with a wedge of lime on each.

This can also be served as a main course. Arrange each half of stuffed avocado in the centre of a warm plate, surrounded by seasoned rice. Garnish each with about four crayfish or a few prawns. Any of the left-over filling can be served on the rice, arranged carefully.

Serves 8

BAKED AVOCADOES WITH BACON AND CRAYFISH

Eastern Caribbean

2 ripe avocadoes about 225g–275g (8–10 oz) each
1 small onion, finely chopped
50g (2 oz) butter
6 rashers of lean bacon, minced or chopped finely
2 teaspoons lime juice
Black pepper, freshly ground
110g (4 oz) crayfish or prawns
Salt to taste
4 lime wedges

1 Halve the avocadoes, remove the stones, scoop out the flesh from the skins, and set both aside.
2 In a small pan sauté the onion in the butter until soft but not brown, add the minced bacon and continue to agitate for about 5 minutes.
3 Remove from heat and cool.
4 Meanwhile press the avocado flesh through a sieve, and in a bowl mix the avocado pulp, lime juice, black pepper and crayfish.
5 Fold in the bacon and onions – mix well, then taste for seasoning.
6 Fill the avocado shells with the mixture.
7 Wrap some foil around each shell for protection but do not cover the stuffing.
8 Bake in a pre-heated oven 200°C (400°F/Gas 6) for about 15–20 minutes.
9 Serve immediately, without the foil of course, and garnish with the lime wedges.

Serves 4

SOUPE AUX POISSONS

FISH SOUP

French speaking Islands

Fish soup is very popular on most islands but more so on the French speaking ones, perhaps because of the tradition of Bouillabaisse. Use the heads of any fish properly cleaned, and make sure the gills etc., are removed – the heads make the best base for a delectable soup.

900g (2 lb) good fish heads & tails
3 tablespoons butter
2 onions, finely chopped
450g (1 lb) tomatoes, peeled, seeded and chopped
3 cloves garlic, finely chopped
4 cloves
2.2 litres (4 pints) water
675g (1½ lb) boneless white fish
2 bay leaves
450g (1 lb) tannias, peeled, washed and cut into pieces
½ teaspoon allspice
2 sprigs parsley, chopped
1 tablespoon chopped chives or spring onions
Small piece of crushed ginger
Juice 1–2 limes or lemons
2 hot peppers, left whole

1 Wash and clean the fish heads and put into a pot with enough water to cover, then bring to the boil.
2 Reduce heat and simmer gently for 15 minutes.
3 Meanwhile melt the butter in a large pot and sauté the onions until transparent but not brown.
4 Add the tomatoes, garlic and cloves and fry for 2 minutes.
5 Pour in the water and add all the other ingredients, except the whole peppers.
6 Bring to the boil, reduce the heat and introduce the liquid from the fish heads with a wooden spoon.
7 Now press out all you can through a sieve from the fish heads and tails.
8 Discard heads and tails.
9 Add the 2 whole peppers and continue to simmer, slightly covered, for about 45 minutes.

10 Taste for salt and seasoning.
11 Turn off heat.
12 Remove the whole peppers without breaking them, search out and set aside any pieces of fish.
13 Now either press the soup through a sieve or liquidize it.
14 Return the pieces of fish to the pot, heat again and serve. Or you can serve the soup with all its bits and pieces – no sieving, no liquidizing – served as it would be served by the country people. It is possibly the best and most classic method.
15 The two whole peppers can be chopped and served on a separate plate.

AVOCADO AND CRAB SOUP

Martinique

2 tablespoons butter
2 medium sized onions, finely chopped
2 cloves garlic, finely chopped
1.1 litres (2 pints) chicken stock
110g (4 oz) ham, minced or finely chopped
½ teaspoon hot pepper, seeded and chopped (*see* Techniques)
Salt to taste
1½ tablespoons flour, made into a paste with a little water
4 ripe small avocadoes
White peppercorns, freshly ground
340g (¾ lb) crab meat
600ml (1 pint) double cream

1 In a heavy pot melt the butter and sauté the onions and garlic until the onions are transparent but not brown.
2 Add the chicken stock, the minced ham, hot pepper and very little salt.
3 Bring to the boil, turn down the heat, thicken with the flour paste and simmer, covered.
4 Meanwhile peel and stone the avocadoes and press the flesh through a sieve.
5 Now add the avocado pulp, pepper and crab meat to the stock, and simmer covered for 10 minutes.
6 Taste for salt and seasoning, add the cream and simmer,

stirring frequently, for about 6–8 minutes or until it is hot right through.

7 Serve hot with buttered toast.

Serves 6–8

CALLALOO SOUP

TARO LEAF SOUP

Eastern Caribbean

Possibly the most famous and most popular of soups throughout the English, French and Patois speaking Islands. There are many versions using crabs and various meats and vegetables. But the following I believe is one of the best.

2 whole crabs, cleaned
2–4 crab claws
225g (½ lb) salt pork, cut into small cubes and soaked for a few hours
½ teaspoon cloves, freshly ground
1.6 litres (3 pints) chicken stock (or 3 bouillon cubes in same quantity of water)
1.25kg (2½ lb) taro leaves*
225g (½ lb) okras, topped and chopped
2 onions, chopped
3 cloves garlic
½–1 hot pepper, seeded and chopped (*see* Techniques)
2 teaspoons fresh thyme
1 sprig parsley
300ml (½ pint) coconut milk (if using creamed coconut from a packet do not use more than one third)
Black pepper, freshly ground
Salt, if necessary, to taste

1 If using fresh crabs, boil, clean and reserve all the white and brown parts and the legs.

* Nowadays these leaves are more readily available from the major open markets, so that substitutes such as spinach need no longer be used. However there is a variety of spinach, known in Spanish as *Acelzas*, which grows throughout the Caribbean, which is confused with true Callaloo, particularly in Jamaica. This, elsewhere in the Caribbean, is known by the Patois name of *Zépina*. It is exported, in cans, to this country and makes an agreeable related dish. Use the leaves of the taro family if you want to sample the best version of this great soup.

2 Crack the claws but leave as whole as possible.
3 Wash the cubed pork and bring to the boil in a large heavy pot together with the cloves, using the chicken stock, and simmer until the pork is tender, then drain and reserve the pork and the stock.
4 Chop and wash the taro leaves or spinach and place the leaves in the pot with the reserved stock, okras, onions, garlic, hot pepper, thyme and parsley.
5 Bring quickly to the boil, lower the heat and simmer covered for about 8 minutes, then cool slightly and liquidize.
6 Return to the heat and bring slowly to the boil.
7 Add the pork, crab and coconut milk, then season with black pepper.
8 Taste for salt and add if needed.
9 Lower the heat and simmer for about 12–15 minutes and serve piping hot.

As a main course, Callaloo is best served with boiled green bananas or plantain.

Serves 6–8

BREADFRUIT VICHYSSOISE

French and Patois speaking Islands

50g (2 oz) butter
2 medium onions, chopped
225g (½ lb) breadfruit, fresh, peeled and diced into small pieces (or canned)
1 clove garlic, finely chopped
900ml (1½ pints) chicken stock (2 bouillon cubes)
¼ teaspoon hot peppers, seeded and chopped (*see* Techniques)
300ml (½ pint) single cream
Salt to taste
White pepper, freshly ground
1 tablespoon chives, chopped

1 Melt the butter in a large heavy pot and sauté the onions until transparent but not brown.
2 Add all the ingredients except the cream and chives. If using bouillon cubes instead of chicken stock, you will need very little salt.

3 Bring to the boil, reduce the heat and simmer covered until the breadfruit is tender, then allow to cool.
4 Put into a blender and process until smooth and creamy – add the cream and continue to blend.
5 Taste for salt and pepper.
6 Refrigerate.
7 Serve chilled, garnished with chopped chives.

Serves 6

BEEF AND VEGETABLE SOUP

Most Islands

675g (1½ lb) stewing beef, cut into cubes
1.75 litres (3 pints) chicken or ham stock (or 2 bouillon cubes)
1 small hot pepper, seeded and chopped (*see* Techniques)
6 cloves, whole
1 sprig thyme
1 sprig parsley
2 bay leaves
Salt to taste
Juice 1 lemon or lime
2 onions, chopped
2 tannias, peeled
1 small dasheen } washed and rubbed with lime
1 small piece of yam } or lemon and cubed
1 sweet potato
2 carrots, scraped and diced
2 tablespoons olive oil
110g (4 oz) chopped cabbage

1 Place the meat in a large pot with the stock, bring to the boil and simmer for about ½ hour.
2 Skim off any scum that forms and add all the spices, herbs, hot pepper, juice and salt, then simmer, covered, for a further 1½ hours.
3 Now add the oil and all the vegetables except the cabbage, and simmer for 20–30 minutes.
4 Taste for seasoning, add cabbage.
5 Cook for 10 minutes more.
6 Remove the bay leaves and serve.

This soup may be served as a main meal, as with several Caribbean dishes of this kind.

Serves 6 or more

PUMPKIN SOUP

Eastern Caribbean

225g (½ lb) pigs' tails or salt pork, soaked overnight
1.1 litres (2 pints) chicken stock
450g (1 lb) pumpkin, peeled, seeded and chopped
2 medium sized onions, finely chopped
2 cloves garlic, finely chopped
1 bay leaf
Black pepper
Salt to taste

1. Cut the meat into small pieces or sections.
2. In half of the amount of stock, bring the meat to the boil, then reduce the heat and simmer until it is tender.
3. Remove the meat from the liquid and set aside.
4. Add the pumpkin to the stock with the onions, garlic and bay leaf and simmer, covered, until tender.
5. Remove from the heat, discard the bay leaf, and pass the soup through a sieve.
6. Return the pot to the stove, adding the remainder of the stock, the cooked meat and pepper.
7. Reheat and simmer, covered, for 10–12 minutes.
8. Taste for salt and serve.

Serves 4–6

RED BEAN SOUP

French and Patois speaking Islands

This is typical of the many soups which, in the Caribbean, often constitute a main meal.

450g (1 lb) red beans, soaked overnight (see notes on technique)
1.75 litres (3 pints) water
170g (6 oz) pigs' tails or salt pork, cubed (*see* Techniques)
1 onion, finely chopped
2 sprigs thyme, tied together

2 sprigs parsley, finely chopped
½ teaspoon ground cloves
Black pepper, freshly ground
¼ hot pepper, chopped (*see* Techniques)
2 chicken bouillon cubes
A few small plain flour dumplings (p. 247)
Salt to taste (beans need a fair amount of salt, but only after they have been cooked)
2 tablespoons oil

1. Wash the red beans and bring to the boil in enough water to cover, then continue to boil rapidly uncovered for 10 minutes.
2. Reduce heat, cover and simmer gently until beans are tender but still whole. Be prepared to add more water.
3. Meanwhile thoroughly wash the pork about 2 or 3 times, then bring to the boil in the water in a large heavy pot with the onion, thyme, parsley, cloves, black pepper and hot pepper.
4. Reduce heat and simmer slowly.
5. When the beans are tender, pour them into the pot with the pork and spices, add the bouillon cubes and the dumplings and continue to simmer, covered, until the pork is tender and the beans are completely cooked and almost falling apart.
6. Taste for seasoning, add the oil, and serve hot with pepper sauce or relish.

Serves 6–8

TANNIA SOUP

English speaking Islands

225g (½ lb) lean beef, cut into small cubes
110g (4 oz) salt pork or beef
1.4 litres (2½ pints) water
900g (2 lb) tannias, peeled, cut into pieces
1 onion, finely chopped
2 tablespoons butter
2 cloves garlic
1 sprig thyme
1 tablespoon parsley, finely chopped
Black pepper, freshly ground
Salt to taste

2 tablespoons chives, chopped
1 sprig parsley

1 Place the meats in a large pot with the water and bring to the boil.
2 Lower the heat, simmer covered for about 20 minutes and skim off any scum that may form on the surface.
3 Add the tannia and all other ingredients except for the chives and parsley.
4 Continue to simmer until meats and tannia are tender.
5 Remove the meats and set aside.
6 Liquidize.
7 Return to heat with meats.
8 Taste for seasoning.
9 Serve sprinkled with chives and parsley.

Serves 6

CHILLED AVOCADO SOUP

Of Hispanic origin

75g (3 oz) butter
1 onion, finely chopped or grated
1 clove garlic, very finely chopped
600ml (1 pint) stock, chicken or ham (you may happen to have one of either)
2 teaspoons flour mixed with 2 tablespoons cold stock
3–4 ripe small avocadoes, weighing 225–275g (8–10 oz) each
1 tablespoon lemon juice
White pepper, freshly ground
Salt to taste
600ml (1 pint) single cream
1½ tablespoons chopped chives or spring onions for garnishing

1 Melt the butter in a pot, sauté the onion and garlic until soft but not browned.
2 Add the stock, bring to the boil, thicken with the flour paste and simmer, covered, for about 6 minutes.
3 Peel and stone the avocadoes and press through a sieve.
4 Stir the lemon juice in to the avocado paste.
5 Add all ingredients to the simmering stock, except the cream and chives, and simmer for a further 5 minutes.

6 Taste for seasoning and stir in the cream.
7 Remove from heat, allow to cool and refrigerate until well chilled.
8 Serve garnished with chives or finely chopped spring onions.

Serves 4

CREAM OF WATERCRESS SOUP

Dominica

Watercress grows like a weed along the slow-flowing streams of some of the islands. Especially Dominica with its streams and rivers, as many as there are days in the year.

3 tablespoons plain flour
5 bunches watercress
2 tablespoons butter
1 onion, finely chopped
450ml (¾ pint) coconut milk
600ml (1 pint) chicken stock (2 bouillon cubes)
½ teaspoon hot peppers, seeded and chopped
½ teaspoon nutmeg, freshly grated
Black pepper
Salt to taste
170ml (6 fl oz) double cream
1 tablespoon chives for garnish

1 Make the flour into a paste with some stock.
2 Wash and clean the watercress, discarding yellow leaves if there are any, and chop finely with a sharp knife.
3 In a large pot sauté the onion in the melted butter, add the watercress and stir until the watercress is slightly limp.
4 Mix in the coconut milk, bring to the boil, turn down the heat and thicken with the flour paste, then simmer covered for about 3 minutes.
5 Now add the stock with all the other ingredients except the cream and chives and simmer, covered, for a further 3 minutes, tasting for seasoning.
6 Allow to cool slightly.
7 Liquidize or pass through a fine sieve.
8 Return to the stove and bring once more to the boil.
9 Reduce the heat and check once again for seasoning.

10 Stir in the cream.
11 Serve garnished with the chopped chives.

Serves 4–6

CUCUMBER AND COCONUT CREAM SOUP

Possibly of African origin

1½ large cucumbers, peeled and grated
425ml (¾ pint) thick coconut cream
1 onion, finely chopped
700ml (1¼ pints) rich chicken or ham stock
55g (2 oz) butter
Black pepper (always try to use freshly ground)
Salt to taste
1 teaspoon fresh fennel leaves, chopped
½ wineglass of sherry
½ green hot pepper, seeded and chopped
1 tablespoon chopped chives (optional)

1. Place the grated cucumber in a pot with the coconut cream, onion, stock, butter, black pepper and salt; simmer gently for 20 minutes.
2. Remove from heat, allow to cool and pass through a sieve, liquidizer or food processor.
3. Return to the heat, add the fennel and sherry and thicken if necessary. Simmer for 6-8 minutes.
4. Taste for seasoning.
5. Pour into a soup tureen, sprinkle with the hot pepper, also the chives if you wish.

Serves 4–6

SOUPE A L'ORANGE

Dominica

This is popular on many of the Islands, but I give here a version of my own.

750ml (1¼ pint) chicken stock
Peel of 1 orange, chopped
5 cloves
Salt, just to taste
2 small sticks cinnamon

600ml (1 pint) freshly squeezed orange juice
4 thin unpeeled orange slices, for garnish

1. Bring the chicken stock to the boil, add the orange peel, cloves, a pince of salt and cinnamon, then simmer for 10 minutes to extract the flavours.
2. Add the orange juice and quickly bring back to the boil.
3. Lower the heat to the minimum and simmer for 5 minutes.
4. Remove from heat and allow to cool completely.
5. Strain through a fine damp cloth.
6. Discard the spices.
7. Refrigerate until quite cold.
8. Serve with a slice of orange in each bowl.

Serves 4

As far away from Dominica as Haiti and Grenada, this recipe is used with powdered gelatine, employed after step 6. This tends to clarify the orange content – thus it is known in those countries as a Consommé.

Fish

I think I could happily live on fish alone. I do like meat, especially pork, but to me there's nothing in this world to compare with freshly caught fish – fresh tuna steak in a court bouillon; just-caught red snapper grilled over charcoal, with just a little salt and lime juice.

In the Caribbean we almost always use lime or lemon when cooking fish. And many of our fish dishes call for marinades – a piece of tuna, swordfish, a few flying fishes or any fish big or small, left to season-up in a lime marinade with spices; then fried and eaten with hot buttered bread and tomato salad.

There are very few tropical fish that are not delicious no matter what cooking method is used – plain boiled, smoked, or poached in an aromatic hot and spicy 'braff' with lots of fresh lime and hot peppers. The waters of the Caribbean are rich in marine life, and some of the most succulent and delicious seafood is caught in those waters – jack-fish, grey mullets, red, pink or white snappers, groupers, kingfisher, eels, lobsters, crabs, dolphin (no relation to the true dolphin or porpoise, which is a mammal) and many, many more besides.

Unfortunately there is no major fishing industry, especially on the smaller islands, and the fishermen, except for a few with outboard motors, still fish in small dug-out canoes the way they learnt from the Carib Indians, or according to the custom they brought with them from the coast of West Africa. During my childhood on Dominica, and up to the early sixties, there was no such thing as imported frozen tuna – alas, today that is what helps supplement the meagre catch of the islands. Still, we have our limes, hot chillis and spices. *Merci Bondieu!* (Thanks be to God!)

It is now possible to buy flying fish, red snappers, groupers and tuna plus many others from markets like Brixton, Balham and Shepherds Bush and a few selected fishmongers. To be honest, there is really no substitute for fish like tuna, dorado, bonito, red snapper, but after years of cooking in England I would suggest that you use any firm white fish of your choice. Discuss your purchases with the salesman.

See Appendix for further information.

The following is a list of fresh fish flown into Britain on ice from the tropical Seychelles, with information where given provided by the suppliers. Most of the fish listed are also caught and used in the Caribbean though some might be recognized under another name. These fish are spectacular in colour, delicious to eat, and the quality is marvellous.

Yellow Fin Tuna *see* **Kingfisher**

Vieille Maconde: A small grouper, well known in Hong Kong, excellent for steaming and baking, and available in portion sizes of about 2 lb. Considered superior to common sea bass in flavour.

Vieille Rouge: A brilliant red grouper, as the creole name suggests, rivals bourgeois and croissant in this respect. Available usually at about 2 to 3 lb. Similar to vieille maconde.

Bonito

Bourgeois: One of the finest of food fishes, with white succulent flesh and good keeping qualities, these are generally large fish from 5 to 12 lb.

Capitaine Rouge: An excellent eating fish with flesh similar to sea bream. Ideal for grilling, baking and steaming. With weights of about 3 to 10 lbs these fish are also ideal for steaks.

Croissant: Known as coral trout in Australia, the creole name comes from the crescent tail of this brilliantly coloured fish, usually weighing from 2 to 5 lb. The sweet white flesh is excellent for baking, grilling or serving cold.

Job Griz

Vara Vara: A fish with brilliant colours and good keeping qualities, in a range of sizes usually from 1 to 4 lb. The smaller ones are ideal for baking or grilling, the large ones, with firm white flesh, are suitable for seafood cocktails, ceviche (Escovitch; pickled fish) and daubes (fish casserole).

Parrotfishes: (scarids, going under the creole name of cacatois). A range of very brightly coloured fish usually from 1 to 3 lb. The flesh of these fish is very delicate, soft and white. Excellent for frying, steaming, fish cakes and pâté. USE QUICKLY, as these fish do not have good keeping properties.

Job Jaune: A deep water snapper with a similar flesh to sea bass, usually about 4 to 6 lb. Excellent cold with salads or in fish soups.

Rabbitfishes: (siganids, in creole cordonnier). Small grey fish of unassuming appearance, but very much appreciated in Hong Kong, the Far East, Eastern Greece and Cyprus. Usually about ½ lb size or slightly larger, making them excellent for frying, grilling or steaming and also in soups.

Lascar
Gueule Longue } All bream family
Madame Berrie

Vielle Platte

Capitaine Blanc

Golden Mullet: (mullids, in creole known as rouget barbes, despite the most common one being yellow). Can be used in all the ways that red mullet is utilized. Usually about 1 lb in weight.

Becune (Barracuda)

True Snappers: (lutjanids, going under the common creole names of bourgeois, therese, job jaune, bordemar and vara vara).

Therese: Similar to bourgeois, but a smaller fish about 1 to 2 lb, with a very delicate flesh, excellent for grilling.

Bordemar: Rivals bourgeois with its brilliant colours and also in size, with weights up to 10 lb. This makes them suitable for steaks and serving cold with mayonnaise.

Sea Bass (serranids: going under the common creole names of croissant, vieille rouge, vieille maconde, also known as groupers).

Emperor Bream: (lethrinids, going under the common creole name of capitaine rouge).

King Carangue: (carangids, in creole carangue). Large fish, generally from 4 to 15 lb related to the crevally and trevally. The flesh is firm with a light taste, ideal for cutting into steaks or other portions, and then grilling or baking. Also excellent for curries, where the flesh is not to be flaked, and can be used in Japanese raw fish dishes. The related yellowtail is also available with weights up to 20 or 30 lb, and similar cooking options.

Kingfisher, Yellow Fin Tuna, Bonito, Wahoo and Sailfish: (scombrids and billfish). All large fish with weights of about 5 lb (bonito) to at least 50 lb (sailfish). All have firm flesh, and are ideal for cutting into steaks or other portions, to be grilled, baked or served cold and for raw Japanese fish dishes. The flesh of tuna and bonito is darker and meatier than the others.

FISH STOCK

900g (2 lb) any inexpensive white fish
1 medium size onion
1 leek
2 sprigs thyme
1 celery stalk
4 sprigs parsley
Juice ½ lime or lemon
1 whole chilli pepper, cooked whole without bursting (*see* Techniques)
Very little salt
1 bay leaf
1 glass white wine (optional)
2 pints water

1. Wash the fish and place all ingredients into a pot.
2. Bring to the boil, then simmer gently for 30 minutes on a low heat, skimming off the foam.
3. Allow stock to cool and remove the chilli pepper.
4. Strain through a cheesecloth placed over a strainer, squeezing the fish pieces with a wooden spoon.
5. Repeat stage 4.
6. Refrigerate.

ACKEE AND SALTFISH

This is certainly becoming known around the world as Jamaica's national dish. Ackee was introduced from West Africa by Captain Bligh of the infamous *Bounty*. Unfortunately it is generally available only in cans outside the Caribbean.

450g (1 lb) salted cod, soaked for at least 8 hours
2 tablespoons oil
75–110g (3–4 oz) lean salt pork, well washed, dried and finely diced
1 large onion, finely chopped
2 cloves garlic, finely chopped
3 tomatoes, blanched, peeled and chopped
½ teaspoon hot pepper, seeded and chopped (*see* Techniques)
½ teaspoon fresh thyme
Black pepper, freshly ground

Salt to taste
1 can, 450g (1 lb) unbroken ackee

1 Put the saltfish into fresh cold water and boil it until tender.
2 Now drain the fish thoroughly, then skin, bone and flake it.
3 Heat the oil in a heavy frying pan and fry the salt pork until just brown, reduce the heat and add the onion and garlic, then sauté until the onions are translucent but not brown.
4 Add the tomatoes, herbs and spices, then sauté further for a minute or two.
5 Now add the saltfish, having thoroughly patted it dry, and the ackee, thoroughly drained and cook for a few minutes until these cold ingredients are heated through.
6 Taste for salt and seasoning.
7 Serve hot, with boiled green bananas, green plantain or breadfruit.

Serves 4–6

SANCOCHE

SALTFISH IN COCONUT MILK

Dominica

I grew up with the belief that the only Sancoche was salted cod cooked with coconut milk. It was not until years later when I returned from England, to travel around the Caribbean, that I discovered how many different Sancoches there are. French, Spanish and English speaking islands all have their own versions. Trinidad Sancoche is prepared with various meats and vegetables and little coconut milk, whilst the Sancoch*o* of the Dominican Republic is either made with pork and sausages or oxtail, both again with various vegetables. But here is one that I grew up with on the island of Dominica and which still today remains one of my favourites.

3 tablespoons oil
2 medium onions, cut into half rings
3 cloves garlic, crushed
1 tablespoon chives, chopped
6 cloves, whole
2 sprigs parsley
1 sprig thyme

Juice ½ lime or lemon
2 tomatoes, peeled and chopped, or a small tin of plum tomatoes
450ml (¾ pint) coconut milk (made from one fresh coconut or ⅓ of a packet of coconut cream)
1 chicken bouillon cube
1 *whole* hot pepper, unpunctured
1.25kg (2½ lb) salted cod (soaked overnight, parboiled, skinned and boned

1. Sauté the onions and garlic in the oil in a pot until the onions are soft and transparent.
2. Add all other ingredients except the salted cod. Place the hot pepper carefully in the pot so that it will not burst – it should be neither at the edge nor in the centre.
3. Bring to the boil and simmer for 15 minutes.
4. Stir and add the skinned and boned saltfish, then simmer for 20 minutes.
5. Taste for salt.
6. Serve with creamed breadfruit and red beans, or plain boiled rice and red beans, or mixed vegetables and red beans. The hot pepper can be served on the side, but it must be removed from the pot absolutely intact.

Serves 4–6

SALTFISH IN TOMATO SAUCE

675g (1½ lb) salt cod, soaked for at least 8 hours
1 tablespoon lemon juice
2 tablespoons vegetable oil
2 tablespoons butter
2 large onions, chopped
450g (1 lb) tomatoes, peeled and chopped, or equivalent of canned plum tomatoes
1 sweet green pepper, seeded and chopped
2 cloves garlic, chopped
1 bay leaf, crushed
½ teaspoon thyme
½ hot pepper, seeded and chopped
Salt to taste

1. Rinse the soaked fish, place into a pot with cold water and bring to the boil.
2. Reduce heat and simmer for 15–20 minutes until the cod is cooked but not falling apart.
3. Have a warm serving dish ready.
4. Drain the cod and leave it to cool.
5. Remove all skin and bones.
6. Arrange in the serving dish, pour the lemon juice over it, then keep warm.
7. Heat the oil and butter in a pot.
8. Sauté the onions until golden brown.
9. Add all the other ingredients, except the cod.
10. Simmer very gently for about 30 minutes.
11. Taste for seasoning.
12. Pour all this over the cod.
13. Serve at once, with creamed yams or breadfruit.

Serves 4

SALTFISH WITH CREAMED YAMS AND PIGEON PEAS

675g (1½ lb) salted cod, soaked overnight
2 tablespoons oil
3 medium size onions, finely chopped
450g (1 lb) tomatoes, peeled and chopped
3 cloves garlic, pressed or finely chopped
½ teaspoon thyme
2 tablespoons chopped parsley
Juice 1 small lemon
Black pepper
2 tablespoons water
Salt to taste
1 sweet red pepper, chopped
225g (½ lb) cooked fresh or canned green pigeon peas (buttered and kept hot)
450g (1 lb) creamed yams (kept hot)
1½ tablespoons chopped chives (for garnish)

1. Rinse the salted cod, then bring to the boil in enough cold water to cover. Turn down heat and simmer, covered, for 15 minutes.

2 Drain, bone, skin and flake the fish. Set aside but keep warm.
3 Heat the oil in a heavy pot and sauté the onions until transparent but not brown.
4 Add the tomatoes, garlic, thyme, parsley, lemon juice, black pepper, 2 tablespoons water and a little salt, then simmer, covered, very slowly for 30 minutes.
5 Strain through a sieve, return to heat, and add the chopped sweet pepper.
6 Taste for seasoning and simmer for a further 10 minutes.
7 Arrange the warm flaked cod in the centre of a serving dish.
8 Surround the cod with the cooked pigeon peas, and arrange the hot creamed yams around the pigeon peas.
9 Pour the sauce over the fish, sprinkle with the chopped chives and serve.

Serves 4

SALTFISH SOUFFLÉ

Dutch Islands

675g (1½ lb) salted cod, soaked for at least 8 hours
225ml (8 fl oz) coconut milk
1 clove garlic, finely crushed
2 tablespoons chives, finely chopped
½ teaspoon freshly ground white pepper
¼ teaspoon ground thyme
1 teaspoon parsley, finely chopped
½ teaspoon cayenne
½ tablespoon nutmeg
Salt to taste
75g (3 oz) unsalted butter
3 tablespoons flour
4 egg yolks
5 egg whites

1 Drain saltfish, then put into fresh water and parboil briefly.
2 Discard water, allow saltfish to cool then remove skin and all bones.
3 Liquidize the saltfish with 150ml (4 fl oz) of the coconut milk, garlic, chives, white pepper, thyme, parsley, cayenne and nutmeg.

4 Taste for salt and add a little if needed.
5 On a very low heat melt the butter in a pan and then stir in the flour. Cook for 2–3 minutes.
6 Now slowly work in the remainder of the milk, continue to stir until thick and smooth.
7 Remove from heat and allow to cool.
8 When cool beat the egg yolks into the milk and flour sauce, then fold in the saltfish mix.
9 Whip the egg whites until stiff and gently fold them in as well.
10 Pour into a buttered 1.75 litre (3 pint) soufflé dish and bake in the middle of the oven at 220°C (425°F/Gas 7) for about 25 minutes until puffed up and lightly brown.
11 Serve immediately.

Serves 4

RED SNAPPER IN GARLIC, TOMATO AND PEPPER SAUCE

All Islands

1 big red snapper, 1.5–1.8kg (3–4 lb)
½ teaspoon salt
Juice ½ lime
Black pepper, freshly ground
3 cloves garlic, finely chopped
1 teaspoon oregano
Flour
5 tablespoons vegetable oil
1 onion, finely chopped
450g (1 lb) tomatoes, peeled and chopped
1 hot pepper, seeded and chopped (*see* Techniques)
1 sweet pepper, seeded and chopped
6 stuffed olives, chopped
1 glass sherry

1 Have a large oblong or oval heat-proof serving dish ready.
2 Scale and clean the snapper (*see* Techniques), leaving head and tail on.
3 Score the fish diagonally on either side, not more than 6 mm (¼ of an inch) deep.
4 Rub into the inside of the fish a little salt, lime juice and

ground black pepper and place a little of the garlic and half the oregano inside the fish.

5 Mix the flour with some black pepper and about half a teaspoon of salt, and coat the fish in the flour.
6 Heat the oil in a heavy shallow frying pan.
7 Fry the fish quickly until golden brown on both sides.
8 Place on the heat-proof dish that you have ready.
9 Check the quantity of oil remaining in the pan, add a little more if needed.
10 Sauté the onion until transparent but not brown.
11 Add the other ingredients and continue to sauté, stirring occasionally for about 5 minutes.
12 Taste for seasoning.
13 Pour the mixture over the fish and bake for 15–20 minutes in a pre-heated oven 190°C (375°F/Gas 5) or until the fish is cooked through.

Serves 4–6

STEWED FLYING FISH

Barbados

I last tested this dish, not in Barbados or anywhere near the Caribbean, but in a friend's flat in Fulham, at Easter 1985. The two of us ate enough for four people, with a dessert of baked bananas and orange to follow.

Allow 1 or 2 flying fish, according to size, per person
Juice 1 lime or lemon
Salt to taste
Black pepper, freshly ground
1 tablespoon olive oil
½–1 hot pepper, seeded and chopped (*see* Techniques)
4 tomatoes, peeled and sliced
3 onions, sliced
2 tablespoons clarified butter

1 Scale the fish (*see* Techniques).
2 Before gutting, wash the fish under running cold water to rid them of any loose surplus scales.
3 Gut and bone the fish (*see* Techniques).
4 After having rinsed the fish under cold water for a second time, pat dry with kitchen paper, towel or a clean cloth.

5 Spread the fish back downwards, squeeze half of the citrus juice on each of them and sprinkle with equal amounts of salt and black pepper.
6 Fold the fishes back into their original shape, then slip the tail of each fish into the mouth, forming a closed loop.
7 Place a pot that has a tight fitting lid on a low heat, pour in the olive oil and arrange the fish across the bottom so that all of them are nicely separated.
8 Cover the fish with the hot pepper, sliced tomatoes and onions and add the rest of the citrus juice and lastly the melted butter.
9 Cover and simmer very gently until the fish is tender.

Serves 4

Serve with coo-coo or rice. Fresh chopped hot peppers or yellow Barbadian pepper sauce are recommended.

CREOLE STEWED SHARK

English, French and Patois speaking Islands

4 shark steaks (about 170g (6 oz) each)
2 cloves garlic, crushed
8 blades chives, crushed
2 sprigs parsley
Juice 1½ limes
½ hot pepper, seeded (*see* Techniques)
Salt to taste
1 tablespoon Island Rum
8 tablespoons water
Oil
Flour
2 small onions, sliced into half rings
2 tomatoes, peeled and sliced
1 sprig thyme

1 Wash the shark in cold water.
2 Mix together 1 clove garlic, the chives, 1 sprig parsley, crushed, juice 1 lime, the hot pepper, some salt, the rum and about 2 tablespoons water. Taste to check that there is enough salt – you can add just a little more as the fish will absorb it.

3 Put the fish in a bowl and pour the marinade mixture over it and allow to stand for 2 hours, turning occasionally.
4 Heat the oil in a frying pan, remove the fish from the marinade, pat slightly dry, coat in flour and fry each piece on both sides until golden brown, then set aside.
5 Fry the onions in the same oil, possibly with a little more added, add the remaining garlic and sauté for 1–2 minutes.
6 Now add the remainder of the ingredients: lime juice, parsley, tomatoes, thyme and salt with about 6 tablespoons of water.
7 Put in the browned fish steaks and simmer covered for about 15 minutes.
8 Taste for seasoning.
9 Serve with mixed vegetables or Riz Creole.

Serves 4

As a child I squirmed at the whole idea of eating shark, but I grew to love it and always will.

BAKED STUFFED FISH

Most Islands

1 whole fish 1.7–1.8kg (3½–4 lb) red snapper, grouper or bass – boned, if you wish (*see* Techniques)
2 tablespoons butter
1 onion, finely chopped
3–4 rashers of lean bacon, finely chopped
2 cloves garlic, pressed or finely chopped
1 tablespoon chives, finely chopped
2 teaspoons parsley, finely chopped
½ teaspoon fresh thyme
1 tablespoon lime or lemon juice
2 cloves, freshly ground
1 tomato, peeled, seeded and chopped
½ hot pepper, seeded and finely chopped (*see* Techniques)
1 tablespoon white wine
2 level tablespoons fresh breadcrumbs
Yolk of 1 hard-boiled egg, mashed
1 tablespoon light rum
Banana leaf or foil
White pepper, freshly ground
Salt, to taste

1 Scale and clean the fish but do not cut off the head or the tail.
2 Melt the butter in a shallow frying pan on a low heat.
3 Sauté together the onion and bacon for about 5 minutes.
4 Add the garlic and chives and fry for a further 2–3 minutes.
5 Add all the other ingredients for the stuffing, except the rum; fold in the mashed egg yolk last and continue to stir until the mixture is well blended.
6 Taste for seasoning.
7 Add the rum and blend in well.
8 Allow to cool.
9 Stuff the fish with the mixture.
10 Butter or oil a piece of banana leaf or foil.
11 Sprinkle the fish with a little ground white pepper and salt and wrap it in the banana leaf or foil.
12 Bake in a pre-heated oven at 190°C (375°F/Gas 5) for about 1 hour.
13 Slightly unwrap the fish, test with a small knife or skewer to see if it is cooked. At the most the fish may need another 10 minutes.
14 Remove the foil or banana leaf and serve the fish on a hot serving dish.
15 Garnish with sliced tomato, citrus wedges and parsley. The banana leaf may be retained as part of the presentation.
16 Serve with creamed yams, red beans and an avocado salad and a creole fish sauce.

Serves 4–6

PÊCHE À LA MATELOTE

CREOLE FRESH FISH

French and Patois Speaking Islands

4–6 steaks – usually tuna, carangue, dorado, bonito or red snapper
Juice 1½ limes or lemons
1 hot pepper, seeded (*see* Techniques)
2 teaspoons salt
Black pepper
Vegetable oil
Flour

2 onions, thinly sliced in rings
3 tomatoes, sliced
4–6 cloves
2 bay leaves
1 generous sprig parsley
1 sprig thyme
Fish stock

1. Place the fish in a large glass or enamel bowl (always use a non-porous utensil for marinating and certainly not a thin plastic one), rub in the citrus juice, the hot pepper, 2 teaspoons salt and a little fresh ground black pepper, and set aside for at least 3 hours.
2. Heat the oil slowly in a frying pan.
3. Discard the marinade, pat the fish dry and coat with flour.
4. Shake to remove any excess flour and fry each piece on both sides until golden brown.
5. Now in the same frying pan with the fish, add all other ingredients with just enough stock or water to make a sauce (the liquid should only reach two thirds of the thickness of the steaks).
6. Simmer slightly covered for about 20 minutes, turning the fish over halfway through the cooking period.
7. Taste for seasoning.
8. Serve accompanied by Riz Creole and mixed vegetables.

Serves 4–6

CURRIED FISH

4 170–225g (6–8 oz) steaks of tuna or bonito *or* 3–4 mackerel, cut into four or five pieces
1 tablespoon sea salt
Juice 2½ limes or lemons
3 cloves garlic, 2 finely chopped, 1 crushed
1 hot pepper, seeded and chopped (*see* Techniques)
1 sprig parsley, crushed
4 tablespoons oil
Flour
2 medium sized onions, cut into ½ rings
1 teaspoon achote liquid
2 tablespoons curry powder

4 cloves, freshly ground
Black pepper, freshly ground
300ml (½ pint) fish stock
1 sprig thyme
150ml (¼ pint) white wine
Arrowroot (optional)

1. Put the fish in a bowl, with some water just to cover, add 1 tablespoon sea salt, juice of 2 limes, the crushed garlic, half the hot pepper with the crushed parsley, and allow to marinate for 3–4 hours or even longer. Discard marinade.
2. Heat 3 tablespoons oil in a large heavy pot, pat the fish dry, coat with flour and fry until lightly brown on both sides.
3. Set the fried fish aside, check the amount of oil left in the pan, add more if needed.
4. Sauté the onions and chopped garlic until lightly brown.
5. Add all the remaining ingredients, except the fish.
6. Simmer, covered, for about 20 minutes.
7. Taste for seasoning.
8. Add the fish and simmer for a further 15–20 minutes.
9. Thicken with a little arrowroot paste if needed.
10. Serve with Riz Creole and fried plantains, with extra chopped and seeded hot pepper for those who need it, or West Indian Hot Pepper Sauce.

Serves 4

COURT BOUILLON À LA CRÉOLE

MARINATED FISH IN TOMATO AND GARLIC SAUCE

French and Patois speaking Islands

2 cloves garlic, crushed, for marinade
Juice of 2 limes
1 hot pepper, seeded but not chopped, for marinade
1 tablespoon salt, for marinade
Water
4 225g (8 oz) fish steaks (tuna, dorado, snapper or any firm fish)
4 tablespoons olive oil
2 cloves garlic, finely chopped, for sauce
Black pepper
8 shallots, finely chopped

2 tablespoons chives, finely chopped
4 medium tomatoes, peeled and chopped
1 teaspoon hot pepper, seeded and chopped (*see* Techniques)
Salt to taste for sauce
1 sprig thyme
1 bay leaf
2 sprigs parsley
1 glass dry white wine

1. In a large bowl put the 2 cloves of crushed garlic, juice of 1½ limes, the whole seeded hot pepper, 1 tablespoon salt and enough water to cover. Stir well, add the fish and allow to marinate in a cool place or a refrigerator for 2–3 hours.
2. Meanwhile in a small bowl beat together with a fork 2 tablespoons olive oil, juice of half a lime, half the chopped garlic and a pinch of black pepper and set aside.
3. On a low heat in a heavy shallow pot or frying pan heat 2 tablespoons of the oil and sauté the shallots until soft but not brown.
4. Add the chives, tomatoes, the remaining garlic, chopped hot pepper, black pepper, salt to taste and the thyme, bay leaf and parsley tied together. Simmer covered for 6 minutes.
5. Taste for salt and pour in the wine, then discard the marinade and add the fish.
6. Pour in about 150ml (¼ pint) water.
7. Simmer for 8 minutes turning the fish once or twice during that time.
8. Pour the seasoned olive oil over the fish and continue to simmer for another 4 minutes or until the fish is cooked. The fish must feel firm when cooked.
9. Discard the tied herbs and serve immediately.

Accompany with Riz Creole or mixed vegetables. Sometimes the fish is served with both.

Serves 4

MARINATED FRIED FISH

All Islands

Juice 2–3 limes
½ hot pepper, seeded (*see* Techniques)
1 onion, sliced for marinade
6–8 blades chives, slightly pounded
Sea salt, about 1½–2 tablespoons
2 tablespoons olive oil (for marinade)
3–4 cloves garlic, slightly crushed but kept intact
1 sprig fresh thyme
2 sprigs fresh parsley
900g–1.8kg (2–4 lb) of any choice from the following: tuna, dorado, snapper, bonito, flying fish, halibut, mackerel and even sprats or fresh sardines)
Water
300ml (½ pint) oil (for frying)
110-170g (4–6 oz) plain flour
2–3 onions, neatly sliced, to be fried for garnish
Lime or lemon wedges for garnish

1. In a bowl large enough to hold the amount of fish you have decided to prepare mix together all the ingredients except the oil for frying and the flour.
2. Add the pieces of fish (if you use sprats, sardines or any such small fish, leave whole).
3. Pour in barely enough cold water to cover the fish, stir a few times and leave to marinate for 5 hours or longer.
4. Heat the oil in a large and heavy frying pan.
5. Pat the fish dry, coat in the flour and fry until crisp and golden brown. Fry only a few pieces at a time.
6. Arrange on a warm serving dish.
7. Fry the sliced onions until they are golden brown and drain on paper towels.

Serve the fish garnished with lime or lemon wedges and the golden fried onions, also watercress if you wish. Accompany with a tomato salad and hot bread.

Fish fried in this way can be eaten either hot or cold.

Serves 4–6

PECHE POCHE

POACHED FISH

French and Patois speaking Islands

300ml (½ pint) water
Juice 2½ limes or lemons
3 cloves garlic, crushed
1½–2 teaspoons salt
3 sprigs parsley
6 blades chives, slightly pounded
2 450g (1 lb) whole fish, cleaned and scaled (small red snappers are ideal for this dish or substitute tuna steaks, halibut or any firm white fish)
300ml (½ pint) fish stock
1 teaspoon hot pepper, seeded and chopped (*see* Techniques)
2½ tablespoons chopped onions
2 bay leaves
1 sprig thyme
4 whole cloves
4 melegueta or allspice berries

1. In a bowl large enough to contain the fish mix together with about 300ml (½ pint) water, juice of 2 limes, 2 crushed cloves of garlic, 1½ teaspoons salt, 2 sprigs parsley and the chives.
2. Add the fish and set aside to marinate for about 2–3 hours, turning the fish over a few times.
3. If you are using whole fish always make a long diagonal cut on either side to allow the 'seasoning up' to penetrate into the fish.
4. Into a large pot put the stock and all other remaining ingredients.
5. Bring to the boil, reduce heat and simmer, covered, for about 8 minutes.
6. Discard the marinade and add the fish.
7. Continue to simmer for a further 10–15 minutes.
8. Taste for salt and other seasonings.
9. When cooked, carefully remove the fish and arrange on a warm, fairly deep serving dish.
10. Pour the liquid all over the fish.

11 Serve with Riz Creole, pigeon peas or, if you prefer, red kidney beans and West Indian mixed vegetables.

Serves 2–4

CREOLE FISH CAKES

French and English speaking countries

Some cooks use potatoes for this dish, instead of breadfruit or yams, following a recipe that came from Portugal and Brazil, known there as *pastéis de bacalhau.*

450g (1 lb) cooked white fish, flaked and mashed
225g (½ lb) mashed breadfruit or white yams
1 small onion, finely chopped or minced
Juice ½ lime
1 teaspoon hot pepper, finely chopped (*see* Techniques)
Salt to taste
1 tablespoon fresh parsley
1 tablespoon chives, finely chopped
Black pepper, freshly ground
2 eggs, beaten
3–4 tablespoons flour, seasoned with salt and black pepper
Oil for frying

1 Mix together the fish, mashed vegetables, onion, lime juice, hot pepper, salt, herbs and spices.
2 Add the beaten eggs and mix well.
3 Taste for seasoning. You may wish to add a little more hot pepper.
4 Flour your hands, shape the mixture into several flat cakes and coat with the seasoned flour, ready to fry in hot oil until golden brown on both sides (if using potatoes, pass the resulting purée from one spoon to another, to make egg shapes ready for deep frying).
5 Serve as a breakfast dish, for snacks or at a party.

Serves 4–6

STUFFED PINEAPPLE WITH PRAWNS AND CHICKEN

Author's recipe

2 medium sized pineapples (try to buy them with some leaves attached)
2 tablespoons olive oil
1 tablespoon chopped onions
1 small clove garlic, finely chopped
1 level teaspoon white pepper, freshly ground
½ teaspoon allspice
2 teaspoons marjoram
Salt to taste
450g (1 lb) shelled prawns
225g (½ lb) cooked and diced chicken breasts
2 tablespoons light rum
1 glass sherry
1 tablespoon lemon juice
2 small tomatoes, peeled and chopped
2 teaspoons arrowroot, mixed into a paste with a little water
20 cooked prawns } for garnish
lettuce leaves }

1 Wash the pineapples, cut each in half lengthwise. Try not to damage the leaves.
2 Carefully cut out the flesh with a sharp knife, without damaging the shells.
3 Cube 1 pineapple into 1cm (½ inch) pieces.
4 Set this aside and also retain the shells of both fruits.
5 Retain the flesh of the second pineapple and store in the fridge for use some other time within the next 2 days.
6 On a low heat in a skillet heat the oil and sauté the onions until transparent but not brown.
7 Add the garlic and white pepper, allspice, marjoram, a little salt and continue to sauté for another 5 minutes.
8 Now add all the other ingredients, except the arrowroot, with the pineapple cubes and simmer for 5 minutes.
9 Taste for seasoning.
10 Thicken with the arrowroot paste, simmer for a further 3 minutes.
11 At once warm the pineapple shells in the oven for about 2–3 minutes.

12 Fill the shells with the contents of the skillet, garnish each shell with 5 prawns and place on serving dishes lined with lettuce leaves.

13 Serve with fried plantain, sweet potatoes, creamed yams and a green salad.

Serves 4

Shellfish and Crabs

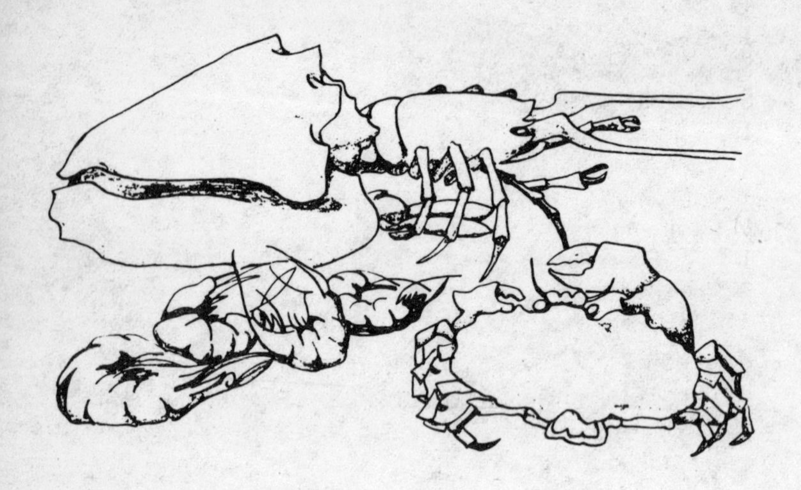

The seas and rivers of the Caribbean were once abundant in lobsters and crayfish; and the lands too in crabs, like those of Montserrat and Dominica. And the cooks of the Islands excelled themselves in their preparation. The clawless lobsters (langost) of the Caribbean seas are the most succulent that I have ever had the pleasure of eating. But, alas, like everywhere else, demand seems to be far outstripping nature. Still, we continue to make the very best use of those that are left, and our many visitors continue to enjoy them, as I am certain you will.

Though it is almost impossible to obtain the land crabs of the Islands, there are many species of lobster from the Mediterranean and crayfish, both salt and freshwater, from the Orient which will do. Naturally a good rum punch before, during or after the meal will help bring you closer to the real thing.

SHELLFISH STOCK

Author's version

This is made from the heads and shells of whatever shellfish you have used in any of the appropriate recipes. Thus it should be made only when needed, for it will not keep too long.

A few rejected shells and heads (or 150ml (¼ pint) cheap shrimps, if you are making the stock expressly)
450ml (¾ pint) water
150ml (¼ pint) white wine
Small sprig parsley
Small sprig thyme
1 bay leaf
1 small onion, chopped
1 clove garlic, crushed
¼ teaspoon pepper sauce
1–2 tablespoons lemon juice
2 tablespoons oil (optional)
Black pepper, freshly ground
Salt to taste

1. In a mortar, lightly pound the heads and shells (or shrimps).
2. Place all the ingredients into a pot. Stir. Place on heat and bring to the boil.
3. Lower heat, and simmer, covered, for about 15–20 minutes.
4. Remove from heat, put through a fine strainer and use.

FALMOUTH HARBOUR LOBSTER

CHARCOAL GRILLED LOBSTER

Antigua

I first sampled this method of preparing lobster on the island of Antigua, while staying with friends on a hill above Falmouth Harbour.

One evening, on the veranda of that Spanish-style house, we set up a coalpot and when the charcoal was glowing, we simply roasted the lobsters, which we had been diving for that afternoon. To roast lobster is to place the whole lobster directly on the fire, but I recommend that you use, in this recipe, a grill over your charcoal.

The Caribbean lobster is called, in French and Patois, *langouste* and is not the same as the lobster you catch and buy in Europe – it is a giant crayfish and has no claws. However the method of preparing langouste is virtually the same for lobster, except that you will have to crack the claws to free the meat.

This dish is served with a spicy lime and garlic butter.

2 lobsters or langoustes
Juice 1 lime
75g (3 oz) butter
1 tablespoon finely chopped chives
2–3 cloves garlic, pressed or finely chopped
Black pepper, freshly ground
¼ teaspoon allspice
Salt to taste
½ teaspoon pepper sauce

1. If you are using a coalpot or charcoal grill, you should start the cooking when the coals are glowing, with no immediate need of further replenishment.
2. Place a clean metal grill over the fire – there should be at least 10cm (4 inches) between the rack and the coals.
3. Arrange the whole lobsters on the grill and cook for about 15–20 minutes, turning from side to side. If you wish, you may butcher the lobsters first by halving them, rather than roasting them whole.
4. Meanwhile take a small mixing bowl and, with a fork, blend the lime juice, butter, chives, garlic, black pepper, allspice, salt and pepper sauce until an almost creamy texture is achieved.
5. Taste for seasoning and set aside – not in the refrigerator, but in a cool place.
6. When the lobsters are cooked, split them lengthways in half and clean (*see* Techniques).
7. Spread the spicy butter over the lobster and bring to the table at once.

Serves 2–4

GRILLADES DE LANGOUSTE *or* LANGOSTA CRIOLLA

LOBSTER CREOLE

French and Spanish speaking countries

2 tablespoons olive oil
6–8 shallots, skinned but left whole
3 cloves garlic, crushed
Juice 1½ limes
2 tomatoes, peeled and chopped
1 hot pepper, seeded but not chopped (*see* Techniques)
1 sweet pepper, seeded and cut into neat thin slices
1 sprig thyme
1 sprig parsley, finely chopped
2 tablespoons chives
1 bay leaf
1 stick celery, cut in 4 lengths
Salt to taste
Black pepper, freshly ground
2–3 green bananas, peeled and cut into pieces
300ml (½ pint) fish stock
150ml (5 fl oz) dry white wine
2–3 fair sized lobsters, uncooked

1 In a heavy large pot, heat the oil and sauté the shallots until slightly transparent but not brown.
2 Add the garlic and all ingredients except the lobsters, wine and stock.
3 Simmer, covered, for 6–8 minutes, add the stock and wine and continue to simmer for another 8 minutes.
4 Meanwhile, if it has not already been done by the fishmonger, cut the lobsters lengthways in half and remove the gravel sac from the heads and the vein running along the back that is attached to it (*see* Techniques).
5 Rinse briefly under cold water and set aside.
6 Taste the stew for seasoning.
7 Add the lobster bodies and simmer covered for 10 minutes.
8 Turn the lobsters in the simmering juice every now and then.
9 Remove the lobsters from the liquid but keep warm in a serving dish.
10 Taste for seasoning again and boil the liquid very fast until reduced by at least a quarter.

11 Remove the bay leaf, hot pepper and thyme.
12 Pour over the lobster and serve at once with cornmeal coo-coo and a green salad.

Serves 4–6

BAKED LOBSTER

English and Patois speaking Islands

675–900g (1½–2 lb) lobster meat (*see* Techniques)
Juice 1 lime
Salt to taste
2 cloves garlic, pressed or finely chopped
150g–170g (5–6 oz) butter
2 medium onions, finely chopped
½ hot pepper, seeded and chopped (*see* Techniques)
50g (2 oz) fresh breadcrumbs
1½–2 teaspoons Worcestershire sauce
Black pepper, freshly ground

1 Place the lobster meat with the lime juice, a little salt and half the garlic in a bowl – allow to marinate for 15 minutes only.
2 Meanwhile melt just 55g (2 oz) of butter in a heavy frying pan over a medium heat, sauté the onions until they are translucent.
3 Add the remaining garlic, hot pepper and half of the breadcrumbs and fry until the breadcrumbs turn a golden brown.
4 Now bring to the pan the lobster, with the marinade, Worcestershire sauce, half of the remaining butter, black pepper and salt. Stir gently for 2 minutes.
5 Taste for seasoning and transfer to a baking dish, sprinkling the rest of the breadcrumbs evenly over the lobster mixture.
6 Dot with the remaining butter and bake in a pre-heated oven 180°C (350°F/Gas 4) for 20–25 minutes or until the breadcrumbs have turned golden.
7 Serve immediately.

Serves 4

LOBSTER AND CRAYFISH STEW

Dutch West Indies

50g (2 oz) unsalted butter
2 medium onions, finely chopped
2 cloves garlic, finely chopped
4 tomatoes, peeled, seeded and chopped
150ml (¼ pint) dry white wine
½ teaspoon annatto liquid (achote)
Juice ½ lime
1 sprig parsley
150ml (¼ pint) shellfish stock
2 tablespoons light rum
½ hot pepper, seeded and chopped (*see* Techniques)
450g (1 lb) lobster meat
Black pepper, freshly ground
Salt to taste
450g (1 lb) crayfish
3 tablespoons grated Edam cheese, otherwise a mature Gouda or Leidsekaas is recommended.

1 In a heavy pot, over a medium heat, melt the butter and sauté the onions and garlic until the onions are transparent but not brown.
2 Add the tomatoes and sauté until soft.
3 Add the wine and other ingredients except the shellfish and cheese and simmer, covered, on a low heat for about 10 minutes.
4 Taste for seasoning; adjust if necessary.
5 Now add the shellfish and simmer on a low heat for about 8 minutes.
6 Sprinkle with the grated cheese and serve.

Best accompanied by boiled rice.

Serves 4–6

CURRIED CRAYFISH

Martinique

This is a simple but delicious dish which is well worth trying. I discovered it in Martinique in 1971–72.

2 tablespoon unsalted butter
1 onion, cut into fine rounds
2 cloves garlic, finely crushed or pressed
1 tablespoon curry powder (Colombo – *see* Techniques)
½ hot pepper, finely chopped (*see* Techniques)
1 teaspoon chopped parsley
150ml (¼ pint) fish stock (or 1 bouillon cube in same quantity of water)
2 tablespoons sherry
1 christophene, finely chopped
Salt to taste
150ml (¼ pint) coconut milk
900g (2 lb) shelled freshwater crayfish (substitute any larger crayfish)
1 tablespoon white Martinican rum
Juice 1 lime or lemon

1. Melt the butter in a heavy pot and sauté the onion until just light brown.
2. Add the garlic, curry powder, hot pepper, parsley, stock and sherry, and simmer, covered, for about 10–15 minutes.
3. Add the christophene, salt and coconut milk and simmer until the christophene is tender.
4. Now taste for seasoning and add the crayfish, rum and lemon juice.
5. Stir and simmer partly covered until the crayfish is cooked, which should take no more than 8–10 minutes.
6. Taste for seasoning.
7. Serve at once with Riz Creole.

Serves 4

CRAB WITH COCONUT MILK

Windward Islands

2 whole crabs (or 4 according to appetite)
1 tablespoon olive oil
2 tablespoons butter
2 cm (¾ inch) piece of root ginger, peeled and sliced
1 onion, cut into half rings
2 cloves garlic, finely chopped
2 sprigs parsley

1 chicken bouillon cube
1 tablespoon lime or lemon juice
Black pepper
6 blades chives, chopped
1 stick of cinnamon
300ml (½ pint) coconut milk (*see* Techniques)
Salt to taste

1. If you are using live crabs, plunge them in boiling water for 10 minutes.
2. Remove crabs from water, allow to cool and prepare according to the method described in the *Techniques* section.
3. Heat the oil and butter in a pot on a low heat, add the ginger, onion and garlic and sauté until the onions are soft and transparent.
4. Add the parsley, bouillon cube, citrus juice, black pepper and chives.
5. Sauté for 10 minutes.
6. Add the crab claws, body and all edible parts, plus the cinnamon stick and coconut milk.
7. Simmer, covered, for a further 15 minutes.
8. Taste for salt and serve with plain rice, dasheen, green plantain and breadfruit.

Serves 4

CRAB GUMBO

CRAB AND OKRAS

Dominica, Martinique, Guadeloupe

On the islands land crabs are used for this dish – but any crab will do.

900g (2 lb) crab meat, white and brown parts
55g (2 oz) butter
10 okras, topped, tailed and sliced
1 onion, chopped
225g (½ lb) tomatoes, peeled, seeded and chopped
½ hot pepper, seeded and chopped (*see* Techniques)
1 tablespoon chives, chopped
150ml (¼ pint) shellfish stock or water
1 bay leaf

1 sprig thyme
1 sprig parsley
Salt to taste

1. If you are using fresh crabs, cook, clean and remove both white and brown meat (*see* Techniques).
2. Melt the butter in a pot and brown the crab meat.
3. Add the okras, onion, tomatoes, hot pepper and chives and sauté for about 8 minutes.
4. Add remaining ingredients and simmer, covered, on a low heat for about 45 minutes.
5. Taste for seasoning.
6. Serve with Riz Creole or plain coo-coo without okra in it, just coconut.

Serves 4

This dish is one of the sources of the famous Gumbos of New Orleans, many of which unfortunately no longer employ okras.

CURRIED CRABS

Dominica

3 medium sized crabs
Juice 1 lime
2 tablespoons coconut oil (substitute vegetable or ground nut oil)
2 medium onions
2.5 cm (1 inch) piece fresh root ginger, peeled and chopped
2 teaspoons hot pepper, seeded and chopped
½ teaspoon cloves, ground
4 cloves garlic, finely chopped
1 fish or chicken bouillon cube
1 bay leaf, crushed
2 tablespoons curry powder
600ml (1 pint) thick coconut milk, which must be freshly made (*see* Techniques)
1 sprig thyme
2 tablespoons medium dark rum
Salt (only if needed after having tasted the sauce)

1. Clean the crabs and retain all edible parts from the body, legs and claws (*see* Techniques).

2 Put these meats into a bowl and pour the lime juice over them.
3 Heat the oil in a heavy pot and sauté the onions until transparent.
4 Add the ginger, hot pepper, cloves, garlic, bouillon cube, bay leaf, curry powder and ½ the coconut milk, then cook, uncovered, for about 5 minutes stirring all the time.
5 Cover and simmer gently for 15 minutes.
6 Now add the crab, the rest of the coconut milk, the thyme and the rum, stir and taste for seasoning.
7 Simmer, covered, on a very low heat for about 20 minutes.
8 Again taste for seasoning.
9 Serve with rice, fried or boiled ripe plantain, boiled breadfruit and dasheen.

Serves 6

MATETE

CRAB WITH RICE

French and Patois speaking Islands

4 tablespoons oil
3 cloves garlic, chopped
4 shallots, chopped
1 chicken bouillon cube
½ hot pepper, seeded and chopped (*see* Techniques)
1 bay leaf
1 tablespoon chopped parsley
1 teaspoon thyme
1½ tablespoons chives, chopped
Juice 1 lime
Black pepper
Salt to taste
340g (¾ lb) rice, well washed
Water
900g (2 lb) crab meat (*see* Techniques)

1 Heat the oil in a large heavy pot, add the garlic and shallots, sauté until soft but not brown.
2 Add all the other ingredients apart from the rice, crab meat and water.
3 Sauté further for about 3 minutes.

4 Add the well-washed rice. Gently stir around a few times, pour in enough water to cover the rice, add a little salt, and bring to the boil.
5 Now add the crab meat, reduce the heat and simmer, covered, until all the liquid has been absorbed.
6 Stir a couple of times to mix well and serve immediately.

Serves 4–6

This dish was originally made by the Caribs, using farine instead of our modern use of rice.

CRAB AND SALTFISH PELAU

Countries with Asian influence

450g (1 lb) salted cod (soaked overnight or for at least 8 hours)
1 tablespoon oil
2 onions, finely chopped
1 clove garlic, finely chopped
2 tablespoons butter
450g (1 lb) rice, well washed
900ml (1½ pints) light coconut milk (*see* Techniques)
1 bay leaf
Black pepper
½ teaspoon hot pepper, seeded and chopped (*see* Techniques)
1 stick cinnamon
Salt to taste
450g (1 lb) crab meat
Juice 1 lime
1 tablespoon chives

1 Parboil the saltfish, bone and skin it, then set aside.
2 Heat the oil in a large pot and sauté the onions and garlic until the onions are soft and transparent but not brown.
3 Add the butter and stir until bubbles form.
4 Mix in the rice and cover every grain with the flavoured butter.
5 Add the saltfish, coconut milk, bay leaf, black pepper, hot pepper and cinnamon, turn down the heat and stir gently.
6 Taste for salt.
7 Now add the crab meat, lime juice and chives, then simmer

covered until the rice is tender and all the liquid has been absorbed.

8 Turn out on to a large serving dish, arrange the seafood attractively over the bed of rice and serve at once.

Serves 6

KESHY YENA

EDAM CHEESE WITH SHELLFISH STUFFING

Dutch West Indies

1.25–1.5kg (2½–3 lb) whole Edam cheese
450g (1 lb) shrimps, crayfish or prawns (fresh and shelled)
50g (2 oz) unsalted butter
1 medium onion, finely chopped
225g (½ lb) tomatoes, peeled, seeded and chopped
Salt (very little)
Black pepper, freshly ground
½ teaspoon cayenne, or good powdered chilli
3 tablespoons freshly made breadcrumbs
2 tablespoons gherkins, finely chopped
6 olives, stoned and chopped
2 tablespoons seedless raisins
2 eggs, well beaten

1 Carefully scrape away the red wax covering from the cheese.
2 Cut a slice, to make a lid, from the top about 4cm (1½ inches) thick.
3 With a sharp-edged spoon or similar implement, scoop out the inside of the cheese, leaving a shell about 2.5cm (1 inch) thick.
4 Place the shell and lid into a bowl with enough cold water to cover and allow to soak for an hour.
5 Grate enough of the scooped-out cheese to render about 225g (½ lb).
6 Shell and clean whatever shellfish you have decided to use and, according to size, cut them into pieces not more than 1–2 cm (½–¾ inch) long.
7 Melt the butter in a heated frying pan.
8 Sauté the onion until transparent but not brown. The creamy sediment of butter browns very quickly; be careful not to allow this to happen. Use a low heat.

9. Add the chopped tomatoes, salt, a little black pepper, ground chilli pepper or cayenne and stir until the mixture is well blended. Do not allow to stick to the pan.
10. Transfer to a mixing bowl and add to it the breadcrumbs, gherkins, olives, grated cheese, shellfish and raisins. Mix thoroughly but avoid breaking up the fish. Add a little salt if needed.
11. Gently fold in the beaten eggs.
12. Remove the cheese shell from the water, drain and pat dry.
13. Stuff the cheese with the seafood mixture.
14. Place the filled cheese into a greased baking bowl which must be deep and just large enough to hold it.
15. Place the lid on top and bake in a pre-heated oven 180°C (350°F/Gas 4) for no more than 30 minutes. The lid by now should be nice and brown.
16. Serve immediately in the same dish.

Keshy Yena is also cooked with a stuffing of poultry or meat.

SEAFOOD SALAD ON SEASONED RICE

A family recipe

340g (¾ lb) rice, well washed
2 whole cloves garlic, slightly mashed but left whole
Salt to taste
Fish or chicken stock, about 900ml (1½ pints)
225ml (8 fl oz) mayonnaise
2 tomatoes, peeled, cooked and finely chopped
1 tablespoon chopped chives
1½ teaspoons chopped parsley
Juice ½ lime or lemon
½ teaspoon hot peppers, finely chopped (*see* Techniques)
Freshly ground white pepper
225g (½ lb) peas (fresh or frozen, cooked)
275g (10 oz) cooked white crab meat
275g (10 oz) cooked white lobster meat
275g (10 oz) cooked crayfish or shrimps
8 large cooked prawns to decorate
4–6 lime or lemon wedges

1. Cook the rice with the garlic and salt to taste in the fish or chicken stock until tender and all the liquid has been absorbed.

2 Set aside to cool.
3 Meanwhile mix together the mayonnaise, chopped tomatoes, chives, parsley, citrus juice, hot peppers and ground pepper.
4 Taste for salt.
5 Fluff up the rice with a fork.
6 Add the peas.
7 Arrange on a serving dish.
8 Now arrange on the rice the various shellfish apart from the prawns.
9 Pour the sauce over the seafood.
10 Decorate with the prawns and citrus wedges and serve.

Serves 4–6

PAELLA CRIOLLA

Spanish speaking Islands

Paella, of course, is very much in evidence on the Spanish speaking Islands, and in many a disguised form on the French, Patois and English speaking Islands too. The ingredients vary from place to place. Land crabs, fresh and seawater crabs, crayfish, bookes, prawns, lobsters, tuna and dolphin fish, red snapper, eels and all kinds of butchered meats and poultry are used, along with rice and locally grown vegetables. But wherever it is made it still remains singularly Spanish in its origin, and no matter how different, even with rum added, it is as delicious as ever.

150ml (¼ pint) olive oil
1 small chicken, cut into serving pieces, marinated in lemon juice and a little salt and garlic
225g (½ lb) salt pork, soaked for at least 6 hours, then cubed
2 onions, peeled and sliced in rings
3–4 large cloves garlic, chopped
1 glass white wine
450ml (¾ pint) shellfish stock
2 teaspoons achote liquid
340g (¾ lb) rice, washed, soaked for 1 hour, then drained very dry
2 bay leaves
Salt to taste
Black pepper, freshly ground

2 red sweet peppers, seeded and sliced
1 hot pepper, seeded and chopped (*see* Techniques)
3–4 firm ripe tomatoes, peeled, seeded and chopped
225g (½ lb) freshly cooked garden peas (substitute frozen)
3 tablespoons light Island rum
340g (¾ lb) white crab meat
12–16 fresh water crayfish tails, unshelled, 5–7 cm (2–3 inches) in length
225g (½ lb) whole prawns

1 Heat the oil in a large heavy frying pan and fry the chicken pieces until golden brown.
2 Remove with a perforated spoon and set aside.
3 Dry the salt pork cubes with a clean cloth or paper towels and fry in the same oil for about 5 minutes, add the onions and garlic and fry until the onions are transparent but not browned.
4 Return the chicken pieces together with the wine, stock, achote, bay leaves, salt and a little black pepper, and simmer, tightly covered, until the chicken is tender; this must be done on a very low heat.
5 Taste for salt. Remove the chicken pieces and keep warm.
6 Now add all the other ingredients including the rum, carefully folding in the rice first, adding the seafood last, and simmer, tightly covered, until all the liquid has been absorbed.
7 Turn out on to a large serving dish, sort out and arrange the shellfish and meats and serve at once.

Serves 6–8

If you wish, you could include, as the original Spanish recipe does, fresh mussels, in season from November.

Poultry

In my youth, chicken was for a special occasion like a christening, a holiday, a feast day; something you ate on Sundays only. Today it is the most common of foods and possibly one of the cheapest of meats. Although now mass-produced, there is nothing to beat a chicken that has pecked off the land, roaming free, be it in England or in the tropics – a fowl for all seasons that has been fed on chopped-up dried coconuts or corn scattered on the ground; the chicken that can start a back-yard fight, and can dodge the swiftest stone thrown at her;* the kind of bird that has been everywhere and pecked at the best or the worst. That's the kind of chicken for any pot. Unfortunately, in most cases we have to make do with mass-produced, pale, tasteless birds; which on the whole have a flavour closer to a poor relative of fish. But still, we have our marinades, our sweet or spicy sauces, curries,

* Apologies to feminist cooks, but cockerels are 'too gamey by half'.

wine and rum sauces to give today's mass-produced bird an extra lift.

CHICKEN STOCK

All Islands

1 boiling fowl, 1.5kg (3 lb) or equivalent in weight, of wings, legs, necks, giblets (not the liver)
1 celery stick, chopped
2 onions, quartered
2 carrots, cut in quarters
Bouquet garni (1 sprig thyme, 2 stalks parsley, 2 bay leaves tied together or wrapped in a piece of cheesecloth)
White pepper
2.2 litres (4 pints) water

1. Place all ingredients in a pot and simmer for 2–2½ hours.
2. Strain through cheesecloth.
3. Cool and refrigerate.

You can 'season up' the boiling fowl and use it in the rice and peas dishes, or in the pelaus, or in any other dish of your choice.

CREOLE CHICKEN

French and Patois speaking Islands

3–4 tablespoons coconut oil (substitute vegetable)
1.5–1.7kg (3–3½ lb) chicken, cut into serving pieces
2 medium onions, sliced
1 tablespoon curry powder
¼–½ teaspoon saffron
3 cloves garlic, finely chopped
1 hot pepper, seeded and chopped (*see* Techniques)
Salt to taste
150ml (¼ pint) chicken stock
2 tomatoes, peeled and chopped
300ml (½ pint) coconut cream (*see* Techniques)
Black pepper, freshly ground

1. Heat the oil in a heavy pot and fry the chicken until brown all over.
2. Add the onions and fry gently for another 2 minutes.
3. Add the curry powder, saffron, garlic, hot pepper, salt and stock.
4. Simmer, covered, on a low heat for 10 minutes; stir at least twice.

5 Now add all other ingredients and continue to simmer, covered, until the chicken is tender.
6 Taste for seasoning (mostly salt).
7 Serve with boiled rice and fried ripe plantains.

Serves 4–6

CHICKEN BROTH

Guadeloupe

I first had this dish in about my twelfth year; it was prepared by Auguste, a chef from Guadeloupe, at the 'Hit Parade Hotel' in Roseau, Dominica, which at that time was owned by my father. I have never forgotten it – it is a simple unsophisticated broth, but very tasty. I have myself prepared it many times over the years, obviously with certain changes. It was at that meal I think, if I remember correctly, that my father said to me that he would rather clothe me than feed me; he did neither, it was left to my mother to do both.

One 1.25–1.5kg (2½–3 lb) boiling fowl
1.7 litres (3 pints) chicken stock
2 onions, chopped
3 tannias, peeled and quartered
2 *whole* hot peppers
2 green bananas, peeled and cut into 4 pieces each
2 large carrots, scraped and cut into pieces
1 red sweet pepper, chopped
2 sprigs parsley
1 sprig thyme
8–10 blades fresh chives
8 cloves
4 cloves garlic, crushed
Juice 1 lime
Black pepper, freshly ground
Salt to taste
Dumplings (*see* Breads and Cakes)

1 Put the whole fowl in a large pot and cover with the chicken stock.
2 Bring to the boil, then simmer until almost tender. This may take anything from 1½ to 2½ hours depending on the age of the bird.

3 Add all other ingredients except the dumplings and simmer, covered, until the bird is completely cooked and nearly falling off the bone.
4 Add the dumplings for the last 15–20 minutes of cooking time.
5 Taste for seasoning.
6 Remove the whole peppers and serve them chopped up on a separate dish.
7 Serve the chicken on a large dish surrounded by the vegetables and dumplings. The liquid can be served in individual soup bowls, possibly spiced with some of the chopped peppers.

Serves 4–6

CREOLE CHICKEN CURRY

French speaking Islands

1 boiling fowl 1.5–1.8kg (3–4 lb) cut into serving pieces
2 tablespoons coconut oil (substitute ground nut oil)
2 tablespoons Poudre de Colombo (*see* Techniques)
2 onions, chopped
3 cloves garlic, finely chopped
2 tablespoons light rum
½ hot pepper, seeded and chopped (*see* Techniques)
1 glass dry white wine
Salt to taste
Juice of 1 lime
1 teaspoon achote liquid
4 cloves, ground
5–7mm (2–3 inch) cinnamon stick
600ml (1 pint) hot chicken stock (or 2 bouillon cubes in same quantity of boiling water)
150ml (¼ pint) thick coconut cream

1 Fry the chicken pieces slowly in the oil in a heavy pot until golden brown.
2 Add all remaining ingredients – except the coconut cream and stock – and fry until bubbles form and all the spices are absorbed.
3 Now pour in the chicken stock and simmer, covered, for 2½–3 hours or until chicken is tender.

4 Add the coconut cream, taste for salt and simmer for a further 15 minutes, skimming off excess fat.
5 Serve with boiled rice or mixed West Indian vegetables, especially pigeon peas.

Serves 4–6

CHICKEN CURRY (2nd version)

English speaking Islands

1.25–1.5kg (2½–3 lb) chicken, cut into serving pieces
2 tablespoons butter
1 tablespoon vegetable oil
2 medium onions, cut into fine half rings
1 clove garlic, finely chopped
Pinch of saffron
2 tablespoons curry powder
Juice 1 lemon
Salt to taste (you may need very little with chicken cube)
1½ chicken bouillon cubes (diluted in 75ml (3 fl oz) hot water)
1 hot pepper, seeded and chopped (*see* Techniques)
300ml (½ pint) rich coconut milk

1 In a heavy pot brown the chicken pieces in the oil and butter; add the onions and garlic, then cook further with the chicken until the onions are slightly brown.
2 Now add the other ingredients except the coconut milk, cover and simmer gently until the chicken is tender. Check occasionally to make certain nothing sticks to the bottom of the pot.
3 Pour in coconut milk; mix well.
4 Taste for salt and simmer for a further 3–5 minutes.
5 Serve immediately.

Serves 4

Riz Creole is best with this dish. If you wish you may serve fried ripe plantains as well.

DYL'S FRIED CHICKEN

St Lucia

This is a simple but delicious recipe given to me by Dylyn Dalton, and like her beef dish (see p.156) sometimes forms part of many of her Sunday lunches. I have actually assisted her in the preparation of it, where again there was Macaroni Pie and salads: a tomato and bean salad and one with Chinese cabbage. The following recipe as part of a larger meal was sufficient for twelve.

One 1.5–1.7kg (3–3½ lb) chicken, skinned and cut into very small pieces, breasts and legs into at least four pieces each
4 tablespoons water
2 chicken bouillon cubes
1–2 tablespoons yellow hot pepper sauce (Dylyn insists on the Barbadian kind)
2 teaspoons garlic powder
6 tablespoons flour
1 egg
Oil for frying

1. In a small pan heat the water and thoroughly dissolve the bouillon cubes.
2. Pour this stock into a glass or similarly non-porous bowl, large enough to hold the chicken, and allow to cool.
3. Add the hot pepper sauce, garlic powder and mix well; blend in the flour to make a smooth batter.
4. Whisk in the egg, using a wire whisk or sturdy fork. Now add the chicken pieces to the mixture and drench them very well. Each piece of chicken must be thoroughly coated with the batter.
5. Set aside in a cool place for 1 hour occasionally turning the meat.
6. Heat the oil in a large frying pan almost to boiling, then reduce the heat slowly whilst frying the battered chicken pieces until golden brown and cooked through. Do not crowd the frying pan. Turn each piece at least three or four times using a long kitchen fork or tongs.
7. Keep the fried pieces warm in a low oven until ready to serve.

Ideal with plain boiled rice and red beans.

Serves 4–6

BARBECUED CHICKEN

A family recipe

4–6 chicken portions, legs jointed and breasts cut into halves
Juice of 1 lime or lemon
2 cloves garlic
1 teaspoon sea salt
2 teaspoons West Indian hot pepper sauce
1 chicken bouillon cube (diluted in 55ml (2 fl oz) of boiling water)
1 medium sized onion, halved and sliced
1 tablespoon soya sauce
1 teaspoon curry powder
3 tablespoons dark rum
2 tablespoons tomato sauce (*see* recipe, p.214)
1 teaspoon thyme
1 small piece fresh ginger, peeled and finely chopped or grated
2 tablespoons vegetable oil

1 Put the chicken portions into a bowl, liquidize all the other ingredients and drench the meat with this mixture then marinate in a cool place for at least 6 hours or overnight, turning over a few times if you get a chance – even at 3 o'clock in the morning! Barbecue the chicken portions or place them with the marinade in a baking tin and roast in a pre-heated oven 200°C (400°F/Gas 6) for 1–1½ hours, turning often.

Serves 4–6

ROAST CHICKEN WITH ORANGE AND PORK STUFFING

Curaçao

One 1.7–1.8kg (3½–4 lb) chicken (with giblets, including the liver)
225g (8 oz) lean pork, finely minced
110g (4 oz) bacon, minced

Liver of the chicken, minced
2 cloves garlic, crushed very fine or minced
Black pepper
1 teaspoon oregano
Grated rind of ½ an orange
1 medium onion, minced
2 teaspoons salt
1 tablespoon butter
4 large oranges
2 tablespoons Mexican or Jamaican honey
150ml (¼ pint) chicken stock
½ teaspoon fresh ground cinnamon
2 teaspoons flour, mixed into a paste with a little water
1 tablespoon light rum

1. Mix together the minced pork, bacon, chicken liver, garlic, black pepper, oregano, grated orange rind, onion and a teaspoon of salt. Mix thoroughly.
2. Melt the butter in a small pan and blend the above mixture by cooking on a low heat for about 5 minutes.
3. Taste for seasoning. Add more if you feel so inclined.
4. Remove from heat and allow to cool, then knead with your fingers for a few minutes.
5. Stuff the chicken with the mixture.
6. Cut one of the oranges in half and seal the parson's nose end of the chicken with it. Save the other half for the garnish.
7. Roast in a pre-heated oven 190°C (375°F/Gas Mark 5) for about 1½ hours or until the juice from the chicken runs clear.
8. While the chicken is in the oven, squeeze and strain the juice of the three oranges you have left and pour this into a saucepan with the honey, chicken stock, and cinnamon, blend well, bring to the boil and reduce to about a third.
9. Thicken with the flour and water paste, then simmer, covered, for about 5 minutes. At this stage, put some of the juice from the roasting pan into your orange sauce. The sauce should be nicely glazed.
10. Add the rum and pour the sauce over the chicken for the last 15 minutes of its cooking time.
11. Place the chicken on a warm serving dish. Garnish with

orange slices and serve with any boiled or creamed West Indian vegetables of your choice, particularly fresh pigeon peas flavoured with chives.

Serves 6–8

CHICKEN, CRAB AND CRAYFISH PELAU

Countries with Asian influence

170g (6 oz) salt pork
1.25–1.5kg (2½–3 lb) chicken, cut into very small serving pieces
3 tablespoons olive oil
2 onions, chopped, but not finely
3 cloves garlic, finely chopped
3 tomatoes, blanched, skinned and chopped
½ hot pepper, seeded and chopped (*see* Techniques)
1 tablespoon Angostura bitters
White pepper
Salt to taste
750ml (1¼ pint) stock, made up with the liquid from the salt pork and 1 wineglass of sherry.
340g (¾ lb) rice, well washed
170g (6 oz) frozen peas
225g (½ lb) white crab meat
12 crayfish
1 tablespoon chopped parsley
1½ tablespoons lime or lemon juice
6 lime wedges for garnish
6 tomato wedges for garnish

1 Cut the salt pork into small cubes, wash two or three times, place into a pot with cold water to cover and cook for about 20 minutes or until tender.
2 Remove from heat, drain and reserve the liquid.
3 While the pork is cooking you can be frying the chicken pieces until golden brown in another heavy pot with the oil.
4 Remove the chicken pieces and set aside.
5 Fry the onions and garlic in the same oil until the onions are transparent but not brown.
6 Return the chicken pieces to the pot with the salt pork,

tomato, hot pepper, Angostura bitters, white pepper and very little salt.

7 Cover and simmer on the lowest heat for about 8 minutes.

8 Meanwhile taste the liquid in which the pork was cooked to make certain that it is not too salty; if it is, pour some into another container but do not discard. Make up liquid to 750ml (1¼ pints) by adding the sherry and then slowly adding water. Taste again for salt.

9 Now pour your stock into the pot and bring to the boil; add the rice and peas and stir once or twice.

10 Simmer, still on the lowest heat, covered, until most of the liquid has been absorbed.

11 Taste for salt again.

12 Add the crab meat, crayfish, parsley and lime juice and a few knobs of butter; but do not mix in the seafood, just leave it on top.

13 Simmer, covered, until all the liquid has been completely absorbed.

14 When the cooking is finished, first remove all the crayfish and set them aside, then turn out on to a heated serving dish.

15 Sort out and arrange the crayfish around the dish, garnish with the lime, tomato wedges and some chopped parsley and serve with whatever you fancy.

Serves 6–8

CHICKEN AND PIGEON PEAS PELAU

French, English Islands

450g (1 lb) fresh pigeon peas, shelled (if dried use 225g (½ lb)) or 1 can (*see* Techniques)
4 chicken portions, jointed
225g (½ lb) salt beef, cut into cubes and soaked for 1 to 2 hours
Black pepper
2 cloves garlic, finely chopped
Salt to taste
2 tablespoons vegetable oil
1 tablespoon butter
1 medium sized onion, chopped
2 tablespoons chopped chives

2 firm tomatoes, chopped
340g (¾ lb) rice, well washed
1 litre (1¾ pints) light chicken stock (2 bouillon cubes in same quantity of water)

1. If you use dried peas, soak overnight, then cook until tender in unsalted water. Reserve the liquid from cooking the peas, to make up the amount of stock required in the recipe.
2. Lightly salt the chicken pieces and place them with the salt beef in a bowl, then rub in black pepper, garlic and a little salt. Set aside for an hour or two.
3. Heat the oil and butter in a heavy pot, add the chicken and beef pieces and fry for about 12 minutes. Avoid burning.
4. Add all the other ingredients except the peas, rice and stock, and simmer covered for about 4 minutes.
5. Now mix the rice and peas together and add them to the pot, stirring carefully.
6. Add the stock and bring to the boil.
7. Cook on a very low heat until the rice is tender and all the water has been absorbed. It is essential at this stage of cooking that the pot is well covered with a close-fitting lid.
8. Just before serving, stir the contents over, twice.

Serves 4–6

CHICKEN AND PEAS

Spanish speaking Islands

1.25–1.5 kg (2½–3 lb) chicken (preferably a boiling fowl), cut into serving pieces
2 tablespoons olive oil
1 tablespoon unsalted butter
2 onions, finely chopped
900ml (1½ pints) chicken stock
1 teaspoon oregano
1 tablespoon chopped olives
Black pepper, freshly ground
Salt to taste
1 glass white wine
675g (1½ lb) pigeon peas (freshly cooked)
½ teaspoon saffron

Flour (about 1 tablespoon mixed into a paste with a little of the wine)
1 teaspoon nutmeg, freshly grated

1. In a heavy pot, fry the chicken pieces in the oil and butter until golden brown.
2. Add the onions and sauté for another 2–3 minutes.
3. Pour in the stock and bring to the boil.
4. Add the oregano, olives, black pepper and salt, to taste.
5. Simmer, covered, until the chicken is tender.
6. Remove from heat and strain the liquid into a bowl. Take out the chicken pieces and set them aside, but keep warm.
7. Return the liquid to the pot and reduce on a high heat to about half the amount.
8. Taste for seasoning.
9. Return the chicken to the liquid together with the white wine, peas and saffron.
10. Thicken with the flour paste and simmer for about 6 minutes.
11. Arrange on a warm dish, sprinkle with grated nutmeg and serve with Riz Creole.

Serves 4–6

POLLO CON FRIJOLES

CHICKEN WITH RED BEANS

Spanish speaking Islands

175g (6 oz) red kidney beans
3 chicken portions, cut into small serving pieces
1½–2 chicken bouillon cubes
3 rashers streaky bacon, cut into slivers
2 cloves garlic
½ teaspoon brown cane sugar
1 medium onion, cut into half rings
4–5 cloves, ground
½ teaspoon thyme
1 sprig parsley, finely chopped
1 tablespoon oil

1. Wash the beans, place in a pot with enough cold water to cover by about 5cm (2 inches).
2. Bring to the boil; then boil further on high heat, uncovered, for about 10–12 minutes.

3 Turn down heat – now cook, covered, until the beans are just tender enough to break between your fingers. Do not allow the liquid to boil away, so add hot water as necessary. But remember that, at the end of this, the sauce must be thick and not watery. No salt of any kind must be added to the beans until they are tender.
4 Add the chicken and all other ingredients except the oil. Cook until chicken is tender. The beans should also by now be very tender.
5 Taste for salt.
6 Pour in the oil; stir a couple of times. Leave on heat for a further 5 minutes.
7 Serve with plain boiled rice or mixed West Indian vegetables if you wish. Pepper sauce is vital to this dish as a condiment.

Serves 2–4

POUL'COCOTTE AUX AUBERGINES

CHICKEN WITH AUBERGINE

Originally from Haiti

3 thick rashers streaky bacon
2 tablespoons oil
5 cloves, whole
550g (1¼ lb) poussin
2 aubergines, about 340g (¾ lb), finely chopped
½ a medium size sweet red pepper, finely chopped
150ml (¼ pint) rich chicken stock (or 1 bouillon cube in same quantity of water)
½ teaspoon grated ginger
1 clove garlic, finely chopped
2 small bay leaves
1 teaspoon Angostura bitters
1 tablespoon lemon juice
2 teaspoons hot pepper sauce
Black pepper

1 In a casserole or heavy pot, fry the bacon in the oil, with the cloves. When the bacon is crisp and brown remove from oil with a perforated spoon or spatula; remove the cloves as well and discard altogether.
2 Having made certain that the poussin is properly trussed,

now gently brown the bird on all sides. Be careful not to break the skin or pierce the flesh.

3 Wash and chop the aubergines, but do not peel.
4 Remove the chicken and set aside.
5 Add all the ingredients to the pot, and cook on a medium heat for about 10 minutes.
6 Now return the chicken to the pot, taste for salt; simmer gently for about 30–35 minutes. The bird should be turned over at least 3 times.
7 Serve with fried sweet potatoes and a salad of your choice.

Serves 2

CHICKEN AND PUMPKIN STEW

Eastern Caribbean

2 salted pigs' tails (*see* Techniques) or substitute 450g (1 lb) salt pork
4 portions of chicken; breasts and legs cut into serving pieces
6–8 cloves, whole
4 cloves garlic, crushed
2 medium onions, chopped
1.4 litres (2½ pints) chicken stock (or 2 bouillon cubes in the same quantity of water)
4 small tannias, peeled, washed and cut into halves
2 green bananas
4–6 pieces of white yam
4–6 pieces of dasheen
1 stalk celery
Juice 1 lime
Cornmeal dumplings (*see* Breads and Cakes)
340g (¾ lb) peeled and chopped pumpkin
2 sprigs of parsley
1 good sprig of thyme
Black pepper
Salt to taste
1 *whole* hot pepper

1 Cut the salt pork or pigs' tails into 3.5 cm (1½ inch) pieces.
2 Put the meat into a pot with enough water to cover and bring to the boil.
3 Cook on a medium heat until the meat is tender.

4 Drain and discard water, setting the pigs' tails aside.
5 In a pot sufficient to hold all, place the chicken, whole cloves, crushed garlic, onions and the stock and bring to the boil. Do not add salt yet.
6 Simmer, covered, for about 10 minutes.
7 Now add all other ingredients. Bring quickly to the boil.
8 Taste for salt.
9 Place the whole hot pepper on top. Cover and simmer gently for another 15–20 minutes. Avoid at all cost bursting the pepper and remove it, still whole, before serving the stew. The pepper can be served on the side for those who wish it.
10 Before removing the stew from the heat, make certain that the yams, green bananas and dasheen are cooked.
11 Taste again for salt and serve immediately. A large slice of lime for each guest is essential.

Serves 4–6

MARINADE DE POUL'CREOLE À LA MUSCADE

CHICKEN WITH GINGER AND MACE

From Grenada to Guadeloupe

1.25–1.5 kg (2½–3 lb) chicken, cut into serving pieces
3 tablespoons dark rum
8 very thin slices fresh ginger
1½ teaspoons freshly ground mace
Juice 1 lemon for marinade
2 teaspoons salt, for the marinade
1 teaspoon West Indian hot pepper sauce
1 teaspoon brown sugar
3 cloves garlic
3 tablespoons oil
1 tablespoon caramel colouring (*see* Techniques)
½ teaspoon fresh ground allspice
Juice and peel of ½ a lemon – for cooking
2 tablespoons tomato purée
1 tablespoon tomato ketchup
300ml (½ pint) stock, made from 1½ chicken bouillon cubes,
Salt to taste
1 level tablespoon arrowroot, mixed with 3 tablespoons water

1 Place the chicken pieces in a large bowl, mix well with half of the rum, ginger, mace, juice of 1 lemon, 2 teaspoons salt, pepper sauce, sugar and 1 garlic clove, crushed. Allow to stand for at least 4 hours (overnight is always better).
2 When ready to cook, remove the chicken pieces from the marinade but do not discard this liquor.
3 Heat the oil in a heavy pot, and having removed as much of the moisture from the chicken pieces as possible and any morsels from the marinade that may be stuck to them, fry the chicken pieces until golden brown.
4 Turn down the heat and pour in the caramel colouring and stir for about 5 minutes.
5 Now add the remaining garlic, the allspice, lemon juice and peel, both tomato ketchup and purée; mix well and simmer, covered, for 7–8 minutes.
6 Pour in both the marinade and the stock; simmer on very low heat until chicken is tender.
7 Taste for salt, then thicken the sauce with the arrowroot paste, add the remainder of the rum, and cook for a further 5 minutes.
8 Serve accompanied by West Indian mixed vegetables and red beans or Riz Creole, fried ripe plantains and a green salad.

Serves 4

This dish tastes even better the following day but a little dark rum must be added just after it is heated up. A Martinican rum is best.

You may also need to adjust the seasoning. Best kept in a very cool place if kept overnight.

POUL'À LA CREME COCO

CHICKEN IN COCONUT MILK

Author's recipe

2 tablespoons oil
1 tablespoon butter
1 onion, chopped
3 cloves garlic, crushed or finely chopped
1.25–1.8kg (3–4 lb) chicken, cut into serving pieces
2 tomatoes, skinned and chopped
Juice ½ lime or lemon

2 chicken bouillon cubes
1 sprig fresh thyme
1 sprig parsley
1 bay leaf
600ml (1 pint) coconut milk (*see* Techniques)
2 cinnamon sticks 9–10 cm (3 inches) long – powdered cinnamon will colour the dish too much
¼ teaspoon grated nutmeg
Ground white pepper
Salt to taste
6 blades chives, chopped

1. In a large pot, fry the onion and garlic in the oil and butter until the onions are slightly transparent but not brown.
2. Add the chicken pieces and gently fry for about 5–8 minutes without browning.
3. Add the tomatoes, citrus juice and bouillon cubes, and mix well.
4. Cover and simmer gently for about 10 minutes. Do not allow to stick or burn.
5. Tie the thyme, parsley and bay leaf together in a piece of muslin, place into the pot with all the other ingredients except the chives.
6. Cook until chicken is tender, but not falling apart.
7. Taste for salt at least 5 minutes before removing from the heat.
8. Garnish with parsley and chopped chives – don't forget to remove the bouquet garni and the cinnamon.
9. Serve with Riz Creole, fried ripe plantain, dasheen and sliced avocadoes. Some slices of fresh hot peppers, seeded of course, would balance the subtleness of this dish very well, especially the aromatic Scots Bonnet (*see* Techniques).

Serves 4–6

CHICKEN WITH PINEAPPLE

Countries with Asian influence

1 medium sized pineapple
4 tablespoons pale brown rum (only the finest Island rum should be used)
1.25–1.8kg (3–4 lb) chicken, cut into serving pieces

Juice 1 lime or lemon
Salt to taste
6–8 black pepper corns
6 cloves, ground
2 tablespoons oil
1 tablespoon butter
2 medium sized onions, cut into half rings
2 cloves garlic, finely chopped
225g (½ lb) tomatoes, peeled and chopped
1 hot pepper, seeded and chopped (*see* Techniques)
3 tablespoons raisins or currants
1 bayleaf
300ml (½ pint) chicken stock (or 1½ bouillon cubes in same quantity of hot water)
½ teaspoon arrowroot for slight thickening (or substitute flour and water paste)
Rind of half the lime or lemon

1 Peel and core the pineapple and cut a third of it into any decorative shape that you wish and put to soak in 2 tablespoons of the rum, then chop remainder of the pineapple and set aside in a dish.
2 Rub into the chicken the citrus juice, a little salt, ground black pepper and cloves.
3 Heat the oil and butter in a shallow but heavy pot and fry the chicken pieces until lightly brown.
4 Remove the chicken pieces and set aside.
5 In the same pot fry the onion and garlic for about 2 minutes.
6 Add the tomatoes, hot pepper, raisins or currants and the bay leaf, then simmer for about 5 minutes stirring occasionally.
7 Return the chicken pieces very carefully to the pan, pour in the stock, mix well.
8 Add the remaining rum and cook on low heat until chicken is tender.
9 After the chicken has been on for about 15 minutes, carefully scoop out about 150ml (¼ pint) of liquid from the pot and place into a small saucepan with the chopped pineapple (not the pieces soaking in the rum) and whatever juice there is; place on heat, bring to the boil, then cook uncovered, stirring occasionally until liquid has reduced to about half.

10 Add the rum in which the decorative pieces of pineapple have been soaking.
11 Thicken if necessary with the arrowroot or a flour and water paste.
12 Pour over the chicken and cook for a few minutes longer.
13 Serve garnished with the pineapple pieces that have been soaking in the rum and sprinkle over with the grated citrus rind.

Serves 4–6

CHICKEN WITH MANGOES AND CASHEW NUTS

Countries with Asian influence

1.25–1.5kg (2½–3 lb) chicken, cut into serving pieces
2 tablespoons light rum
Juice ½ a small lemon
½ teaspoon Angostura bitters
1 glass white wine
½ teaspoon fresh thyme, ground
2 cloves garlic, pressed
50g (2 oz) tamarind pulp (*see* Techniques)
½ teaspoon black pepper, freshly ground
Salt to taste
1 teaspoon allspice, freshly ground
½ teaspoon saffron or turmeric
170g–225g (6–8 oz) unsalted cashew nuts
2 ripe mangoes, peeled, stoned and sliced

1 Blend together the rum, lemon juice, Angostura, wine, thyme, garlic, tamarind pulp, a little black pepper, salt, half of the allspice, and the saffron.
2 Place the chicken pieces into a heavy pot or casserole; pour the blended mixture over the chicken, let stand 4–5 hours.
3 Add the cashew nuts, place on a low heat and simmer gently, covered, for about 20 minutes.
4 Now place the sliced mangoes on top of the chicken, dust with the remaining allspice and black pepper, and cook for 10 minutes.

5 Taste for salt.
6 Serve immediately.

Serves 4

I found that the nicest accompaniments to this delicious dish were green salad, with a lime or lemon dressing and plain boiled rice.

FOWL SWEET WITH RAISINS

Countries with Asian influence

1.25–1.5kg (2½–3 lb) boiling fowl, cut into serving pieces
3 tablespoons coconut oil (substitute vegetable or sunflower oil)
2 onions, chopped
1 tablespoon wine vinegar (red)
Salt to taste
2 tablespoons tomato purée
2 cloves garlic, chopped
1 heaped teaspoon brown sugar
6 cloves
1 sweet pepper, seeded and chopped
½ hot pepper, seeded and chopped (optional)
300ml (½ pint) stock (1½ bouillon cubes in same quantity of water)
½ teaspoon grated nutmeg
Black pepper
1 tablespoon flour for paste (with two tablespoons water)
110g (4 oz) raisins

1 In a heavy pot fry the chicken pieces in the oil until golden brown. Set aside. If there is too much oil in the pot, use your discretion and discard some, leaving enough to fry the onions. Boiling fowl sometimes produce a lot of fat. You can retain and store the fat in the refrigerator.
2 Fry the onions in the remaining oil until transparent but not brown.
3 Return the chicken pieces to the pot together with the vinegar, a little salt and the tomato purée.
4 Turn heat down and sauté for 2–3 minutes.
5 Add all the other ingredients except the flour paste and the

raisins and bring slowly to the boil, then simmer for about 1½ hours.

6 Thicken with the flour paste – it must not be too thick, so use your own judgement.
7 Now add the raisins and simmer for a further 15 minutes.
8 Taste for seasoning and continue to simmer until chicken is tender.
9 Serve accompanied by Caribbean vegetables.

Serves 4–6

I have tried the above dish with olives and about 110g (4 oz) chopped bacon. The taste was different but delicious.

CHICKEN AND ORANGE SALAD

Curaçāo

3 large chicken breasts
1 tablespoon chicken stock
2 cloves garlic, crushed but left whole
Small sprig parsley
4 cloves, left whole
2 teaspoons orange rind (use the one to be juiced)
White peppercorns, freshly ground
1 tablespoon dry sherry (optional)
Salt to taste
3 oranges, peeled and segmented with all seeds and pith removed
Juice 1 orange
1–2 teaspoons lemon juice
2 teaspoons orange liqueur
2 tablespoons olive oil
Sugar (optional)

1 Cook the chicken breasts in just barely enough water to cover, with the stock, garlic, parsley, cloves, orange rind, a little pepper, sherry, and enough salt to bring out the flavour. Simmer very gently until tender.
2 Meanwhile peel and prepare the oranges. Always prepare any soft fruits over a bowl so as to collect the juices.
3 Make a dressing with the orange juice, lemon juice, orange liqueur, olive oil, white pepper, salt and sugar and mix well.

4 When the chicken is cooked remove from the heat, and allow it to cool in the liquid, turning the chicken pieces over occasionally.
5 When cool remove from the liquid, take one tablespoon of the liquid and add to the salad dressing. The rest can be refrigerated for future use.
6 Bone the chicken, then cut (do not chop) the meat into small cubes.
7 Place the chicken cubes into a bowl and pour the dressing over them. Mix in well and set aside for 1 hour.
8 Arrange half the orange segments in the bottom of a salad bowl, layer the dressed chicken and decorate with the remainder of the orange segments.

Serves 4

CANARD CREOLE

CREOLE DUCK

Prepared on several of the Islands

1.8–2.25kg (4–5 lb) duck, cut into serving pieces
Juice 1 lemon
4–6 cloves, freshly ground
Black pepper, freshly ground
Salt to taste
2 tablespoons olive oil
1 tablespoon butter
2 tablespoons rum
1 onion, in sliced half rings
2 cloves garlic, crushed
2 tomatoes, blanched, peeled and chopped
1 tablespoon chopped chives
1 tablespoon tomato purée
2 tablespoons caramel colouring
1 teaspoon thyme
1 glass red wine
Flour paste
2 tablespoons orange liqueur

1 Put the duck into a bowl with the lemon juice, 2 or 3 cloves, black pepper and salt. Mix well and allow to stand for about 1 hour.

2 Heat the oil and butter in a large pot and fry the duck until brown.
3 Now flambé with the rum.
4 Add the onion and garlic and sauté for about 3 minutes.
5 Now add all the other ingredients except for the orange liqueur and flour paste.
6 Simmer, covered, until tender.
7 Thicken with the flour paste if required.
8 Taste for seasoning and pour in the liqueur.
9 Cook for a further 10 minutes.
10 Serve with plain boiled local vegetables.

Serves 4

STEWED DUCK WITH PIGEON PEAS

Author's recipe

Duck is not common on the islands, but quite a few of the wealthier people keep their own in yards or in the country. But over the years, especially with Caribbean people travelling as much as they now do and the influx of tourism, there is a growing demand and use for duck. So it is now more available in supermarkets – frozen of course. The following is one of my own recipes.

1.8–2.25kg (4–5 lb) duck, firmly trussed
2 tablespoons butter
1 tablespoon vegetable oil
1 tablespoon rum, warmed
900ml (1½ pints) clear chicken stock
340g (¾ lb) fresh pigeon peas (or 1 can of green pigeon peas, drained)
8 shallots, peeled but left whole
225g (½ lb) young carrots, scraped and cubed
1 small christophene, peeled, cored and cubed
2 cloves garlic, finely chopped
2 bay leaves
2 tablespoons chives, chopped
1 sprig fresh thyme
Juice 1 lemon
1 glass sherry

Black pepper, freshly ground
Salt to taste

1 Melt the butter with the oil in a heavy pot and brown the duck on all sides.
2 Pour in the warmed rum, and flambé.
3 Add the stock and simmer covered for about half an hour, carefully turning the duck a few times.
4 Remove the duck and place in a colander over a bowl to catch any juice.
5 Skim off the fat from the liquid in the pot, then boil and reduce it to about a third.
6 Return the duck to the pot.
7 Skim off any further fat from the bowl over which the duck has been drained, and add that liquid to the pot.
8 Surround the duck with all the other dry ingredients and pour in the lemon juice and sherry.
9 Simmer covered until tender, basting frequently without disturbing the vegetables too much.
10 Taste for seasoning.
11 Remove the bay leaves and the thyme.
12 Serve with fried ripe plantains, Riz Creole and a green salad.

Serves 4–6

Pork

Though many young people who grew up between the end of the sixties and the eighties are members of the Rastafarian movement and therefore non-pork eaters, pork remains, I think, the favourite meat of the Caribbean. There are many recipes for pork and a variety of ways of preparing them. I have tried in this book to include as many as possible that can be prepared in Europe without too much difficulty in finding the right ingredients. In the Islands almost every part of the animal is made use of, including the head and trotters which are used for souse, and the blood and intestines for the making of the most mouth-watering black pudding. A suckling pig spit-roasted or seasoned with herbs and spices then wrapped in banana leaves and cooked buried in a charcoal pit is one of the greatest culinary delights. Smoked pork, *Cochon parfumé*, forms part of a large stew prepared at Christmas and Carnival time on the island of Dominica.

But all the pork dishes are tempting and delicious when prepared. Picture a small wooden cabin with a verandah and a pitched roof covered with cedar shingles, perched almost on the edge of a deep gorge with a white cascading waterfall; and towering trees festooned with liana vines, slim graceful 'balisias' (a flowering member of the banana family) with their pink, yellow and deep red claw-like flowers, whose leaves are used to protect bread baked in wood-fired ovens. Imagine, in your mind's eye, a forest of tall tree ferns, and scattered here and there anthurium lilies, and birds of paradise. It has just been raining as it almost always does a thousand feet or more up in the rain forest. The leaves of the plants and trees glisten as the late morning sun filters through. The air is cool and scented with orange and grapefruit blossoms. You can hear the sounds of the Siffleur Montagne – a bird not to be heard anywhere else but in the rain forest of Dominica. A short walk away there is a glimpse of the sea in the distance; a view over rolling hills and more rich and vibrant vegetation. One sips a rum punch of fresh orange juice and ripe pawpaw. No more congenial atmosphere in which to experiment with a newly discovered dish; a joint of pork gently simmering in rum with coriander and spices – a new aroma drifts out to mingle with that of the forest. That is how I first prepared the first dish in this section, on a small estate, Ramelton, on the island of Dominica, which belongs to an American friend of mine and was loaned to me for a few weeks.

DAUBE DE COCHON RAMELTON

BRAISED PORK WITH CORIANDER AND RUM

1.5–1.8 kg (3–4 lb) middle shoulder of pork, skinned with some of the fat removed
2 tablespoons vegetable oil
2 tablespoons caramel colouring
3 tablespoons dark Island rum
1 teaspoon hot pepper, seeded and chopped (*see* Techniques)
½ teaspoon grated lemon rind
5 cloves, ground
3 cloves garlic, very finely chopped (or use a garlic press)
1 teaspoon fresh ground coriander
1 tablespoon fresh coriander leaves
2 tablespoons lemon juice
5 tablespoons chicken stock (using 2 bouillon cubes)
Very little salt

1 In a heavy pot with a tight-fitting lid, large enough to hold the joint of pork, heat the oil and brown the pork on all sides.
2 Add the caramel and half the rum and continue to sear on a medium heat until the pork is a rich brown. Do not allow to burn.
3 Now add all the other ingredients, except the remaining rum, cover tightly and simmer on the lowest heat until the meat is tender; about 2½–3 hours.
4 Turn over the joint as often as possible, but do not leave uncovered for too long.
5 5 minutes before serving add the rest of the rum.
6 Taste for salt and serve, accompanied by fried ripe plantains and boiled christophene with a fruit and vegetable salad.

Serves 4

ROAST SUCKLING PIG

4.5kg–5.4kg (10–12 lb) prepared suckling pig (be certain to have your butcher leave enough flesh and skin on the belly for sewing)
Juice 1 lime
2 tablespoons sea salt

4 cloves, ground
2 teaspoons black pepper, freshly ground
3 tablespoons oil

1 Wash the suckling pig under cold water and thoroughly dry inside and out. The pig should not spend too much time in the water, so this task should be done as quickly as possible.
2 Rub the inside of the pig with the lime juice, then mix together the salt, cloves and black pepper and sprinkle the inside with half of the mixture.
3 Set aside while you prepare a STUFFING of:

Heart, liver and kidneys of the pig
3 tablespoons butter
2 onions, finely chopped
3–4 cloves garlic, finely chopped
340g (¾ lb) fresh bread crumbs
1 hot pepper, seeded and chopped (*see* Techniques)
4 tablespoons chopped chives
1 large sprig parsley, finely chopped
½ teaspoon thyme
½ teaspoon allspice
4 tablespoons Island rum
Juice ½ a lime
Salt to taste

1 Clean and wash the liver, heart and kidney.
2 Pat dry, then chop or mince all three.
3 Melt the butter in a pan on a low heat, add the chopped onions and garlic and sauté until the onion is transparent but not brown.
4 Add the offal and continue to sauté, mixing well, for about 6 minutes.
5 Remove from heat.
6 When cool, add the other ingredients, mixing well.
7 Taste for salt and seasoning. If the stuffing is too dry, add up to 2 tablespoons water or milk.

Now return to the main procedure:

4 Fill the ribcage and belly of the pig with the stuffing.
5 Roll a piece of foil into a ball the size of a small orange and place this in the pig's mouth.

6 Seal the belly with skewers or sew with a kitchen needle and strong thread or twine.
7 Tie each pair of legs together and fold beneath the pig.
8 Now place belly downwards on a trivet in a fairly shallow pan.
9 Brush the back with oil and sprinkle the remainder of the ground cloves, sea salt and black pepper all over.
10 Place the pan in the centre of a pre-heated oven at 160°C (325°F/Gas 3) for about 2 hours.
11 It is advisable to protect the pig's ears and tail with foil for the first 1½ hours of cooking.
12 To check if the dish is done, insert a thin sharp knife into the thigh – the juices should run clear and not pink.
13 Remove the pan from the oven and allow to cool for about 12 minutes.
14 Place the pig on a heated platter and replace the foil in the mouth with an orange.
15 Remove any skewers and serve with a sauce suitable for roast pork.

Sufficient for a party

ROAST PORK CALYPSO

Jamaica

This is excellent for a Sunday lunch or formal dinner.

1.5kg–1.8kg (3–4 lb) loin of pork, with the chine bone sawn through by your butcher
4 tablespoons Island rum
1½ teaspoons ground ginger
3 cloves garlic, finely chopped
2 tablespoons brown sugar
2 tablespoons lime juice
6 cloves, freshly ground
Black pepper
Salt to taste
2 bay leaves, ground in a mortar and pestle
½ hot pepper, chopped (*see* Techniques)
450ml (¾ pint) chicken stock (2 bouillon cubes in same quantity of water)

2 teaspoons arrowroot, blended with 1 tablespoon chicken stock

1 Score the loin of pork to form a diamond pattern and rub salt into the cuts.
2 Place on a rack in a roasting pan in a pre-heated oven 200°C (400°F/Gas 6).
3 Meanwhile, prepare a basting sauce with 2 tablespoons of the rum, all the ginger, garlic, sugar, lime juice, cloves, black pepper, salt and ground bay leaves, chopped pepper and a little stock.
4 When the crackling is brown and crisp, turn the oven down to about 180°C (350°F/Gas 4) and start basting the pork regularly with the sauce, just a little at a time, until the pork is cooked. Allow 30 minutes roasting per pound. The juice of the loin should run clear and not pink, when a skewer, blade tip or fork is inserted.
5 Remove from oven and transfer the pork to a heated serving platter. Add the stock to the pan.
6 Taste liquid in roasting pan for seasoning, mainly salt, adjust if you need to, place on a high heat and bring to the boil.
7 Skim off any excess fat.
8 Thicken with the arrowroot paste, stirring to prevent any lumps forming.
9 Simmer for about 2 minutes.
10 Add the remaining rum.
11 Pour into a sauceboat.

Serves 6–8

Mixed vegetables and pigeon peas, plus a raw cabbage salad, are ideal to accompany this dish.

A passion fruit punch beforehand is highly recommended.

PIERNA DE PUERCO RELLENA

STUFFED LEG OF PORK

Spanish speaking Islands

1.8kg–2.45 kg (4–5 lb) boned leg of pork
2 cloves garlic, finely chopped or pressed
110g (4 oz) pistachio nuts
Salt to taste

75g (3 oz) minced chicken
75g (3 oz) minced bacon
75g (3 oz) fresh breadcrumbs
1 whole clove garlic, cut into slivers
4 cloves, freshly ground
1 onion, finely chopped
6 green olives, stoned and finely chopped
½ teaspoon thyme
1 bay leaf, finely crushed
Black pepper, freshly ground
2 tablespoons rum
300ml (½ pint) chicken stock

1 Have your butcher score and bone the pork.
2 Insert a knife at several points where the skin has been scored, each cut deep enough to take a sliver of garlic and a pistachio with a little salt.
3 Save half the nuts for the stuffing.
4 Rub the pork all over with salt.
5 Combine all the other ingredients except 1 tablespoon of rum and the stock.
6 Taste for seasoning.
7 Stuff the cavity of the leg, bring together with a skewer or two, put on a rack in a greased baking pan and bake in a preheated oven at 220°C (425°F/Gas 7) until the skin crackles.
8 Lower heat to 190°C (375°F/Gas 5) until cooked. Allow 30–35 minutes to the pound.
9 When done remove from baking pan but keep warm.
10 Pour the chicken stock into the same pan, bring to the boil, then lower the heat.
11 Taste again for seasoning.
12 Simmer for about 6 minutes, then add the remaining rum and serve this sauce separately with the roast. You may add a little hot pepper sauce to the gravy if you so wish.
13 Bring to the table with West Indian vegetables and red beans.

Serves 6–8

CARNE DE PUERCO A LA NARANJA

PORK WITH ORANGE

Spanish speaking countries

1.5kg (3 lb) boned shoulder of pork, cubed
2 tablespoons oil
2 tablespoons caramel colouring (*see* Techniques)
3 cloves garlic, crushed
7.5 cm (3 inch) stick of cinnamon
6 blades chives, chopped
Peel of 1 orange, in thin strips
Peel and juice of ½ a lemon
1 teaspoon allspice
1 sprig fresh thyme
2 bay leaves
2 bouillon cubes (chicken)
450ml (¾ pint) fresh orange juice
Black pepper
Salt to taste
1 tablespoon flour, mixed with 3 tablespoons orange juice
2 tablespoons orange liqueur

1. Heat the oil in a large pot, add the pork pieces and fry until just brown, pour in the caramel and continue to fry until a rich brown.
2. Mix in all the other ingredients, except for the orange liqueur and flour paste but including the bouillon cubes, and simmer, covered, on a low heat until the pork is tender.
3. Thicken with the flour paste, stirring to prevent any lumps from forming.
4. Taste for salt.
5. Add the orange liqueur and simmer for a further 5 minutes.
6. Remove the bay leaves.
7. Serve with West Indian vegetables, Riz Creole and red beans. Garnish the dish with slices of orange if so desired.

Serves 4–6

BELLY OF PORK WITH CHICKEN LIVER

Author's recipe

675g (1½ lb) belly of pork (cut away as much of the fat as possible)
450g (1 lb) white beans, soaked overnight
2 cloves garlic, pressed or finely chopped
½ hot pepper, seeded and chopped (*see* Techniques)
5 whole cloves
Small sprig fresh tarragon
2 tablespoons chives, chopped
2 bay leaves
Black pepper, freshly ground
Salt to taste
450g (1 lb) fresh or frozen chicken liver
2 tablespoons olive oil
1 tablespoon white wine vinegar
1 tablespoon butter

1 Cook the beans in enough water to cover for about 20 minutes.
2 Cut the pork into cubes and add to the beans with all the herbs and spices, but with no salt. Simmer, covered, for about 30 to 40 minutes. Add more liquid if needed.
3 Add salt to taste and simmer for another 15 minutes.
4 Now add the rest of the ingredients including the chicken liver and continue to simmer until the beans and pork are tender.
5 Serve with Riz Creole and a green salad.

Serves 4–6

PORC ET CHOU-CHOU AUX EPICES

SPICED PORK WITH CHRISTOPHENE

French Islands

675g (1½ lb) shoulder of pork (in a piece)
2 tablespoons olive oil
1 tablespoon sugar
1 onion, sliced
1 christophene, peeled, cored and sliced
150ml (¼ pint) water

Callaloo soup – ABOVE ingredients; BELOW prepared dish

ABOVE Avocado and saltfish; BELOW smoked herring and souse

Baked stuffed red snapper – ABOVE ingredients; BELOW prepared dish

Fried red snapper and sprats (*foreground*); courtbouillon (*left*) and coo-coo (*right*)

ABOVE Lister's stewed beef, chicken in coconut cream, and red beans; BELOW Port Royal lamb with foo-foo

ABOVE Chicken marinade with rice and pigeon peas;
BELOW Stuffed pineapple with fruit

ABOVE LEFT Okra and hot peppers (Scot's bonnet); ABOVE RIGHT plantain, yam and sweet potatoes; BELOW LEFT dasheen and yellow yam; BELOW RIGHT christophene (*right*) and tannia

1 Yellow Fin Tuna, tunny, thon: a member of the mackerel family; has a firm flesh not unlike meat. Ideal for steaks.

2 Vielle Maconde: a small Grouper of up to 900g (2lbs), and excellent for steaming or baking.

3 Vielle Rouge: another Grouper and similar to vielle maconde.

4 Bonita: a smaller member of the tuna family.

5 Bourgeois: a red snapper with a white succulent flesh; one of the finest of food fishes. Weighs between 5 to 12 lbs.

6 Capitaine Rouge: another excellent eating fish similar to sea bream. Ideal for stuffing and baking whole, also for steaks and grills. 3 to 10lbs.

7 Croissant: one of the groupers or sea bass; has a sweet white flesh which is delicious even served cold. 2 to 5lbs.

8 Job Griz: a snapper; can be grilled, baked or used in stews and soups.

9 Vara Vara: a red snapper with a firm white flesh ideal for Escovitch and daubes.

10 Parrotfishes: from 1 to 3lbs in weight; best served fried.

11 Job Jaune: a deep water snapper with a similar flesh to sea bass.

12 Rabbitfish: goes under creole name of cordonnier. Average weight about 250g (½lb); best again for frying or grilling.

13 Lascar
14 Gueule Longue
15 Madame Berrie
} All members of the bream family

16 Vielle Platte: a large grouper related to the bass.

17 Capitaine Blanc: another excellent fish similar to Capitaine Rouge.

18 Golden Mullet: also known in creole as rouge barbes, even though the most common one is yellow. Delicious marinated, then fried or grilled.

19 Barracuda, Becune: very popular in the Caribbean fried, or in stews and soups.

The name of the suppliers can be found at the back.

1 sprig parsley or fresh coriander leaves
1 clove garlic
8 allspice berries, freshly ground
1½ bouillon cubes (chicken or pork)
1 teaspoon pepper sauce
Juice ½ lemon
1 teaspoon rum

1. Heat the oil in a heavy pot and put in the shoulder.
2. Sprinkle the sugar over the pork and brown it, adding the onion and the christophene.
3. Now add all the other ingredients except the rum.
4. Allow to simmer gently until tender.
5. Taste for seasoning and add the rum.
6. Serve accompanied by dasheen and green bananas.

Serves 2

DAUBE DE PORC ÉPI AUBERGINE

PORK STEW AND AUBERGINES

Martinique

1.5kg (3 lb) fillet of pork, left in one piece
2 tablespoons vegetable oil
2 tablespoons butter
3 medium sized onions, finely chopped
1 level teaspoon allspice
1 bay leaf
2 tablespoons water
Black pepper, freshly ground
Salt to taste
1.25–1.5kg (2½–3 lb) small aubergines (preferably those called Chinese, which are pale and curved)

1. Heat the oil in a heavy pot and sauté the fillet of pork until a golden brown.
2. Lift the pork from the pot and set aside.
3. Add the butter to the pot which should be on a low heat.
4. When the butter has melted, line the bottom of the pot evenly with the chopped onions.
5. Spread over the onions all the remaining ingredients except for the aubergines.

6 Return the fillet to lay on the ingredients in the pot.
7 Cover, and simmer gently for 45–60 minutes. Turn the pork at least three times during the cooking period. Check to make certain that nothing sticks to the bottom of the pan. This dish must be prepared without any other liquid apart from the 2 tablespoons of water.
8 After the hour is up, cut the aubergines lengthways, then slice them into half moons and add quickly to the pot. Cover tightly and cook on a moderate heat for a further 15–20 minutes.
9 Taste for salt.
10 Sweet potatoes are essential with this simple but delicious Creole dish.

Serves 6–8

COCHON PARFUMÉ ÉPI POIS ROUGES

SMOKED HOCK WITH RED BEANS

French and Patois speaking Islands

2 smoked hocks, about 900g (2 lb) each in weight
340g (12 oz) red beans, soaked overnight
1 onion, cut into half rings
3 cloves garlic, chopped
6–8 cloves, ground
½ teaspoon nutmeg
2 sprigs thyme
2 bay leaves
1 teaspoon brown sugar
Black pepper
150ml (¼ pint) stock from the hock
Salt to taste
2 tablespoons chives (for garnish)

1 Soak the hocks overnight, changing the water at least twice.
2 Discard the water when ready to cook and cover with enough fresh cold water, bring to the boil in a heavy pot and cook on a medium heat for 1 hour.
3 Taste to see how salty the liquid is; if in your opinion there is too much salt, which is possible even after the meat has been soaked, discard half of the liquid and replace with an equal amount of boiling water.

4 Cook the hocks until tender but still fairly firm.
5 Now the red beans should be put on to boil in another pot (*see* Techniques).
6 When the hocks are just right and the red beans are tender but not broken, remove the meat from the heat, drain the liquid, reserving 300ml (½ pint), return the pork to the heat and pour in the red beans.
7 Add all other ingredients except the salt and chives, bring to the boil and add 150ml (¼ pint) of stock.
8 Simmer, covered, for about 15–20 minutes, taste for salt and seasoning and continue to cook until the beans and hocks are tender.
9 If to your taste there is too much liquid, cook uncovered for the last 10 minutes. However, remember that beans, being starchy, tend to stick to the bottom of the pot. If on the other hand there is not enough liquid, there is still that 150ml (¼ pint) left over from the stock.
10 Transfer to a large decorated serving dish, sprinkle with the chopped chives and serve with Riz Creole and dasheen or yams.

Serves 4–6

PORK PELAU WITH RICE AND CABBAGE

Countries with Asian influence

450g (1 lb) salted pigs' tails
450g (1 lb) salted pig's snout or the same amount of salt pork, unsmoked
2 medium sized onions, chopped
2 cloves garlic, chopped
1 red sweet pepper
1 teaspoon hot pepper, chopped and seeded (*see* Techniques)
1 sprig thyme (or ½ teaspoon dried)
½ teaspoon fennel seeds
¼ teaspoon allspice
1 tablespoon lime juice
Black pepper
Just a little salt, to taste
225g (½ lb) long-grained rice

450g (1 lb) white cabbage
2 tablespoons butter

1 Cut the meat into suitable pieces and wash thoroughly, then allow to soak for at least 6 hours changing the water as often as is convenient.
2 When ready to cook, drain and wash the pieces of meat, place into a pot with enough water to cover, then bring to the boil.
3 Cook, covered, on a low heat for about 15 minutes.
4 Taste for salt; if there is too much salt, discard some of the water and make up with an equal amount of boiling water. The water or liquid must just cover the meat and no more.
5 Now add all the other ingredients, except the rice, butter and cabbage.
6 Bring to the boil, then simmer, covered, for about 1¼ hours.
7 Test the meat to see how tender it is; if fairly tender and not chewy, add the rice and simmer, tightly covered, for another 10 minutes.
8 Now spread the cabbage on top of the rice, and cook, covered, until all the liquid has been absorbed.
9 Stir to mix the cabbage and rice in with the meat.
10 Turn out on to a serving dish and serve with knobs of butter on top.

Serves 4

PORK WITH PINEAPPLE

Curaçāo

1.5–1.8kg (3–4 lb) loin of pork, with the chine bone cut through by your butcher
4 cloves, ground
Black pepper
Salt to taste
1 medium size ripe pineapple
75g (3 oz) butter
1 tablespoon brown sugar
1 clove garlic, slightly crushed
½ teaspoon nutmeg
300ml (8 fl oz) chicken stock
1 glass sherry

1 tablespoon arrowroot, made into a paste with a little water
6 red cherries

1. Wipe the joint and score the rind almost down to the flesh.
2. Mix the ground cloves, black pepper, some salt and the cinnamon together and rub into the cuts of the scored rind. Rub some salt all over the rind as well.
3. Place on a rack in a roasting pan, and roast in a pre-heated oven 200°C (400°F/Gas 6) until the crackling is nice and crisp, then turn down to 180°C (350°F/Gas 4) and continue to roast until the joint is tender and the juices run clear.
4. In the meantime, peel and core the pineapple, retain a third of it for garnishing and cut that third into spear-point shapes. Cut the rest into attractive small pieces ready for the sauce.
5. Melt the butter in a small pan, add the sugar, garlic and nutmeg, then the pineapple pieces.
6. Cook, covered, for about 7 minutes making sure the sugar does not burn.
7. Add the stock and the sherry and simmer for a further 10–12 minutes.
8. When the joint is done, remove from the oven and place it on a warm serving dish; keep warm.
9. Put the roasting pan on a low heat, pour in the pineapple sauce and simmer for a few minutes.
10. Taste for seasoning, especially salt.
11. Thicken with the arrowroot paste. Do not leave to cook now for any longer than about 3–4 minutes. You may remove the crackling and serve it on the side, or leave it on the joint, whichever you prefer.
12. Pour the pineapple sauce over the joint.
13. Garnish with the pineapple spears and a cherry pinned down by a cocktail stick on six of the spears.
14. Serve with any West Indian vegetables of your choice.

Serves 4–6

QUICK AND SPICY PORK CHOPS

Author's recipe

2 pork chops, preferably with kidneys attached
1 tablespoon butter
1 tablespoon oil

1 clove garlic, finely chopped
¼ teaspoon ground cloves
Black pepper
1 glass white wine
2 teaspoons lemon juice
1 chicken bouillon cube
1 tablespoon rum
1 bunch watercress
1 small carton fresh double cream

1 Heat the oil and butter in a heavy frying pan, then quickly brown the chops on both sides without burning.
2 Turn the heat down and add the garlic, cloves, pepper, white wine, lemon juice and the bouillon cube.
3 Stir and cook, uncovered, until the liquid has reduced, but do not cook for any longer than about 8 minutes.
4 Add the rum and watercress, then stir in the cream. But stir quickly and continuously to prevent the cream from curdling. Cook for a further 3 minutes.
5 Serve garnished with watercress and accompanied by boiled rice, seasoned with fennel, and perhaps a few slices of avocado.

Serves 2

COUNTRY BRAFF

SMOKED PORK, TUNA AND VEGETABLE STEW

Dominica

450g (1 lb) smoked pork, cut into reasonable pieces, soaked overnight
450g (1 lb) fresh tuna (substitute dolphin fish, sword fish, bonito or any such firm fish), cut into six pieces
4–6 small tannias, cut into halves
3 green bananas, each cut in half
4–6 small pieces of white yam
4–6 small pieces of dasheen
6 okras, topped but left whole
½ hot pepper, seeded (*see* Techniques)
2 onions, chopped
3 cloves garlic, finely chopped
Juice 1 lime

6 whole cloves
2 bouillon cubes
1 sprig thyme
1 sprig parsley
Black pepper, freshly ground
Salt to taste
Piece of banana leaf

1 Thoroughly wash the pork and place in a pot with enough cold water to cover.
2 Bring to the boil.
3 Having peeled and washed the vegetables add them to the pot with all the other ingredients except the fish.
4 Cover with the banana leaf, then the lid, place a heavy object, like a brick, on top to increase the pressure, and simmer, covered, until the pork is just about cooked.
5 Uncover, taste for seasoning.
6 Place the fish on the stew, replace the banana leaf, the lid, the weight and cook for another 10–15 minutes.
7 Serve from the pot.

Serves 4–6

Other Meats

Though not as plentiful or popular as pork or chicken, and indeed goat on several of the English-speaking Islands, Caribbeans still make use of all other meats. And with the increase in tourism and the appearance of large supermarkets with their commercial freezers, Caribbeans are able to buy many meats that were not readily available to them before.

The following recipes have either been devised by myself, or are those I have picked up on my travels throughout the Islands, or are ones given to me by many friends.

BEEF STOCK

900g–1.5kg (2–3 lb) cheapest beef, minced
2 medium sized onions, minced
1 carrot, minced
1 clove garlic, minced
1 stalk celery, minced
2 sprigs parsley, minced
1 sprig thyme, minced
1 bay leaf, minced
2 egg whites, beaten
1 tablespoon salt
1.75 litres (3 pints) water

1 Bring all ingredients except the egg whites to the boil in the water.
2 Simmer for 1 hour, skimming off all the foam and excess fat.
3 Add egg whites to stock in order to bring the last fatty substances to the surface.
4 Bring to the boil, simmer 10 minutes.
5 Now skim off the egg whites.
6 Strain through a cheesecloth.
7 This may have to be repeated.
8 Cool and refrigerate until needed.

LISTER'S BEEF AND CHRISTOPHENE STEW

I will always remember this as being one of the favourite beef dishes of my mother (she is named Lister) which she loved cooking outside in the yard, on a coalpot underneath a Julie mango tree. It formed part of many a gargantuan but excellent Sunday lunch.

We West Indians love to suck and chew bones: hence the beef on the bone.

675g (1½ lb) lean stewing beef, cut into cubes
450g (1 lb) beef on the bone, chopped into pieces
3 tablespoons oil
1 tablespoon brown sugar (substitute caramel colouring)
2 medium sized onions, sliced into half rings
3 cloves garlic, crushed flat but not chopped
½ teaspoon nutmeg

3 ripe tomatoes, sliced
2 carrots, cubed
6 whole cloves
1 hot pepper, seeded and chopped (*see* Techniques)
6 blades chives
1 sprig parsley } tied together as a bouquet garni
1 sprig fresh thyme
300ml (½ pint) beef stock (2 bouillon beef cubes)
150ml (¼ pint) dry red wine
2 tablespoons tomato sauce (*see* p.215)
Black pepper
Salt to taste
1 tablespoon flour mixed with a little stock
1 large christophene, peeled, cored and sliced

1 Heat the oil in a heavy pot or casserole, add the sugar but do not disturb until it begins to caramelize. When the sugar begins to turn a golden brown swirl it round in the oil.
2 Put in the meat at once and stir until the meat is a rich dark brown.
3 When the meat is browned, add the onions, garlic, nutmeg and tomatoes and cook for about 6 minutes.
4 Now add all the other ingredients, except the christophene and the flour paste, then cover and simmer gently for 1½ hours.
5 Taste for seasoning.
6 Thicken with the flour paste, add the christophene and cook for a further 30 minutes or until the meat is tender.
7 Serve with red kidney beans, West Indian vegetables and a salad of cabbage and shredded carrots.

Sometimes on a Sunday, especially when guests were expected, this stew would be accompanied by various other dishes, including both chicken and fish, also by slices of avocado, stuffed ripe plantains and macaroni pie. This could be part of a meal prepared for as many as twelve people, but alone would serve four or six.

JUG-JUG

Barbados

As already mentioned, many cultures have contributed to the cuisine of the Caribbean, and Scotland was no exception. This is the Bajan (Barbadian) version of the Scottish Haggis. After the Monmouth Rebellion of 1685, many Scots were exiled to Barbados by the infamous and feared Judge Jeffreys. Cromwell had sent many Irish there before, hence the 'Redlegs' of today.

170g (6 oz) salt pork, soaked for at least 6 hours or longer
170g (6 oz) salt beef, treated as the pork
450g (1 lb) fresh pigeon peas (or equivalent, if canned, when drained)
2 medium size onions, finely chopped or grated
110g (4 oz) guinea corn (millet), ground
6–8 blades chives, chopped (or about 3–4 spring onions)
2 teaspoons fresh thyme leaves
1 tablespoon parsley, chopped
50–75g (2–3 oz) butter
Black pepper, freshly ground
Salt to taste

1. Wash the meats in fresh water and cut into cubes.
2. Put them into a pot with just enough water to cover (you may have to add a little more water during cooking).
3. Bring to the boil.
4. Lower the heat and simmer, covered, for about 45 minutes or until the meat is fairly tender.
5. Add the pigeon peas (if you are using canned peas, add them when the meats are cooked, and cook for only another 5–6 minutes), then simmer until the peas are tender.
6. Remove the pot from heat, drain and reserve the liquid.
7. Make a purée of the meats and peas in a blender, or pound in a mortar with a pestle.
8. Return about half the liquid or less to the pot (you can always add more if needed), then add all other ingredients, except the purée and the butter, and simmer on a low heat, stirring constantly. The mixture should become fairly stiff in about 10 minutes.
9. Now stir in the puréed meats and peas and simmer on a very low heat for about 20 minutes. Stir as often as possible to

prevent sticking or burning. The mixture must be almost dry at the end of the cooking.

10 Blend in 40g (1½ oz) of the butter.
11 Turn out into a mould greased with butter. Pack well.
12 Now turn out on a warm serving dish.
13 Spread the balance of the butter all over and serve hot.

Serves 4–6

In Barbados this is principally a Christmas dish.

JERKED BEEF

St Lucia

This recipe was given to me by my friend, Dylyn Dalton, from St Lucia, now living in London.

1.5kg (3 lb) topside, cubed
3 tablespoons vegetable oil
Water
3 teaspoons pepper sauce
4–5 cloves garlic, pressed
1 teaspoon turmeric
2–3 beef bouillon cubes
Black pepper, freshly ground
Salt to taste, if at all

1 In a heavy large pot heat the oil until almost smoking.
2 Put in the cubed beef and fry until brown.
3 Now lower the heat to just above medium, add all other ingredients (the water should barely cover the meat) and mix well.
4 Continue cooking, lower the heat and simmer until tender, about 1½–2 hours, depending on the quality of the meat. Stir often. You may have to add a little, very little, water, now and then. But always allow any liquid to evaporate.
5 Reduce rapidly. The beef must be served when tender, nice and dry, having absorbed all the liquid and flavours of the spices.
6 Serve with rice and a green salad or with boiled West Indian vegetables and greens quickly steamed in a little water, with butter and salt.

Serves 6

CREOLE SPICED BEEF

French and Patois speaking Islands

900g (2 lb) good stewing beef, cut into cubes
Juice 2 limes or lemons
4 cloves garlic, pressed
2 teaspoons cinnamon, freshly ground
4–6 cloves, ground
2 teaspoons freshly grated ginger
1 hot pepper, seeded and chopped (*see* Techniques)
Salt to taste
3 tablespoons butter
3 bay leaves
½ teaspoon nutmeg
1 tablespoon dark rum
2 teaspoons annatto liquid
Black pepper, freshly ground

1 Blend together the citrus juice, garlic, cinnamon, cloves, ginger, hot pepper and about 2 teaspoons salt.
2 Put into a bowl with the meat and mix together very well.
3 Set aside in a cool place for at least 24 hours. The longer the better. This marinade will conserve the meat even for 3 days.
4 In a heavy pot melt the butter, add the meat pieces with all of the marinade and sauté for about 10 minutes.
5 Add all other ingredients and simmer, tightly covered, over a very low heat for about 2–2½ hours or until tender, stirring occasionally.
6 This dish is ideal with creamed yams, potatoes, and a green salad.

Serves 4–6

SPICED GRILLED STEAKS

The idea for this dish came from the kitchen of Anna Green in Dominica. Though she entertains lavishly, this dish shows her flair for simplicity.

2 rump or entrecôte steaks (about 225g (8 oz) each)
2 tablespoons butter
2 teaspoons lemon juice
¼ teaspoon allspice

1 clove garlic, finely chopped
Dash of pepper sauce
1 tablespoon tomato sauce (*see* p. 215)
4 tablespoons port
2 teaspoons arrowroot (made into a paste with 1 tablespoon of the port)
1 tablespoon rum
Black pepper, freshly ground
Salt to taste
¼ teaspoon freshly grated nutmeg

1 In a small pan, quickly heat a mixture of the butter, lemon juice, allspice, garlic, pepper sauce and tomato sauce.
2 Cover and leave on a very low flame while you begin to grill the steaks (always light the grill a couple of minutes before you start grilling); 2 minutes each side for rare, 3 minutes for medium and 5 minutes for well done.
3 At the last minute turn your butter mixture into a sauce with the port, arrowroot and port paste, then pour in the rum and blend well.
4 Place the steaks on a serving dish, pour the sauce over them and sprinkle with black pepper, salt and grated nutmeg.
5 Serve with a tomato salad garnished with chopped fresh coriander leaves, and creamed yams brushed with butter.

Serves 2

BOEUF AU POIVRE A LA CREOLE

CREOLE PEPPERED BEEF

French Islands

900g (2 lb) rump steak, in one piece but not more than 2.5cm (1 inch) thick
1 clove garlic, slightly crushed
½ hot pepper, seeded but not chopped (*see* Techniques)
1½ teaspoons black peppercorns, freshly ground
1 tablespoon oil
2 tablespoons butter
150ml (¼ pint) dry white wine
4 tablespoons double cream
Salt to taste
1 tablespoon pale brown Island rum

1 tablespoon brandy
1½ tablespoons finely chopped chives
1cm (½ inch) cube of well-chilled butter pressed gently with the chopped chives

1. Have a warm serving dish ready.
2. Rub both sides of the steak with the garlic and hot pepper; discard the pepper and garlic.
3. Coat either side of the steak with the freshly ground black pepper by spreading first then pressing in gently with the palms of your hands.
4. Heat the oil and butter in a heavy frying pan and fry the steak for 3–5 minutes on each side, according to taste.
5. Remove the steak and place it on the serving dish.
6. Spoon out excess fat from the frying pan but leave any bits of peppercorns there may be.
7. Pour in the wine and cream, add a little salt and a pinch of black pepper, bring to the boil, stir continuously and allow to thicken.
8. Turn down the heat, pour in the rum and brandy and taste for seasoning.
9. Pour over the steak and garnish with the seasoned butter.
10. Serve immediately with christophene au gratin, a salad, boiled potatoes and dasheen.

Serves 4

SALT BEEF PELAU

Montserrat

900g (2 lb) salt beef (soaked overnight)
2 tablespoons butter
1 onion, finely chopped
2 cloves garlic, chopped
340g (¾ lb) rice, washed several times and drained
170g (6 oz) unsalted cashew nuts
1 tablespoon chives
1 hot pepper, seeded and chopped (*see* Techniques)
1 teaspoon thyme
½ teaspoon lemon rind
900ml (1½ pint) stock (retained from boiled beef)

Black pepper
Salt to taste

1. Cut the salt beef into 4cm (1½ inch) cubes, wash thoroughly, put into a heavy pot and bring to the boil.
2. Simmer, covered, for about 1¾ hours.
3. Drain the meat and set aside, but reserve the liquid.
4. In the same pot sauté the onion and garlic in the butter, but do not brown.
5. Add the rice, stir and simmer, uncovered, for about 3 minutes. Be careful that the rice does not stick to the pot.
6. Check the stock liquid for salt; if too salty adjust with cold water.
7. Now add the meat and all the ingredients and pour in enough of the liquid (about 900ml – 1½ pints) to cover the rice.
8. Bring to the boil, turn down the heat, and simmer, covered, until all the liquid has been absorbed.
9. Turn out onto a warm dish and serve.

Serves 6

MARINATED BEEF IN GARLIC AND VINEGAR

Dominica

1.25kg (2½ lb) braising beef, cut into 4cm (1½ inch) cubes
3–4 tablespoons vinegar
1 teaspoon dry mustard
3 cloves garlic, crushed through a garlic press
2 bay leaves
Salt to taste
3 tablespoons olive oil
1 onion, finely chopped
110g (4 oz) salt pork, cut into fine small pieces (optional)
2 tomatoes, peeled and chopped
6 green stuffed olives, quartered
1 sprig thyme
1 teaspoon hot pepper, seeded and chopped
300ml (½ pint) good beef stock
Black pepper
1 tablespoon flour, made into a paste with 3 tablespoons stock

1 Put the meat into a bowl with a tight-fitting lid.
2 Liquidize or thoroughly blend the vinegar, mustard, garlic, 1 bay leaf and about 1 teaspoon salt, then pour this over the meat, rub in well and leave tightly covered to marinate overnight in a cool place.
3 Have a casserole ready. Drain the meat but reserve any liquid there may be from the marinade.
4 Heat the oil in a heavy frying pan and fry the meats until brown. You may have to fry a few pieces at a time.
5 Transfer all the meat to the casserole.
6 Now fry the onion in the frying pan and add a little more oil if needed.
7 Add all the other ingredients, including any liquid from the marinade, with the flour paste, mix well and set to cook in a pre-heated oven 180°C (350°F/Gas 4) for about 2 hours or until the meat is tender.
8 Discard the thyme and bay leaf and serve accompanied by baked sweet potatoes and pigeon peas and rice.

Serves 4–5

OXTAIL STEW

Antigua, Dominica

1–2 oxtails, cut into serving pieces
1 tablespoon butter
1 clove garlic, finely chopped
2–3 carrots, sliced
2 medium onions, sliced
300ml (½ pint) beef stock
2 glasses red wine
1 stalk celery, sliced
Salt to taste
½ teaspoon hot pepper sauce
1 bay leaf
1 sprig parsley
¼ teaspoon nutmeg
Black pepper
1–2 tablespoons flour, mixed with a little water

If your oxtail has not been prepared properly by your butcher, you will have to blanch it in seething water which has been boiling for a while, then with the sharpest knife or even a razor cut slightly lengthwise into the surface of the meat to loosen the thin skin which can then be peeled off. Blanching also removes fat and blood from next to the bone.

1 Heat the butter in a heavy pot and fry the oxtail until brown. Remove from pot. Set aside.
2 Fry the garlic, carrots and onions until just slightly brown. Drain off any excess fat.
3 Stir in the stock with a wooden spoon. Add the oxtail, wine, celery, salt, hot pepper sauce, herbs and spices and simmer, covered, until tender.
4 Taste for seasoning, then thicken with the flour paste. Simmer for a further 5–8 minutes. Serve with West Indian boiled vegetables or Riz Creole.

Serves 4–6

CARNE DE VACA SALADA CON FRIJOLES

SALT BEEF AND RED BEAN STEW

Spanish speaking Islands

900g–1.5kg (2–3 lb) salt beef, soaked overnight and cubed
340g (¾ lb) red beans, soaked for at least 8 hours
2 medium sized onions, chopped
1 teaspoon fresh thyme leaves
2 tablespoons chopped chives
6 cloves, ground
1 teaspoon marjoram
150ml (¼ pint) coconut milk
½ teaspoon hot pepper, seeded (*see* Techniques)
½ teaspoon mace
Black pepper
Salt to taste

1 Put the pieces of cubed meat into a pot of cold water and bring to the boil.
2 In another pot, cook the beans until just tender.
3 Simmer the meat for approximately 15 minutes, then discard the water and start again.
4 After the salt beef has been on for a further 15–20 minutes, taste the liquid for salt.

5 If it is still too salty, pour away half the liquid and add some boiling water, then continue to simmer until the meat is fairly tender, but not falling apart.
6 Remove the meat, reserving the liquid, and add the meat to the beans.
7 Now add all other ingredients.
8 Cook uncovered for a few minutes to allow evaporation.
9 When the liquid has reduced pour in some of the liquid in which the meat was cooked to just about cover, giving a quick stir.
10 Taste for salt and seasoning.
11 Thicken if necessary with a little flour paste – leave on the heat a further 6 minutes.
12 Check for the tenderness of both meat and beans and serve. Riz Creole is the ideal companion to this dish.

Serves 4–6

BEEF WITH RICE AND PIGEON PEAS

Most Islands

900g (2 lb) stewing beef, cubed
225g (½ lb) salt pork, cubed
2 tablespoons vegetable oil
600–900ml (1–1½ pints) beef stock (2 bouillon cubes in same quantity of water)
450g (1 lb) fresh pigeon peas, or 1 can, drained
2 onions, chopped
2 cloves garlic, finely chopped
1 teaspoon allspice
1 teaspoon hot peppers, seeded (*see* Techniques)
1 teaspoon oregano
1 tablespoon tomato purée
Salt to taste
340g (¾ lb) white rice, washed several times
1 sweet pepper, seeded and coarsely chopped
1½ tablespoons chives, freshly chopped

1 Heat the oil in a heavy pot and fry the beef and then the pork until golden brown.
2 Pour in the stock and simmer, covered, for about 1 hour.
3 If you are using fresh pigeon peas, add them now along with

all the other ingredients except the rice, chives and sweet pepper.

4 Simmer for another 30 minutes or until the peas are just tender but not completely cooked.
5 Taste for seasoning.
6 Now add the rice, sweet pepper and chives. If you are using canned pigeon peas, now is the time when they should be added to the rice.
7 Simmer, tightly covered, until all the liquid has been absorbed.

Serves 6

BOEUF CREOLE

POT ROAST BEEF IN ONIONS AND TOMATOES

French speaking Islands

1.5kg (3 lbs) stewing beef (one whole piece)
2 tablespoons olive oil
Black pepper
Salt to taste
¾ teaspoon nutmeg, freshly ground
1 hot pepper, chopped and seeded (*see* Techniques)
675g (1½ lb) onions, sliced
675g (1½ lb) tomatoes, sliced
2 bay leaves
225g (½ lb) salt pork, diced
8 olives, stoned and chopped

1 Grease the bottom of a heavy pot with the oil.
2 Rub the joint with a mixture of black pepper, salt, nutmeg and some of the hot pepper.
3 Any of the spices that are left over should go into the pot when adding the meat.
4 Line the bottom of the pot with the onions, then the tomatoes and bay leaves, and place the joint on top of that.
5 Now surround the beef with the diced salt pork, the rest of the hot pepper and the olives.
6 Place on a low heat and simmer, covered, for 3 hours or until the beef is tender.
7 Taste for seasoning.
8 Cook for a further 10 minutes. No liquid must be added.

The meat and vegetables will give out their own. It is important that the heat is kept to the minimum.

9 Bring to the table and cut slices from the meat in the pot.

Serves 6

BAKED PAWPAW WITH SPICY MEAT

Jamaica

450g (1 lb) best minced meat
3 green pawpaws weighing in all about 2.25kg (5 lb)
1 tablespoon butter
1 tablespoon oil
1 onion, finely chopped
1 clove garlic, finely minced
3 tomatoes, peeled and chopped
¼ teaspoon allspice
Black pepper
Salt to taste
4 tablespoons grated Parmesan cheese

1 Cut the pawpaws in half lengthways, scoop out and discard the seeds. With a spoon carefully scrape out as much of the flesh as possible, but leave enough to hold the skin firm. Be careful not to damage the skin; and remember that the enzyme from the pawpaw can cause irritation. Set the pawpaw shells and flesh aside.
2 Place a shallow pan on a very low heat, melt the butter with the oil, add the onion and garlic and sauté until the onions are transparent but not brown.
3 Add the meat and continue stirring until the meat is well mixed in and there are no lumps left.
4 Turn up the heat to moderate and add all the ingredients, except the cheese, but including the flesh of the pawpaw.
5 Stir until the mixture is thick and most of the liquid has evaporated.
6 Taste for salt.
7 Now fill each pawpaw shell with an equal amount of the mixture.
8 Place the shells in a baking dish and pour in enough boiling water to come to just about halfway up the shells.

9 Bake in a pre-heated oven 190°C (375°F/Gas 5) for about half an hour.
10 Remove from the oven, spread an equal amount of cheese on each; return to the oven and continue to bake for 5-10 minutes or until the pawpaw is cooked. Test with a knife or skewer.
11 Serve immediately. You may if you wish sprinkle on some more Parmesan cheese, just before serving.

Serves 6

STEWED BEEF IN VEGETABLE PURÉE

I believe this Creole dish originated from New Orleans, though it is now to be found on the French speaking islands.

900g–1.5kg (2–3 lb) rump (substitute topside, but it will need a longer cooking time)
Black pepper, freshly ground
Salt to taste
½ teaspoon grated nutmeg
2 cloves garlic, finely chopped
2 tablespoons vinegar
3 tablespoons olive oil
3 medium sized onions, skinned and left whole
2 medium sized potatoes, peeled and left whole
2 celery stalks, cut into 4 or 5 pieces
2 carrots, scraped and washed
225g (½ lb) tomatoes, chopped
1 aubergine, cut into about 4 pieces
1 small christophene, peeled and cored (cut into large pieces)
½ a small cucumber, peeled and cut into large pieces
2 bay leaves
1 teaspoon thyme
½ hot pepper, seeded and chopped (*see* Techniques)
600ml (1 pint) beef stock (use 2 bouillon cubes)
2 glasses white wine
3 tablespoons dark rum

1 Season the whole piece of meat with black pepper, salt, nutmeg, garlic and vinegar. Allow to stand for two to three hours. Start the preparation early in the morning if you can.

2 Heat half of the oil in a heavy frying pan.
3 Pat the meat dry, but retain the marinade to add to the pot.
4 Fry the meat until golden brown on all sides.
5 Place the meat and all other ingredients except the rum into another large pot. Retain the oil, you will need it again.
6 Cover and cook slowly until the meat is tender (about 1½ to 3 hours depending on what cut of meat you have used).
7 Remove from heat, allow to cool and take the meat out of the pot.
8 Liquidize all that is left and pour the puréed mixture back into the pot.
9 Bring to the boil, turn down heat and simmer, uncovered, for a short time.
10 Meanwhile cut up the meat into cubes.
11 Place a frying pan with the rest of the olive oil on a high heat and, when hot, add the meat.
12 Turn a few times.
13 Quickly heat the rum and pour over the meat, then flambé.
14 Arrange the meat on a warm serving dish, pour the purée over the meat and serve. You may, if you wish, serve this dish with a vegetable of your choice, creamed, fried or boiled. But not rice.

Serves 6–8

CREOLE BEEFBURGER

My childhood days were spent in total ignorance of anything called a 'burger', be it ham, beef or any other. The term *junk food* did not then exist. But like everything else, including mass tourism, the beefburger came to the Caribbean and we decided to do something about it. And this is what we did and still do.

900g (2 lb) beef
1 medium size onion, minced or grated
2 cloves garlic, pressed
2 teaspoons hot pepper sauce
1 teaspoon fresh thyme leaves
1 tablespoon parsley, very finely chopped
1 teaspoon dry mustard powder
½ teaspoon nutmeg, freshly grated

Black pepper, very little
Salt to taste

1 Buy good lean beef and mince it yourself or get your butcher to mince it for you.
2 Using a large bowl, combine all the ingredients.
3 Taste for seasoning.
4 Flour your hands, make four or eight equal balls, then shape into burgers.
5 They can be grilled over charcoal or underneath any domestic grill.
6 The length of time for grilling depends on whether the choice is for rare to medium (2–3 minutes), medium (3–4 minutes), or well done (5–6 minutes), on either side.
7 If you are using a grill, any liquid in the grill pan can be quickly made into a sauce by adding a little water or red wine, tomato sauce, more black pepper and salt, after the burgers have been taken out. The sauce can be thickened with a little flour and water paste or arrowroot.
8 Serve with sauté potatoes (sauté in butter and a little oil), with a green salad of cucumber, a firm lettuce and spring onions or chives.
9 The salad dressing should be made with vegetable oil, lemon juice, juice of ½ an orange, a little brown sugar, dry mustard, salt, black pepper and wine vinegar, made to your taste.

Serves 4

With this dish, try freshly baked buttered mastiff bread (*see* Breads).

BEEF OR MUTTON CURRY

Though similar to a recipe from Trinidad, this is one of my own recipes.

1.7g (3½ lb) lean beef or mutton, cut into 3.5cm (1¼ inch) cubes
5 tablespoons vegetable (or coconut) oil
2 onions, finely chopped
3 cloves garlic, pressed or finely chopped
6 cloves, freshly ground
1 teaspoon turmeric

2 tomatoes, peeled and chopped
Juice 1 lime or lemon
1 teaspoon fresh thyme leaves
2 bouillon cubes
2½ tablespoons curry powder
1 cinnamon stick 8cm (3 inches) long
225g (½ lb) potatoes, peeled and quartered according to size
600–900ml (1–1½ pints) water
Salt to taste (remember when using bouillon cubes use less salt)

1 Heat the oil in a heavy pot and brown the meat a few pieces at a time. Set aside.
2 In the same oil fry the onions until lightly browned.
3 Turn the heat down, and return the meat to the pot together with the garlic, ground cloves, turmeric, tomatoes, citrus juice, thyme and the bouillon cubes, then cook for about 6 minutes. Do not allow to stick to the pot.
4 Add the curry powder and about 4 tablespoons of water. Mix well and simmer gently, covered, for a few minutes. Stir occasionally.
5 Now add the cinnamon stick, potatoes and about 600ml (1 pint) of water.
6 Bring slowly to the boil, lower the heat and simmer, covered, until the meat is tender. Do not allow to burn.
7 Check the quantity of liquid during the cooking period. Add more water if needed, but not too much as this must be a fairly thick and dry curry at the end. Taste for seasoning; mostly salt.
8 Serve with Roti, and/or with plain rice and Dhal.

Sufficient for about 15 Roti or as a dish for 6 with rice

POT AU FEU

French Islands

900g (2 lb) beef (any cheap cut will do)
1 boiling fowl
1 whole hot pepper
2 cloves garlic
sprig thyme
sprig parsley

2 bay leaves
Black pepper
Salt to taste
Juice 1 lemon
4 tannias, peeled and washed with lime or lemon, cut into small pieces
6 sticks celery
3 carrots, sliced
1 small but firm cabbage
2 onions, sliced
Dumplings (*see* Breads)

1. Place beef and chicken in enough cold water to cover and bring to the boil.
2. Turn down the heat, allow to simmer for about 10 minutes, then skim, removing all the scum from the top and any that may be stuck to the side of the pot.
3. Add the herbs and spices and ½ the lemon juice.
4. Simmer, covered, for about 1½ hours.
5. Skim again if necessary.
6. Taste for seasoning and remove the whole hot pepper, being careful not to burst it.
7. Add the vegetables, the tannias first, then the dumplings, and return the pepper.
8. Simmer further until meats and firmer vegetables are tender.
9. Remove the whole pepper.
10. Remove meats from pot, sprinkle with the remaining lemon juice, carve and serve with vegetables.

Serves 6–8

PEPPERPOT

Guyana

This dish is one of Guyana's most famous dishes. Pepperpot is supposed to keep indefinitely. There are even stories of pots being kept going in one family for generations by simply being boiled each day with meats and the other condiments added to them when necessary. Always throw in cooked meats and avoid onions, garlic or any vegetables that may cause fermentation. The pepperpot stew is preserved by the cassareep so it is essential now and then to add a little of this particular ingredient to the pot. But even if you do not wish to hand down to your future heirs a large bubbling pot of stew, it is worth trying even just once, as it is a most wonderful and delicious dish.

900g (2 lb) stewing beef, cut into cubes
1 boiling fowl, cut into serving pieces
225g (½ lb) salt beef, cubed
3 pig's trotters
1 calf's foot
675g (1½ lb) oxtail
150ml (¼ pint) cassareep (*see* Techniques)
2 hot peppers, seeded and chopped (*see* Techniques)
10 whole cloves
2 tablespoons vinegar
2–3 bay leaves
Juice 1 lime or lemon
1 tablespoon brown sugar
2 sticks cinnamon (optional as there is already cinnamon in the cassareep)
Salt to taste

1. Unless you possess a heavy meat cleaver it is best to get your butcher to cut up the trotters, oxtail and calf's foot for you, into comfortable small serving pieces.
2. Wash all the meats under cold running water, then blanch them in seething water and rinse again. Now put them into a large pot with enough cold water to cover and bring to the boil. One or two of the meats may cook before others but that does not matter with this dish.
3. Reduce the heat and simmer for about 30 minutes. Skim off any scum that forms as often as possible.
4. Add the cassareep and continue to simmer for a further 30–40 minutes. Skim again if necessary.
5. Now add all the other ingredients and simmer, covered, until all the meats are tender.
6. Taste for seasoning.
7. Serve with plain boiled West Indian vegetables and boiled rice, or hard dough bread (*see* recipe for Mastiff bread).

Serves 10 or more

GARBURE LOUBIÈRE

Dominica, specifically from the village Pointe Michel

This is a dish I once put together at a small house I rented on the island of Dominica. The name of the Estate was Loubière in the village of Pointe Michel. I have prepared it several times since for parties, especially during my time with a touring theatre company round the north and the borders of Scotland.

340g (¾ lb) lean braising beef, cubed
340g (¾ lb) boned shoulder of lamb, cubed
340g (¾ lb) boned shoulder of pork, cubed
Oil for frying
Salt to taste
Black pepper, freshly ground
1 large stick of cinnamon
225g (½ lb) carrots, scraped and cut into rounds
225g (½ lb) shallots, skinned but left whole
1 large sweet pepper, coarsely chopped
110g (¼ lb) bacon, coarsely chopped
4 cloves garlic, finely chopped or pressed
1 sprig thyme
900ml (1½ pints) chicken stock (or 2 bouillon cubes in same amount of water)
300ml (½ pint) coconut cream (or ½ a block in same amount of water)
450g (1 lb) can cannellini beans, drained

1 Have ready a large pot to hold all the ingredients.
2 Heat the oil in a large heavy frying pan and fry the beef until lightly brown.
3 Using a perforated spoon transfer the beef to the waiting pot.
4 Repeat the same procedure with the lamb, then the pork. If when you come to fry the pork there are any burnt pieces in the pan, strain the oil, wipe the pan clean, and return the hot oil to the pan.
5 Now sprinkle over the meats a little salt and some black pepper and also put in the cinnamon stick.
6 Add the carrots, shallots and sweet pepper, then the bacon, followed by all other ingredients, except the beans.
7 Simmer, covered, until the meats are tender. Taste for

seasoning. Add the beans and simmer for a further 4–5 minutes or until the beans are well warmed through.

Serve with creamed yams, breadfruit or mashed potatoes.

Serves 6–8

PORT ROYAL LAMB

Jamaica

900g–1.5kg (2–3 lb) stewing lamb, cut into 4cm (1½ inch) cubes
2 tablespoons vegetable oil
600ml (1 pint) chicken stock
1 tablespoon vinegar
300ml (½ pint) orange juice
½ teaspoon hot pepper sauce
2 teaspoons grated orange rind
1 bay leaf
¼ teaspoon allspice
Salt to taste
3 egg yolks, beaten
Black pepper

1 In a heavy pot or casserole, fry the lamb pieces in the oil until brown.
2 Remove the lamb pieces from the oil, discard the oil and add to the pot the stock, vinegar, orange juice, hot pepper sauce, orange rind, the bay leaf, allspice and salt.
3 Bring to the boil, add the lamb pieces and simmer, covered, for about 1½ hours or until the lamb is tender. Test a piece. If too tough, leave for a few minutes longer.
4 Remove the lamb from the pot and transfer to a heated serving dish, but keep warm in the oven loosely covered by foil.
5 Reduce the heat under the casserole, skim off all excess fat, then strain through a fine sieve.
6 Return the liquid to the casserole, measuring so that if the quantity is more than 600ml (1 pint), it can be reduced on a high heat with the lid off the casserole.
7 Lower the heat.
8 Thoroughly beat the egg yolks; add some of the hot liquid to

the yolks and continue beating, then very slowly add this to the casserole. But be careful not to pour it in too quickly, nor to allow it to boil, or else the sauce will curdle. Stir constantly while pouring.

9 Taste for salt and other seasonings.

10 Pour the sauce over the lamb pieces. Do not let the dish stand for too long. It should be served as soon as possible.

Serves 4–6

ROAST LAMB LE CARAÏBE

1.5–1.8kg (3–4 lb) leg or shoulder of lamb
Salt to taste
2 tablespoons rum
½ teaspoon allspice
Black pepper
½ teaspoon cinnamon, freshly ground
2 tablespoons olive oil
2 teaspoons caramel colouring
Juice 2 oranges
1 onion, grated
2 cloves garlic, left whole uncrushed
½ teaspoon mace, freshly ground
1 bay leaf
1 bouillon cube
1 tablespoon brandy, warmed
½ teaspoon hot pepper, seeded and chopped (*see* Techniques)

1 Mix together the following: salt, 1 tablespoon rum, allspice, black pepper and the cinnamon.

2 Make several fairly deep insertions in the joint with a sharp knife; now in each deep cut put some of the mixture until it is all used up. Allow the joint to stand for 1 to 2 hours.

3 Heat the oil in a heavy casserole, add the caramel and fry the joint on all sides until nice and brown.

4 Pour in the orange juice and leave on a medium heat, uncovered, for about 5 minutes, turning the meat a few times. Do not allow to dry or burn.

5 Add all the other ingredients, except the brandy, and pot roast, covered, in a pre-heated oven 180°C (350°F/Gas 4) until tender. Turn the lamb over a few times.

6 Remove from oven, place on top on medium heat uncovered for about 5 minutes, discarding the bay leaf and garlic.
7 Flambé the lamb with warmed brandy and serve immediately, garnished with slices of lemon and oranges.

Serves 4–6

This was one of the most popular Sunday roasts at the old 'Le Caraïbe' restaurant in Fulham, which I once managed. It was always served accompanied by fried ripe plantains, fried sweet potatoes, baked Irish potatoes, one or two boiled vegetables such as dasheen, and a salad depending on what was available in the markets at the time of the year.

DAUBE DE MOUTON

POT ROAST SHOULDER OF MUTTON

Guadeloupe

1.8kg (4 lb) shoulder of mutton, trimmed but left whole
2 tablespoons oil
3 onions, cut into half rings
3 medium green tomatoes, sliced
3 medium ripe tomatoes, sliced
½ teaspoon cumin seeds
2 cloves garlic, chopped
2 bay leaves
2 teaspoons rosemary
2 tablespoons water
Salt to taste
3 small tannias, cut into about 4cm (1½ inch) pieces
2 large carrots, cut into 1cm (½ inch) pieces
1 stick celery, cut into 4cm (1½ inch) lengths
1 small christophene (optional) peeled, cored, and cubed
1 hot pepper, seeded and chopped (*see* Techniques)
2 bouillon cubes
2 small aubergines, cubed; but do not peel
1 red sweet pepper, seeded and sliced
225g (½ lb) Kenya or French beans, topped and tailed but left whole
½ teaspoon nutmeg, freshly ground

1 In a large pot heat the oil and fry the mutton joint until brown.

2 Remove the joint and set aside, turn down the heat, lay the onions evenly on the bottom of the pot; then the sliced tomatoes, mixing both green and ripe; lastly, the cumin seeds, garlic, bay leaves, rosemary, the water and just a little salt.
3 Return the mutton to the pot, cover and simmer on the lowest possible heat for about 2 hours. (If using gas always check to make certain that it does not go out – the lower the flame the more likely it is to do so.)
4 Now add the pieces of tannia, carrots, celery, christophene, and hot pepper, in that order, round the joint.
5 Remove some of the liquid from the pot and use this to dissolve the bouillon cubes, then pour back into the pot and simmer, covered, for another 12 minutes.
6 Add the aubergine, sweet pepper, beans and nutmeg.
7 Taste for salt.
8 Cook slowly for a further 30 minutes or until the meat is tender and the last vegetables are cooked then taste for salt again.
9 Serve on a dish with the mutton surrounded by the vegetables.

Serves 6

SPICED LAMB CHOPS

Grenada

4–6 large lamb chops
½ teaspoon allspice
1 teaspoon freshly ground thyme leaves
1 teaspoon freshly ground rosemary leaves
Juice ½ lime or lemon
1 clove garlic, pressed
½ teaspoon black pepper
2 tablespoons olive oil
1 teaspoon hot pepper sauce
Salt to taste
4–6 generous knobs of garlic butter

1 Mix or blend together the allspice, thyme, rosemary, citrus juice, garlic, black pepper, oil, pepper sauce and add enough salt to taste.

2 Place the chops into a dish and rub the mixture well into the chops.
3 Cover and set aside in a cool place for 4 hours or longer.
4 Heat the grill to the hottest point, place the chops on a rack in a tray and grill for 4, 5 or 6 minutes on each side, according to taste.
5 Serve immediately with a knob of garlic butter on each chop, accompanied by an avocado salad and any green salad of your choice.

Serves 4–6

STEWED NECK OF LAMB

This is one of my own inexpensive dishes.

900g (2 lb) neck of lamb, cut into convenient pieces
2 tablespoons oil
1½ tablespoons caramel colouring (*see* Techniques)
1 teaspoon curry powder
1 teaspoon dried mustard
2 teaspoons hot pepper sauce
200–225g (7–8 oz) tin plum tomatoes
1½ chicken bouillon cubes
1 tablespoon red wine vinegar
6 whole cloves
2 cloves garlic
3 medium onions, cut into fine rings
1 tablespoon chopped mint leaves
2 teaspoons dried rosemary
1 teaspoon brown sugar
300ml (½ pint) water

1 Heat the oil in a heavy pot and fry the lamb until brown.
2 Add the caramel colouring and continue to fry until a very rich dark brown. Do not allow to burn. Sprinkle the curry powder and dried mustard over the lamb and fry for about 5 minutes more.
3 Add the pepper sauce, tomatoes, bouillon cubes and vinegar. Stir.
4 Simmer, covered, for about 10 minutes.
5 Now add all the other ingredients and simmer, covered, until the lamb is tender.

6 Taste for seasoning. Add salt if needed.
7 Serve with West Indian vegetables.

Serves 4–6

CURRIED LAMB

Countries with Asian influence

1.5kg (3 lb) shoulder of lamb or mutton, cut into cubes
2 tablespoons ghee (clarified butter)
2 onions, finely chopped
3–4 cloves garlic, chopped
3 tomatoes, peeled and chopped
4 ground cloves
¼ teaspoon ground cinnamon
½ teaspoon thyme
½ teaspoon turmeric
¼ teaspoon nutmeg
¼ teaspoon coriander
2 tablespoons curry powder or poudre de Colombo
juice of 1 lime or lemon
Black pepper
Salt to taste
300ml (½ pint) chicken stock (use 2 bouillon cubes in same quantity of water)
300ml (½ pint) coconut milk

1 In a heavy pot heat the ghee and sauté the onions and garlic until just lightly brown.
2 Add all the ingredients except the stock, meat and coconut milk, and stir into a nice thick paste. Do not allow to burn. This should not take more than 5 minutes.
3 Now add the meat pieces, stir and cook, covered, on a low heat for about 10 minutes.
4 Add the stock and coconut milk, and simmer until the meat is tender.
5 Taste for salt; stir and simmer for about 4 minutes.
6 Serve with Riz Creole, fried plantains and pigeon peas. Lime or lemon wedges are also a nice touch, and of course sliced hot peppers.

Serves 6

CHULETAS DE CORDERO

LAMB CHOPS WITH CUCUMBER AND TOMATOES

Spanish speaking Islands

4–6 large lamb chops (or 8–12 small ones)
1 clove garlic, chopped
2 tablespoons sofrito
1 teaspoon oregano
1 tablespoon chives, chopped
4 peppercorns *or* allspice berries, freshly ground
½ teaspoon hot pepper, seeded (*see* Techniques)
1½ teaspoons lemon juice
1 tablespoon light rum
Salt to taste
4–5 ripe but firm tomatoes, thinly sliced, unpeeled
1–2 cucumbers, washed and cut into 1cm (½ inch) thick rounds, unpeeled
2–3 tablespoons olive oil

1 First butter a deep oven-proof baking dish large enough to hold whatever quantity of chops you have.
2 Now mix together the garlic, sofrito, oregano, chives, pepper or allspice, hot pepper, lemon juice, rum and salt to taste.
3 Line the baking dish with half the tomatoes, evenly spread, then half of the cucumbers on top of the tomatoes.
4 Now spread half the spiced mixture on the cucumbers and set aside.
5 Heat the oil in a frying pan and brown each chop on both sides until golden.
6 Place the chops evenly in the prepared baking dish, spread the remaining half of the spiced mixture over the meat, then add the rest of the cucumbers and tomatoes.
7 Cover with foil, then bake in the centre of a pre-heated oven 200°C (400°F/Gas 6) for about 25–30 minutes.
8 Serve accompanied by a green salad and creamed yams.

Serves 4–6

CURRIED GOAT

I must say that I do not know of one island, among the English speaking Islands, where curried goat is not popular, especially during Bank Holidays and other festivities. Goat is available from most Halal butchers. But be certain that you are getting goat and not mutton. I have also been able to order goat from local butchers with a few days' notice.

1.25kg (2½ lb) goat, bones as well (if it is not already butchered, saw the meat into small pieces to avoid splintering of the bones)
Juice 2 limes
1½ tablespoons mild curry powder
1 teaspoon turmeric
Salt to taste
3 cloves garlic, finely chopped or pressed
4–6 allspice, freshly ground
6 cloves, freshly ground
2 onions, finely sliced
1 teaspoon hot pepper, seeded and chopped (*see* Techniques)
Sprig thyme
Sprig parsley
750ml (1¼ pints) chicken stock (or 2 bouillon cubes in same quantity of water)

1. In a large bowl put the goat, lime juice, curry powder, turmeric, about 2 level teaspoons salt, 2 cloves garlic, allspice and cloves to marinate. Allow to stand in a cool place for 4 hours or longer.
2. Turn out into a heavy large pot with a close-fitting lid. Make sure that you scrape off all the marinade liquid into the pot.
3. Sauté on a medium heat for about 8–10 minutes.
4. Add all the remaining ingredients. Stir. Bring to the boil.
5. Simmer, covered, on a low heat until the meat is tender.
6. Taste for seasoning.
7. Serve with boiled rice.

Serves 6

This recipe comes from two friends, resident in Dominica, Alison Southwell and Lyn Giraud.

CREOLE RABBIT STEW

Haiti

Rabbit as part of the animal life in the Caribbean has never been very plentiful but rabbits are now available frozen and obtainable from supermarkets.

1 rabbit, cut into serving pieces
3 tablespoons oil
2 teaspoons brown sugar (or 2 tablespoons caramel colouring, *see* Techniques)
4 shallots, sliced into quarters
2 cloves garlic, finely chopped
2 carrots, scraped and sliced
Tomato purée
Rind of half an orange, shredded
4 cloves, ground
1 teaspoon oregano
Sprig parsley
Juice 1 orange
1 glass white wine
300ml (½ pint) chicken stock
Flour paste
Black pepper, freshly ground
Salt to taste

1. In a heavy pot heat the oil, add the sugar and allow to brown slightly, but without burning. If it begins to smoke lift from heat for a few seconds.
2. Now add the rabbit pieces mixing in well with the browned sugar (caramel).
3. Fry until golden brown.
4. Add the other ingredients, bring to the boil, thicken with flour paste.
5. Simmer for 45–60 minutes or until tender.
6. Taste for seasoning about two thirds of the way through cooking time.
7. Serve with Riz Creole and a salad.

Serves 4–6

RABBIT STEW

Aruba

900g–1.5kg (2–3 lb) rabbit, cut into serving pieces
Salt to taste
Juice 1 lemon
Black pepper, freshly ground
3 tablespoons butter
2 tablespoons caramel colouring (*see* Techniques)
2 onions, in half rings
2 cloves garlic, finely chopped
4 rashers smoked bacon, chopped
6 cloves
1 sprig thyme
1 sprig parsley
1 glass red wine
2 tablespoons dark rum
300ml (½ pint) chicken stock
Flour mixed into a little of the stock, for thickening

1. Season the rabbit with some salt, half the lemon juice and pepper. Allow to stand for about 1 hour.
2. Melt the butter in a pot and lightly brown the rabbit.
3. Add the caramel colouring and fry until golden brown, add the onions and brown slightly for 2–3 minutes.
4. Now stir in all the other ingredients except for the flour paste.
5. Cover and simmer for 30 minutes longer.
6. Thicken with flour paste if needed.
7. Taste for seasoning and simmer until tender.
8. Serve with pigeon peas and Riz Creole or with fried ripe plantain and other vegetables.

Serves 4–6

MARINATED FRIED LIVER

Trinidad

675g–1kg (1½–2 lb) calves' liver, thinly sliced
1 lemon or lime, for scrubbing the liver
Juice ½ lemon
1 clove garlic, crushed

6 blades chives, crushed
6–8 sage leaves, crushed
½ hot pepper, seeded but not chopped (*see* Techniques)
1 tablespoon Trinidad rum
White pepper, freshly ground
Salt to taste
Coarse cornmeal
Oil for frying

1 Slice the liver very thinly.
2 Rinse the liver in cold water, then rub gently with the lime or lemon cut in half, squeezing a little of the juice on both sides of each piece of liver.
3 Rinse very lightly again under cold water and pat dry to remove any excess water.
4 Mix together in a large bowl the lemon juice, crushed garlic, and chives, then add the rest of the ingredients, except the cornmeal and oil.
5 Lay the liver in the marinade and allow to stand for about two hours. Occasionally turn the liver slices, so they become well married to the marinade.
6 Meanwhile make a sauce with the following:

2 tablespoons margarine
2 onions, cut into rounds
2 tomatoes, peeled and chopped
1 teaspoon oregano
2 cloves garlic, finely chopped and pressed
300ml (½ pint) stock
2 teaspoons vinegar
1 tablespoon tomato sauce (*see* p. 215)
4 allspice berries, freshly ground
Black pepper, freshly ground
Salt to taste
Flour mixed with a little stock for thickening

1 Melt the margarine in a small pot on a heat high enough to sauté the onions but not to burn the margarine.
2 Fry the onions until golden brown.
3 Add all the other ingredients, except for the flour paste and simmer, covered, for about 10 minutes.
4 Taste for seasoning, then thicken.

5 Simmer, covered, for a further 10 minutes.
6 Keep warm, until needed.

After about one and a half hours, return to the main process of the dish:

6 Mix the coarse cornmeal with a little salt and white pepper.
7 Remove the liver from the marinade and wipe off any of the herbs that may cling to the slices. Coat the meat with the seasoned cornmeal.
8 Heat the oil in a heavy frying pan, and fry the liver slices until brown on both sides.
9 Arrange the fried liver in a heated dish and pour the sauce over.
10 Garnish with watercress and slices of lemon.
11 Serve with plantain foo-foo or creamed yams and a salad.

Serves 4

FÍGADO GUISADO

STEWED LIVER IN RUM AND SPICES

Cuba

675g–900g (1½–2 lb) calves' or lambs' liver, sliced evenly
1 tablespoon lime juice
Salt to taste
Black pepper
1 teaspoon nutmeg
3 tablespoons oil
110g (4 oz) plain flour
300ml (½ pint) chicken stock (1 bouillon cube in same quantity of hot water)
1 teaspoon brown sugar
2 tomatoes, chopped
1 clove garlic, finely chopped
1 teaspoon grated orange rind
1 tablespoon sofrito
2 tablespoons rum

1 Having sliced the liver, arrange the slices in a dish.
2 Pour over each slice a little lime juice, and sprinkle with salt, black pepper and nutmeg.
3 Allow to stand for 1–2 hours.

4 Heat the oil in a heavy frying pan, coat each side of the liver with flour and fry until brown.
5 Stir in the stock, sugar, tomatoes, garlic, orange rind, sofrito and taste for seasoning.
6 Now pour in the rum, stir and simmer, covered, for not more than about 6 minutes. If just by chance the flesh is still on the red side, allow another 2 minutes' cooking time.
7 Serve with Riz Creole.

Serves 4

ROGNONS

HAITIAN KIDNEY CASSEROLE

8–12 pigs' kidneys, skinned, halved and cored
50g (2 oz) margarine or butter, coloured with achote (*see* Techniques)
2 onions, finely chopped
225g (½ lb) bacon, diced
2 sweet peppers, seeded and thinly sliced (*see* Techniques)
½ small cucumber or christophene, peeled and cubed
2 cloves garlic
6 cloves, freshly ground
1 teaspoon achote
1 glass red French wine
2 tablespoons Haitian rum (or any Island rum you have in store)
3 tablespoons tomato ketchup
300ml (½ pint) stock (you can use beef or chicken)
Black pepper
Salt to taste
2 tablespoons flour mixed with a little water

1 Melt the butter in a heavy pot over a moderate heat, with care lest it burn.
2 Gently brown the onions, then add the kidneys and bacon. Sauté for about 8 minutes.
3 Add all other ingredients except for the flour paste, and simmer, covered, on a low heat for about 10 minutes.
4 Thicken with the flour paste, then cook for a further 5 minutes.

5 Taste for seasoning.
6 Serve very hot with Riz Creole.

Serves 4–6

Vegetables, Rice and Salads

Early Saturday morning, and the trucks with their gaily painted wooden carriages are making their way from villages all over the Islands to the open market places of the capitals or main towns. The carriages are packed with human life, the tailboards and roofs laden with the most colourful and exotic of tropical produce – yams and taros, sweet potatoes, avocadoes, plantains both ripe and green, bunches of bananas, citrus fruits, breadfruits and scented herbs and spices. Soon everything will be displayed on large leaves, sacking or baskets. There will be noise and bustle, then the haggling and the buying. West Indians make a great fuss when choosing any produce either for the pot or to be eaten without cooking. 'I work for the money so I don't want to pay for no breadfruit that "blessé" (bruised)' or 'If you don't cut a piece from the dasheen how can I see if it good? Is not like I asking you for me to feel-up your zaboca (avocado).'

There are many who can't afford to eat meat or fish with each meal. And since the advent of tourism their local streams and rivers have been almost depleted of crayfish, which now fetches quite an exorbitant price at the big hotels. So even more so today they have learnt to make the very best of vegetables and ground provisions. And they do not have to depend overmuch on nuts and pulses either, even though beans and peas are indeed widely grown and very popular.

As for Caribbean soups, they make a very substantial meal on their own. Callaloo, pumpkin, cream of tannia, okra, avocado soup – all can be prepared without either meat or fish and taste just as good. The same applies to the many vegetable stews, and dishes such as baked breadfruit, or 'Foo-Foo' (in Dominica Ton-Ton), which is green plantain pounded and flavoured with chives, garlic, lime juice, salt, pepper and sometimes Annatto-coloured lard.

Today in market places and the larger shopping centres all over the world, these exotic fruits and vegetables are becoming more readily available. So like us you too, I am certain, will learn to make imaginative use of them.

BAKED CREAMED YAMS

Most Islands

1.25–1.5kg (2½–3 lb) white yam
1 lime or lemon
75g (3 oz) butter
2–3 tablespoons single cream or milk
Black pepper, freshly ground
Salt to taste
1 tablespoon chives, finely chopped

1. Peel and cut the yam into reasonable pieces for boiling.
2. Wash several times in fresh water and rub with a piece of lime or lemon.
3. Bring to the boil in enough salted water to cover, with a little extra citrus juice squeezed.
4. Simmer on a medium heat until tender. Do not overcook.
5. Drain the yams thoroughly and mash them.
6. Mix in 50g (2 oz) of the butter, then the cream and the black pepper.
7. Taste for salt.
8. Mix in the chives.
9. Butter 2 or 3 shallow oblong oven-proof dishes and mould an equal amount of the creamed yam in each.
10. Dot with butter and bake in a pre-heated oven 200°C (400°F/Gas 6) until golden brown.
11. Serve hot with a dish of your choice or as recommended.

Serves 4–6

CREAMED DASHEEN, YAM, BREADFRUIT OR SWEET POTATOES

675g (1½ lb) any of the above
1 medium onion, grated
100g (4 oz) butter
110ml (4 fl oz) cream, or cream and milk
½ teaspoon freshly grated nutmeg
Black pepper

1. Peel and boil the vegetables (*see* Techniques).
2. Mash with a fork, mouli or food processor.
3. Combine all the ingredients and work into a smooth cream.

4 Taste for seasoning.
5 Put into a pie or baking dish.
6 Coat with melted butter and bake in a pre-heated oven 220°C (425°F/Gas 7) for 15 minutes.
7 Serve with meat, poultry or fish dish.

Serves 4

FRIED RIPE PLANTAINS

Allow one plantain per 2 persons or, if very large, for 3 if accompanied by other vegetables.

1 Top and tail the plantains.
2 Cut in half and make 3–4 slits lengthways down each half.
3 Peel (*see* Techniques).
4 Slice lengthways into 3 or 4 slices.
5 Heat oil in a frying pan and fry each side until golden brown.
6 Serve with meat or fish or with fried bacon, as a snack or for breakfast.

JACKET BAKED TANNIAS

4–6 tannias
½ lime or lemon for cleansing
Salt to taste
Black pepper, freshly ground
1–2 tablespoons chives, finely chopped
Lime or lemon juice
50–70g (2–3 oz) softened butter
1–2 tablespoons parsley, finely chopped

1 Pre-heat the oven to 190°C (375°F/Gas 5).
2 Thoroughly wash the skin of the tannias, using a brush to scrub off any excess dirt (I keep a nail brush handy for such a purpose).
3 Rinse and rub with the citrus half, pat dry.
4 Bake in the oven for about 1½ hours or until a sharp thin knife inserted will go through without difficulty.
5 Remove from oven.
6 Cut tannias in half.
7 Carefully loosen the flesh with a fork without damaging the skin.

8 Sprinkle each with salt, pepper, chives, then squeeze a little lime or lemon juice and spread a generous amount of butter on each half.
9 Return to the oven for about 5–6 minutes.
10 Serve hot, garnished with parsley; grated cheese sprinkled over the hot tannias makes a good change.

Serves 4–6

BAKED WHOLE SWEET POTATOES

1 Preheat oven to 180°C (350°F/Gas 4).
2 Wash and scrub the potatoes.
3 Stick a fork into them. This prevents them exploding.
4 Initially, wrap the sweet potatoes in foil, so that the skins do not harden too quickly. Unwrap them after half the cooking time.
5 Place in the oven and bake for a total of about 1½ hours or until soft through.
6 A very thin knife or skewer should go through the potatoes without effort, when they are done.
7 Serve hot with butter, salt, and black pepper.
8 For a snack a little grated cheese may be served in each potato, when split or halved.

SWEET POTATO BAKES

450g (1 lb) cooked sweet potatoes
140g (5 oz) strong white flour
2 tablespoons chives or spring onions, finely chopped
2 tomatoes, peeled and chopped
1 clove garlic, pressed or finely chopped
1 tablespoon melted butter
½ teaspoon allspice
Black pepper
Salt to taste
1 teaspoon baking powder, sifted with the flour

1 Preheat oven to 190°C (375°F/Gas 5).
2 Mash the potatoes into a smooth paste.
3 Add all the other ingredients and mix well, by kneading very gently – but for not too long.

4 Roll out on a floured board to about 1–2cm (½–¾ inch) thick.
5 Cut into rounds not more than 7.5cm (3 inches) in diameter.
6 Place them on a greased baking sheet and bake until brown and crisp.

Serves 4–6

COL FRITO

FRIED CABBAGE

Spanish speaking Islands

1 small cabbage, shredded
2 tablespoons olive oil
1 tablespoon butter
2 rashers bacon, chopped
1 teaspoon fennel
6 capers
4 chopped green olives
2 teaspoons vinegar
Black pepper
Salt to taste
1 large clove garlic, thinly sliced crosswise

1 Wash the shredded cabbage and pat dry in a clean cloth.
2 Heat half of the oil and butter in a small saucepan.
3 Put in the bacon and fry until crisp, add the cabbage and other ingredients except the garlic and cook until tender but still firm.
4 Quickly heat the remaining oil and butter in a skillet and brown the garlic, then pour this over the contents of the saucepan.
5 Serve with boiled rice, ham or boiled gammon.

Serves 4

OKRA IN TOMATO SAUCE

675g (1½ lb) okra, topped and tailed but left whole
2 tablespoons butter
1 onion, finely chopped
675g (1½ lb) tomatoes, blanched and chopped

150ml (¼ pint) light vegetable stock (or 1 bouillon cube in same quantity of water)
2 tablespoons chives, finely chopped
1 teaspoon aniseed, powdered (if fresh, use whole, *not* the star variety)
2 teaspoons lime or lemon juice
Black pepper, freshly ground
Salt to taste

1. Melt the butter in a saucepan, sauté the onion until soft but not brown – add the tomatoes and stock.
2. Simmer, covered, for no more than about 25 minutes.
3. Remove from heat and press with a spoon through a fine sieve.
4. Place the okras in the same saucepan, pour the tomato sauce over the okras.
5. Add all remaining ingredients and simmer, covered, until the okras are tender.
6. Taste for seasoning.
7. Serve hot with Riz Creole or Creamed Vegetables.

Serves 4

COO–COO

Barbados and other English speaking Islands

In West Africa rice is ground to a very fine meal and cooked until all the water has disappeared. This dish is called foo-foo and is used almost as an implement, to wrap pieces of meat and vegetables in the fingers: you have a bowl of water beside the plate, for moistening the fingers, since foo-foo is sticky. It is served as a side-dish usually, but sometimes it is simply dumped on the side of your plate.

In crossing the Atlantic four hundred years ago, this dish changed its name and contents, and also to some extent its style, with possible influence from Amerindian cooking.

Now called coo-coo, which means side-dish in a number of African languages, it is served plain, as a mixture of cornmeal and water (there having been little rice grown in the West Indies until the 19th century), or with coconut. In some Islands, particularly Dutch ones, this simple version is known as Funchi, a Papiamento name.

The addition of okra not only enriches coo-coo enormously, but removes it even further from the dish traditionally eaten with the fingers.

Foo-foo has become, in the Caribbean, a dish made with pounded green plantain or breadfruit, even sweet potato, sometimes formed into small cakes or balls.

Both of these Creole developments from African recipes are essential to Caribbean cooking and are indispensable to many fish and light meat dishes.

225g (8 oz) okra
600ml (1 pint) water
125g (5 oz) cornmeal (preferably finely ground)
Butter
Salt to taste

1. Wash the okra, cut off the tops and slice the pods into small pieces.
2. Bring the water, with salt added, to the boil, drop in the okras and simmer, covered, for 10–12 minutes.
3. Gradually pour in the cornmeal, stirring constantly – then, for about 6 minutes, continue to stir until the mixture is thick and smooth and begins to leave the side of the pot.
4. Turn out on to a dish, spread with butter and serve.

Serves 4–6

TOMATE AVEC AUBERGINE

TOMATO WITH AUBERGINE

French and Patois speaking Islands

675g (1½ lb) tomatoes, peeled and sliced
675g (1½ lb) aubergines, peeled and chopped
3 tablespoons butter
1 onion, finely chopped
1 teaspoon oregano
6 capers
1 sweet pepper, sliced
½ teaspoon mace, freshly ground
Black pepper, freshly ground
Salt to taste

1 Have a heat-proof serving dish ready and buttered.
2 Put the chopped aubergine into a pot of salted boiling water. Cook for about 8–10 minutes. Drain, then mash into a pulp.
3 Heat the remaining butter in a shallow frying pan.
4 Sauté the onion until transparent but not brown.
5 Add the mashed aubergine, oregano, capers, sweet pepper, mace, black pepper and salt to taste.
6 Sauté, uncovered, for about 5 minutes.
7 Taste for seasoning.
8 Layer the buttered dish with half of the tomato, spreading the mashed aubergine evenly over.
9 Layer with the remaining tomatoes.
10 Bake in a pre-heated oven 190°C (375°F/Gas 5) for 25–30 minutes.
11 Serve immediately.

Serves 6–8

CHRISTOPHENE WITH TOMATOES

2 large christophenes, peeled, cored and cubed
450g (1 lb) tomatoes, peeled and coarsely chopped
2 tablespoons butter
1 clove garlic, chopped fine
A few leaves of basil, chopped fine
Black pepper, freshly ground
Salt to taste
1 tablespoon chives, chopped
110g (4 oz) grated cheese
75g (3 oz) buttered breadcrumbs

1 Have a warm baking dish ready.
2 Melt the butter in a pot, add the cubed christophenes with a little salt and simmer for about 15 minutes, stirring occasionally.
3 Remove from the pot and arrange in the baking dish.
4 Put all the other ingredients, except the chives, cheese and breadcrumbs in the pot, with a little more butter if needed.
5 Cook until well blended to the consistency of a thick paste.
6 Taste for salt and other seasonings.
7 Pour the sauce evenly over the christophenes.

8 First sprinkle with the chives, then the cheese and finally the buttered breadcrumbs.
9 Place under a hot grill until a rich golden brown.
10 Serve immediately. This can be served as part of a main meal to accompany a meat dish.

Serves 4

CHRISTOPHENE AND BACON

Author's recipe

2 christophenes, peeled, cored, cooked then cubed
1 tablespoon olive oil
1 tablespoon butter
2 rashers lean bacon, chopped
1 onion, chopped
Black pepper
Salt to taste (you may need none at all)

1 Heat the oil and butter in a frying pan, then lightly fry the bacon, add the onion and fry until transparent but not brown.
2 Now add the christophenes, pepper and a little salt if needed.
3 Sauté for 8–10 minutes, and serve hot. This goes well with any chicken dish.

Serves 4

STUFFED CHRISTOPHENE 1

2 christophenes about 450g (1 lb) each
1 tablespoon oil
1 tablespoon butter
1 onion, finely chopped
1 clove garlic, pressed or finely chopped
110g (4 oz) crab meat, white and brown
1 medium tomato, peeled and chopped
1 tablespoon chives, chopped
Small sprig of parsley, chopped
½ teaspoon pepper sauce
½ teaspoon allspice
½ teaspoon oregano
1 teaspoon Worcestershire sauce
Black pepper

Salt to taste
4 tablespoons grated hard cheese

1. Have salted water on the boil.
2. Cut the christophenes in half lengthwise.
3. Drop the christophene halves into the boiling water, turn down the heat and simmer for about 6 minutes.
4. Remove christophenes and allow to cool, then core and scoop out about ¾ of the flesh from each half, leaving enough to hold the shells firm. Discard the core.
5. In a shallow pot, sauté the onion and garlic in the oil and butter, but do not brown.
6. Add all the ingredients including the christophene flesh, but not the cheese, and cook, uncovered, until the mixture is of a thick consistency.
7. Taste for seasoning.
8. Stuff the christophene shells.
9. Arrange in a greased baking dish and bake in a pre-heated oven 190°C (375°F/Gas 5) for about 20 minutes.
10. Sprinkle with cheese and bake for a further 8–10 minutes.
11. Serve immediately.

Serves 4

STUFFED CHRISTOPHENE 2

This version uses no meat.

4 very large christophenes
2 tablespoons butter
1 small onion, finely chopped
½ small sweet red pepper, finely chopped
1 half-ripe tomato, blanched, peeled, seeded and chopped
4 small spring onions, green and white parts, chopped evenly
2 teaspoons lemon juice
55–75g (2–3 oz) fresh or frozen peas
6 fresh basil leaves, chopped, or 1 teaspoon if they are dried
1 tablespoon double cream
½ teaspoon turmeric
Salt to taste
White peppercorns, freshly ground
2 eggs, beaten

1 Bring a pot of salted water to the boil, cut the christophenes in equal halves (do not peel yet) and plunge into the boiling water.
2 Cook gently for about 10 minutes.
3 Test for tenderness by pricking with a knife.
4 Drain and rinse them under cold water immediately.
5 Leave to drain further and cool for a few minutes.
6 Carefully remove the core (*see* Techniques) and discard.
7 Now peel. Be gentle and scoop out as much of the flesh as possible and reserve it; but leave enough to hold the shell together.
8 Set aside but keep warm.
9 Melt the butter in a frying pan, add the onion, sweet pepper, tomato and spring onions, and sauté gently until soft, but without the onions browning.
10 Pour in the lemon juice and stir.
11 Add the peas, basil, a little salt, some white pepper and the pulp removed from the christophenes.
12 Beat the cream, turmeric, salt and white pepper with the eggs.
13 Pour over the vegetables and stir, very gently, until the eggs are mixed in with the contents of the pan and lightly scrambled.
14 Place the christophene halves on a serving dish and fill with the vegetable and egg mixture.
15 Garnish with some chopped chives if you so wish and serve with a really good bread of your choice or of your own baking.

Serves 4

STUFFED PUMPKIN

1 pumpkin
1 tablespoon olive oil
1 tablespoon butter
3 medium onions, finely chopped
2 cloves garlic, finely chopped
900g–1.25kg (2–2½ lb) lean beef, finely minced
225g (½ lb) tomatoes, peeled and chopped
1 sweet pepper, finely chopped

110g (4 oz) raisins
1 hot pepper, seeded and chopped (*see* Techniques)
2 teaspoons marjoram
1 tablespoon lemon juice
75ml (3 fl oz) beef stock (1½ bouillon cubes in same quantity of hot water)
Black pepper
Salt to taste
4 hard boiled egg yolks, mashed
4 tablespoons grated cheese

1. Cut the top off the pumpkin (about 5cm (2 inch)) and reserve the lid.
2. Scoop out the seeds and fibrous parts.
3. Bring a large pot of water to the boil, carefully drop in the pumpkin and its lid, reduce the heat and simmer, covered, for about 20 minutes or until the pumpkin can be pierced by a small knife or skewer with the shell remaining fairly firm.
4. Remove from the water, being very careful not to damage it.
5. Turn upside down and drain.
6. Meanwhile, in a pot, sauté the onions and the garlic in the butter and oil until the onion is transparent but not brown.
7. Add the meat and fry until there is no blood and no lumps.
8. Add all the other ingredients except the cheese and mashed egg yolks.
9. Continue to cook for about 10–12 minutes. The mixture should be of a thick well-mixed consistency.
10. Blend in the egg yolks. Taste for seasoning.
11. Carefully fill the pumpkin with the stuffing and cover with the lid.
12. Place in a casserole just large enough to hold the pumpkin. If it tips to one side, pack crumpled foil around it for support.
13. Bake in a pre-heated oven 190°C (375°F/Gas 5) for 1 hour.
14. Remove the lid, sprinkle the cheese over the filling and bake for a further 15 minutes, without the lid.
15. The pumpkin is best allowed to cool for a short time. Cut into segmented wedges when serving. A salad is sufficient as an accompaniment.

Serves 6–8

COLOMBO DE GIRAUMON

CURRIED PUMPKIN

Martinique

450g (1 lb) pumpkin
2 tablespoons oil
1 medium onion, finely sliced
1 clove garlic, finely chopped
2 teaspoons curry powder
½ teaspoon hot pepper, seeded and chopped (*see* Techniques)
½ teaspoon cloves, ground
Juice ½ lemon
Salt to taste
2 tomatoes, chopped

1. Peel and cut the pumpkin into 2.5cm (1 inch) cubes.
2. Heat the oil in a heavy pot and add the onion.
3. Fry until transparent but not brown.
4. Add the garlic, curry powder, hot pepper, cloves, lemon juice and salt.
5. Cook further for about 1 minute.
6. Now add the pumpkin and tomatoes. Great care must be taken that no burning occurs.
7. Lower the heat and cook for 20 minutes, stirring frequently until the pumpkin is tender.
8. Serve immediately – this dish can be accompanied by boiled rice or roti bread, or it can also be part of a meal with meat or fish.

Serves 4–6

BREAD COO-COO

½ breadfruit, peeled and cored
225g (½ lb) salt beef or pork, soaked for a few hours
½ teaspoon hot pepper, seeded and chopped (*see* Techniques)
1 tablespoon chives
1 teaspoon thyme
Black pepper, freshly ground
Salt to taste
55g (2 oz) butter

1. Wash the salt meat and place in a pot with just about enough water to cover.

2 Bring to the boil and simmer for about 20 minutes.
3 Cut the breadfruit into about 3 or 4 pieces and add to the pot with the meat.
4 Simmer, covered, until the breadfruit is tender.
5 Drain but reserve the liquid.
6 Mince the meat and mash the breadfruit.
7 Return to the pot with a little of the liquid, the hot pepper, chives, thyme, and black pepper.
8 Stir over a low heat until all the liquid has been absorbed.
9 Taste for seasoning.
10 Add the butter and cook for a few more minutes. Do not allow to stick to the bottom of the pan. Use more butter or liquid if necessary, for the coo-coo must bind well.
11 Turn out onto a warm dish. Shape and serve dotted with more butter. It must still be hot when served.

Serves 4

FRIED BREADFRUIT

English speaking Islands

This is a favourite for breakfast.

Breadfruit, well matured
Lime juice
Oil for frying
Butter
Black pepper, freshly ground
Salt to taste

1 Peel and core the breadfruit (*see* Techniques).
2 Parboil in salted water with the lime juice for 12–15 minutes.
3 Drain and allow to cool.
4 Cut into slices not more than 1½cm (¾ inch) thick.
5 Heat the oil in a frying pan and fry the breadfruit slices on both sides until golden brown.
6 Drain on kitchen paper.
7 Spread with butter.
8 Sprinkle with pepper and a little salt and serve hot.

BAKED BREADFRUIT

1 whole breadfruit
1 tablespoon oil
1 small onion, finely chopped
225g (½ lb) salt beef or pork, finely minced
2 tablespoons chives, finely chopped
½ teaspoon hot pepper, finely chopped (*see* Techniques)
1 teaspoon fresh thyme
Black pepper, freshly ground
Salt to taste
50g (2 oz) butter or margarine
Melted butter, for basting

1. Thoroughly wash the breadfruit and parboil in salted water with the skin still on.
2. Drain and allow to cool.
3. Heat the oil and sauté the onion until transparent but not brown.
4. Add the minced meat and fry for a few minutes until slightly brown.
5. Add all the herbs and spices with a little salt and cook for a few more minutes.
6. Remove from heat and allow to cool.
7. Blend in the butter while still warm.
8. Taste for seasoning.
9. Carefully peel the boiled breadfruit and remove the centre core with a sharp knife (think of coring an apple but without cutting through to the other end).
10. Stuff the empty part of the breadfruit with the mixture, place in a greased baking dish and bake in a pre-heated oven 180°C (350°F/Gas 4), basting with the melted butter, for 40–50 minutes.

Serves 6–8

WHITE BEANS IN HOT DRESSING

225g (½ lb) white beans (haricots, cannellini or fasoul), soaked for a few hours
1 onion, finely chopped
2 cloves garlic, finely chopped

2 teaspoons thyme leaves
6 whole cloves
1 tablespoon white vinegar
1 teaspoon sugar
Black pepper
Salt to taste

1 Rinse the soaked beans.
2 Place them in a saucepan with enough cold water to cover by about 5 cm (2 inches).
3 Bring to the boil.
4 Simmer, covered, until beans are tender but still whole.
5 Add all other ingredients and simmer, covered, until well cooked. Remember never to add salt to dried pulses until they are fairly soft.
6 Taste for seasoning.
7 Serve hot as part of a main meal, or cold with salads and cold meats.

Serves 4

FAOUINADE DE ZABOCA

AVOCADO AND FARINE

French and Patois speaking Islands

1–2 avocadoes, depending on size
170g (6 oz) farine (*see* Glossary)
Juice ½ lime or lemon
Salt to taste
1 tablespoon oil (optional)

1 Peel, stone and cut up the avocadoes and put into a bowl.
2 Add all the other ingredients, a little at a time, and with your fingers mix into a paste.
3 Shape on a serving dish.
4 Serve with Féroce de Morue (Fierce Saltfish) or any similar smoked herring or salted fish dish.

Serves 4

FÉROCE DE MORUE

225g (½ lb) salted cod, soaked overnight (change water as often as possible)
1 hot pepper, cut in half and seeded (*see* Techniques)
55–75ml (2–3 fl oz) oil

1 Having soaked the salt cod, pat as dry as you can with kitchen towels.
2 Grill until almost burnt.
3 Remove skin and bones, then shred.
4 Rub the hot pepper into the fish.
5 Marinade in oil for about 1 hour, then serve with the Faouinade de Zaboca.

Serves 4–6

FOO-FOO

POUNDED PLANTAINS

English and French speaking Islands

4 large green plantains
Salt
1–2 tablespoons butter
Black pepper

1 Peel and boil the plantains (*see* Techniques) until tender and drain.
2 Place in a large mortar, with the salt, butter and pepper, and dip the pestle in cold water. This you will have to do several times to prevent sticking.
3 Pound the plantain into a smooth paste.
4 Taste for salt and pepper.
5 Serve warm.

Serves 4

The foo-foo, if too cold, can be warmed in a covered dish in the oven. Brush with melted butter if you so wish. Serve with any fish, meat or poultry dish.

MACARONI PIE

English speaking Islands

The best macaroni for this dish is called shortcut and comes from Jamaica – it is widely available.

225g (½ lb) cooked macaroni
1½ tablespoons olive oil or clarified butter (ghee)
2–3 tablespoons butter
110g (4 oz) hard cheese, grated
1 onion, finely sliced
2 tomatoes, blanched, peeled and sliced (optional)
Black pepper, freshly ground
Salt to taste
2 eggs
275ml (½ pint) milk
6 slices fried bacon (optional)

1. Pre-heat the oven to 190°C (375°F/Gas 5).
2. Pour the olive oil or ghee into a skillet and heat gently, then add some spices of your choice from the list in this book and cook them until bubbles form and the proper blending has taken place.
3. At the same time, put the cooked macaroni into a saucepan over a medium heat, with a liberal sprinkling of water.
4. Agitate the macaroni and pour the contents of the skillet over it, then continue to keep the saucepan on the move so that each cut of pasta is nicely coated and 'seasoned up'.
5. Lightly butter an ovenproof dish and heat it in the oven a little.
6. Line the bottom with the fried bacon, then a layer of macaroni mixed with some of the cheese, then make a second layer of onions and tomatoes and sprinkle with some pepper and salt.
7. Repeat this process but finish with a layer of macaroni.
8. Beat the eggs with the milk and pour over.
9. Now dot the dish with butter and bake for about half an hour.
10. You may serve decorated with the slices of bacon, grilled.

Serves 6–8

This forms an indispensable part of a Sunday or feast day lunch, but is ideal as a lighter meal in itself.

RICE

These are some of the various rice dishes on the Islands. Rice in one form or another accompanies many of the meat, poultry and fish dishes and has become a major part of the staple diet of the Islands.

RIZ CREOLE

450g (1 lb) long grain rice
2 teaspoons salt
1.1 litres (2 pints) water

1 Wash and rinse the rice several times or until the water runs clear.
2 Place the rice, salt and water in a pot, bring to the boil, stir once.
3 Cover with a tight-fitting lid and simmer gently until two-thirds done (about 15 minutes).
4 Remove from the heat and rinse in cold water. Do not handle the rice too much.
5 Drain thoroughly and put back into the pot and dry uncovered on a low heat until heated right through.
6 Serve.

Serves 6

Some Caribbean cooks (mostly the Latin ones) prefer not to rinse the rice. They coat each grain with butter, by frying a piece of onion, finely chopped, in softened butter, then tossing the rice in that, before adding enough boiling water to cover. At the end of the cooking the pot is left slightly uncovered for about five minutes more. This version is called Arroz Crillo or Arroz de Mantequilla. In French Creole kitchens, the cooked rice is left in the pot, off the stove, wrapped in a damp towel until the meal is ready to serve, with the result that the rice is smothered in steam.

SEASONED RICE FOR FISH

450g (1 lb) long grain rice
50g (2 oz) butter
2 cloves garlic, finely chopped
850ml (1½ pints) of fish stock

Juice ½ lemon
White pepper, freshly ground
Salt to taste

1 Heat the butter in a heavy pot, add the rice and garlic, fry until the butter has been absorbed by the rice. Do not allow the rice to burn or brown.
2 Add the stock and the rest of the ingredients, bring to the boil, reduce the heat to the lowest possible level and simmer, tightly covered, until the rice is tender and all the liquid has been absorbed.

Serves 6

RICE AND PIGEON PEAS

450g (1 lb) long grain rice
450g (1 lb) fresh pigeon peas, *or* 225g (½ lb) dried *or* one can
2 tablespoons vegetable oil
2 medium onions, finely chopped
2 cloves garlic, finely chopped
1 teaspoon thyme
2 tablespoons parsley, chopped
Black pepper
Salt to taste

1 If you are using dried pigeon peas, soak them overnight. If canned, simply drain and add to the rice just before cooking.
2 Boil the pigeon peas, fresh or dried, in enough water to cover. Do not add salt. When just tender, drain and reserve the liquid for cooking the rice.
3 In a large heavy pot, sauté the onions and garlic in the oil until lightly brown and add all the other ingredients including the peas but not the rice.
4 Simmer covered on a very low heat for about 10 minutes.
5 In the meantime, bring the rice quickly to the boil in another pot and simmer, covered, for 6 minutes.
6 Now add the rice to the pigeon peas.
7 Simmer, covered, until the rice is tender and all the liquid has been absorbed.

Serves 8–10

This is a basic recipe. Herbs can be added to the peas when they are cooked, or introduced with other spices at the third stage. Fresh ingredients from your own garden can be used at step six or seven.

RED BEANS AND RICE

225g (½ lb) long grain rice
225g (½ lb) red beans, soaked for 6 hours
Salt to taste
2 cloves, ground
1 clove garlic, finely chopped
1 medium onion, finely chopped
½ teaspoon hot pepper, seeded and chopped (*see* Techniques)
1 sprig thyme
1 tablespoon chives, chopped

1 Wash the beans two or three times.
2 In a large saucepan, with enough water to cover, bring to the boil for 10 minutes.
3 Reduce the heat and simmer, covered, until the beans are almost tender.
4 Add a little hot water whenever necessary.
5 When the beans are tender add some salt, the cloves, garlic, onion, hot pepper, thyme and chives.
6 Wash the rice several times, drain and add to the beans.
7 Mix carefully and simmer, covered, until all the liquid has been absorbed and the rice is tender but firm.

Serves 6

SALADS

In most of the English speaking islands the salad is a small but interesting affair, offered on the side of a plate with a main dish, consisting of finely chopped raw vegetables, sometimes hidden in a lettuce leaf and usually dressed very lightly. But in French, Patois and Spanish speaking countries, *la salade*, *la ensalada*, becomes a major part of the meal, with resourceful use of a wide range of ingredients, served in a large bowl and dressed in a number of exciting ways. Other salads than the few listed here can be found in the hors d'ouevres, fish and poultry sections.

SALADE A LA CARAÏBE

1 ripe but firm avocado, peeled, stoned and sliced
1 bunch of watercress
1 small white cabbage, finely shredded
1 sweet pepper, seeded and finely sliced
1 baby cucumber, peeled and sliced
1 small ripe mango, peeled, stoned and finely sliced
6 spring onions, cleaned and neatly chopped
5 tablespoons olive oil
Juice 2 limes, or to taste
Juice 1 lemon
1 clove garlic, pressed
Black pepper, freshly ground
Salt to taste

1. Set the avocado and watercress aside, then put all the other vegetables into a salad bowl.
2. Blend the oil, citrus juice, garlic, pepper and salt.
3. Pour half the dressing over the salad vegetables, toss.
4. Arrange the avocado and watercress on top of the bowl.
5. Pour over the balance of the dressing, and serve.

Serves 6–8

CHILLED AVOCADO SALAD

2 avocadoes
Juice ½ lime or lemon
2 tomatoes, blanched, peeled, seeded and chopped
2 small onions, finely chopped
1 clove garlic, pressed
½ teaspoon hot pepper sauce
Salt to taste
White pepper, freshly ground

1. Peel, stone and mash the avocadoes, mixing in the citrus juice.
2. Add these to a serving bowl with all the other ingredients, mixing carefully.
3. Taste for seasoning.
4. Chill for at least 1 hour, then serve.

Serves 4

This dish can be served with mango or another salad and hot buttered bread, as a breakfast or as part of a main course.

MIXED FRUIT AND VEGETABLE SALAD

1 teaspoon sugar
2 tablespoons olive oil
Salt to taste
A little black pepper
2 oranges, peeled and pipped, with the pith beneath the peel removed
2 pink grapefruits, prepared as the oranges
2 slices pineapple, cubed
Small head firm lettuce, shredded
2 firm ripe bananas
½ cucumber, peeled, seeded and cubed (reserve the juice)
Bunch watercress

1. Blend together any juice collected from the citrus fruits and cucumber with the sugar, olive oil, salt and black pepper.
2. Toss in a salad bowl with the oranges, grapefruit, pineapple and lettuce. This must be done very gently so as not to break up the citrus fruit.
3. Mix in the bananas and cucumber.
4. Garnish with the watercress and serve.

Serves 6–8

This is an excellent accompaniment to ham dishes, or may include strips or cubes of ham as a light lunch or as part of a larger meal.

GREEN MANGO SALAD

4–6 green but almost ripened mangoes
Juice 2 limes, or to taste
1 clove garlic, pressed or finely chopped
1 teaspoon sugar
4 tablespoons oil
½ teaspoon hot pepper, seeded and chopped (*see* Techniques)
1 tablespoon chives, chopped
Salt to taste

1 Peel, stone and slice the mangoes and put them into a salad bowl.
2 Mix thoroughly all the other ingredients and pour this dressing over the mangoes.

Serves 4

SAUCES AND SALAD DRESSINGS

Like marinades, sauces are very popular among the peoples of the Caribbean, and it is not unusual to hear someone ask for more 'juice' or 'gravy'. Very few dishes are served without a sauce, either extracted or prepared separately. There are hot and spicy sauces, mild and sweet ones. We have some using fiery hot peppers; yet delicate accompaniments, which use coconut milk and subtle herbs and spices, come from many districts. These range from the clever curries exclusive to families of Asian origin, through the Creole sauces to be tasted in French and Patois speaking islands, to the characteristic Sofrito found in Cuba and Santo Domingo.

In countries where English is little spoken, many developments may be discovered as dressings for salads, some of which are covered in this book. You will notice, however, that in the Caribbean the fresh flavours of citrus juices are mostly preferred to the tang of the various vinegars used in Europe.

SAUCE CREOLE

CREOLE SAUCE

Martinique

To accompany lobsters, prawns and crayfish.

1 medium onion, finely chopped
150ml (¼ pint) tomato purée
Juice 1 lime
½ hot pepper, seeded and chopped (*see* Techniques)
1 sprig of parsley
1 tablespoon celery, finely chopped
Salt to taste
Black pepper

1 Combine all the ingredients in a bowl and blend thoroughly.

This sauce is best served at once, but you can cover it tightly and keep it in the refrigerator until needed, but only over the next seven days.

Serves 3–4

2nd Version

To accompany meats or poultry.

3 tablespoons oil
1 medium onion, finely chopped
1 clove garlic, finely chopped
1 sweet pepper, seeded and chopped
3 medium tomatoes, chopped
150ml (¼ pint) chicken stock
300ml (½ pint) dry white wine
2 level tablespoons plain flour, mixed with a little wine or stock
Small bunch of chives (tied)
2 teaspoons hot pepper sauce
2 teaspoons lime juice
Black pepper
Salt to taste

1. Heat the oil in a saucepan and sauté the onion, garlic and sweet pepper until the onion is transparent but not brown.
2. Add the tomatoes and fry for another 3 minutes.
3. Now pour in the stock and wine.
4. Bring to the boil.
5. Reduce the heat and gradually thicken with the flour paste, stirring constantly.
6. Add all the other ingredients.
7. Simmer gently, partly covered, for about 5 minutes.
8. Taste for seasoning.
9. Serve.

Serves 6–8

SOFRITO

Spanish speaking islands

1 teaspoon lard
110g (4 oz) salt pork, diced
3 medium onions, finely chopped
5 cloves garlic, finely chopped
2 sweet peppers, seeded and chopped
¾ teaspoon liquid annatto (achote)
110g (4 oz) ham, finely cubed
225g (8 oz) tomatoes, peeled, seeded and chopped
3 teaspoons coriander leaves, finely chopped
½ teaspoon oregano
Black pepper, freshly ground
Salt to taste

1. Rub the inside of a large heavy frying pan with the lard and fry the salt pork over a moderate heat until the pork is crisp and brown and has rendered all its fat. Stir frequently to avoid burning.
2. Remove the pork pieces from the fat with a perforated spoon or similar implement. (Either discard the pork pieces or reserve for some other use.)
3. To the fat add the onions, garlic and sweet peppers and fry until soft but not brown.
4. Stir in the annatto liquid, then the cubed ham.
5. Now add all other ingredients and simmer, tightly covered, over a low heat for 30 minutes. Stir from time to time to prevent any sticking and burning.
6. Pour into sterilized jars and refrigerate. This will keep for about 2 weeks and is sufficient for about 450ml (¾ pint).

SALAMAGUNDI SAUCE

4 tomatoes, peeled and chopped
½ christophene, peeled, cored and finely chopped
2 medium onions, finely chopped
½ hot pepper (*see* Techniques)
1 carrot, peeled and thinly sliced
2 sweet red peppers, chopped
300ml (½ pint) chicken stock
1 tablespoon vinegar

Salt to taste
Black pepper

1 In a heavy saucepan cook the tomatoes until soft.
2 Add all other ingredients and simmer for 20 minutes.
3 Taste for seasoning and simmer for a further 10–12 minutes.

Serves approximately 6

SHRIMP AND AVOCADO SAUCE

For any white fish, hot or cold.

75g (3 oz) butter
Pulp of 2 ripe avocadoes
Juice 1 lemon or lime
1 tablespoon parsley, chopped
White pepper, freshly ground
Salt to taste
6 tablespoons double cream
110g–170g (4–6 oz) shrimps, shelled and freshly cooked

1 Melt the butter in a saucepan on a low heat, add the avocado pulp, citrus juice, white pepper and salt to taste.
2 Cook for 2 minutes.
3 Now add the cream and shrimps, stirring to blend in well.
4 Taste for seasoning.
5 Serve with any white fish, or with flying fish.

Serves 4–6

SAUCE FOR SUCKLING PIG

2 tablespoons oil
1 onion, grated
3 cloves garlic, pressed or finely chopped
2 teaspoons grated ginger
½ teaspoon ground coriander
2 tablespoons chopped chives
2 teaspoons brown sugar
3 tablespoons tomato purée
2 tablespoons plain flour, mixed into a paste with stock
600ml (1 pint) chicken stock
4 cloves, ground

1 hot pepper, seeded and chopped (*see* Techniques)
1 tablespoon wine vinegar
1 tablespoon lime or lemon juice
1 tablespoon fresh orange juice
2 tablespoons dark rum
Salt to taste

1 In a heavy saucepan heat the oil and sauté the onion, garlic, ginger, coriander and chives for about 3–4 minutes.
2 Add the sugar and tomato purée, cook on a low heat for a further 3 minutes.
3 Stir in the flour paste.
4 Now gradually pour in the stock, stirring constantly.
5 Add all the other ingredients, and simmer, half covered, for 6–8 minutes.
6 Taste for seasoning and simmer for a further 5 minutes.
7 Allow to cool.
8 Pour into an electric blender and blend at high speed.
9 Warm again before serving.

Sufficient for a 5.5–7kg (12–15 lb) pig

TOMATO SAUCE

3 tablespoons oil
1 onion, finely chopped
3 cloves garlic, chopped
900g (2 lb) tomatoes, peeled and chopped
½ hot pepper, seeded and chopped (*see* Techniques)
4 whole cloves
6–8 peppercorns, freshly ground
2 tablespoons vinegar
1 tablespoon lime or lemon juice
2–3 teaspoons light brown cane sugar, or to taste
Salt to taste

1 Heat the oil in a heavy pot.
2 Add the onions and garlic and cook them until they are soft, about 3 minutes, without browning.
3 Introduce the tomatoes and all other ingredients. Blend in well.
4 Cook over low heat, stirring from time to time, until the mixture is thick and well blended.

5 Taste for seasoning, and continue to cook for a further 5–8 minutes.
6 Remove from heat. Pass through a sieve.
7 Pour into sterilized jars and store.

HOT PEPPER SAUCE

This is a very hot sauce – one of my own recipes.

225g (½ lb) hot peppers (mixture yellow, green and red Scots Bonnet – *see* Techniques)
3 cloves garlic, chopped
1 onion, finely chopped
6 cloves, freshly ground
2 teaspoons turmeric
Juice 2 limes
275ml (½ pint) malt vinegar
2 teaspoons salt
1 tablespoon cane sugar

1 Wash the peppers and remove stalks and seeds (*see* Techniques).
2 Roughly chop the peppers and place into a saucepan with all the other ingredients.
3 Bring to the boil, then cook on a moderate heat for about 3 minutes, stirring frequently.
4 Pour into a blender and blend to a smooth purée (or pass through a sieve and discard whatever pulp is left).
5 Return the purée to the pan, bring quickly to the boil. Boil for about 1½ minutes, stirring constantly.
6 Pour into sterilized jars and store. Will keep for weeks, sometimes even months.

Makes approximately 550ml (20 fl oz)

QUICK HOT SAUCE

2 hot peppers, seeded and finely chopped (*see* Techniques)
2 cloves garlic, finely chopped
1 onion, grated
1 tablespoon chives, finely chopped
3 tablespoons lime juice
1 tablespoon vinegar

1 tablespoon water
½ teaspoon sugar
Black pepper
Salt to taste

1. Place the hot peppers, garlic, onion, and chives in a bowl or heat-proof jar.
2. Bring to the boil the lime juice, vinegar, water, sugar, black pepper and salt.
3. Boil rapidly for about 2 minutes.
4. Taste for salt.
5. Pour the hot liquid over the chopped pepper mixture.
6. Cool and serve.

Makes approximately 110ml (4 fl oz)

MOLHO DE LIMÃO E LARANJA

ORANGE AND LEMON SAUCE

A recipe from the Portuguese speaking community in Guyana

Juice and peeled rind of 1 orange
Juice and rind of 1 lemon
150ml (¼ pint) chicken stock
1 teaspoon brown cane sugar
1 tablespoon butter
Black pepper
Salt to taste
Flour paste for thickening
2 tablespoons dry Madeira (known as Sercial)

1. Peel off the rind of both the orange and lemon as thinly as possible, preferably in one long spiral.
2. Bring the chicken stock to the boil, add both rinds and simmer, covered, on a low heat for about 6 minutes.
3. Strain the liquid.
4. Return to heat together with the citrus juices and bring slowly back to the boil.
5. Add the cane sugar, butter, pepper and salt to taste.
6. Simmer for about 5 minutes.
7. Thicken with the flour paste.
8. Simmer for a further 5–6 minutes.

9 Taste for seasoning.
10 Pour in the Madeira and serve.

This sauce goes well with roast pork or duck.

Serves 4

WINE AND ORANGE SAUCE

Spanish and French speaking Islands

2 full glasses claret
Juice 2 oranges
1 stick cinnamon
Zest of 1 lemon
4 whole cloves
1 bay leaf
1–2 teaspoons cane sugar
Black pepper, freshly ground
Salt to taste
2 teaspoons arrowroot mixed with a little water

1. Pour the claret wine and orange juice into a small pan and bring quickly to the boil.
2. Lower the heat and add the cinnamon, lemon peel, cloves, bay leaf, sugar, black pepper and salt.
3. Simmer, covered, for about 10 minutes.
4. Taste for seasoning.
5. Thicken with the arrowroot paste, stir and simmer for a further 3 minutes. Strain before serving.

Serve with roast pork or any duck recipe.

Serves 6–8

LIME OR LEMON DRESSING

Juice 1½ limes or lemons
75ml (3 fl oz) olive or vegetable oil
½ teaspoon sugar
Small clove garlic, finely chopped
2 teaspoons vinegar
Salt to taste
Black pepper

Place all the ingredients in a bowl and beat with a fork or whisk until the salt and sugar have melted and the oil is blended in.

This dressing is clearly for green salads.

AVOCADO DRESSING

2 ripe avocadoes
Yolks of 2 soft boiled eggs, carefully scooped out
2 tablespoons oil
2 teaspoons lemon juice
1 teaspoon white wine vinegar
White pepper, freshly ground
Salt to taste
2 teaspoons chives, finely chopped

1. In a bowl thoroughly blend the egg yolks with the oil, lemon juice, vinegar, white pepper and salt.
2. Peel and stone the avocadoes, then mash into a pulp and add to the egg mixture, together with the chives.
3. Blend thoroughly.
4. Taste for seasoning.

Serve with any vegetable or green salad; also recommended to accompany salt fish, any fish served cold, freshly baked breakfast bread or a cold chicken dish.

MANGO RELISH

1kg (2 lb) green mango flesh, cut in thin slices
675g (1½ lb) brown cane sugar
600ml (1 pint) malt vinegar
170g (6 oz) tamarind pulp (available from most Asian shops)
1 hot pepper, seeded and chopped (*see* Techniques)
6 cloves, freshly ground
4 allspices, freshly ground
110g (4 oz) seedless raisins
50g (2 oz) fresh ginger, grated
Juice 2 limes
2–3 tablespoons sea salt
170g (6 oz) tamarind pulp (available from most Asian shops)

You may need about 1.75kg (3½ lb) of firm green mangoes to get 1kg (2 lb) of flesh after peeling and stoning. Be sure to ask the stall or shop keeper which are the best mangoes for chutney.

1. In a heavy saucepan combine the sugar and vinegar and bring to the boil.
2. Reduce the heat and simmer for about 10 minutes.
3. Stir in the tamarind pulp, then all the other ingredients except the mangoes, and mix well.
4. Now add the mango slices and simmer for about 30 minutes, or until the mango slices are transparent. Do not overcook or allow the mango slices to fall apart and become too much of a purée.
5. Seal in sterilized jars and serve with cold or hot meat dishes and colombos.

Ice-Cream, Sweets and Fruit Desserts

Caribbean people on the whole have a great love of sweet things. But nothing I think is more popular than ice-cream. Every home that can afford an ice-cream tub has one, and even the poorest will save up their pennies to acquire one. On Sundays and holidays it is not uncommon to see several members of a family churning away at an ice-cream maker, a bag of ice and quantities of rock salt at their feet, all vying with each other for passing trade. Ice-cream is sold in cornets or customers may bring a glass, bowl or cup to have them filled with the delicious flavours (coconut, mango, banana, soursop, coffee and so on) that can all be bought from one ice-cream seller or another.

Today, imported mass-produced ice-cream can be purchased from the large supermarkets; although home-made remains the most popular – as it should.

The base for most Island ice-cream is home-made custard of eggs and milk.

Even under the tropical sun, hot puddings are popular (see next chapter), and naturally there are dozens of desserts made from the abundance of exotic fresh fruits – almost everything again is laced with rum and liqueurs.

There are other sweets like guava cheese and coconut 'tablets' (pralines), mousses, pancakes, fritters, peanut and cashew nut pralines. I have tried to give as varied a cross-section of recipes for desserts and puddings as it is possible to do within the confines of this book.

BASIC RECIPE FOR ICE-CREAM CUSTARD (1)

1.25 litres (2¼ pints) single cream
6 egg yolks
170g (6 oz) caster sugar

1 On a medium heat bring the cream to the boil in a saucepan, or make use of a double boiler if you have one, and stir occasionally.
2 Remove from heat – but keep warm.
3 Whisk the egg yolks and sugar until creamy.
4 Now gently mix the whisked yolks and sugar into the hot cream.
5 Return to a low heat and cook for about 10–15 minutes or until the mixture turns into a creamy custard. Do not boil too quickly and remember to stir to prevent lumps from forming. Also do not let mixture stick to the bottom of the saucepan.
6 Allow to cool before adding whatever flavouring or pulp of any fruit you wish.
7 Freeze (*see* next recipe).

For Vanilla Ice-Cream
Simply add about 1 level teaspoonful of vanilla extract or substitute vanilla sugar for caster sugar (*see* Techniques).

Serves 10–12; with pulp fruit added will serve 16–18

BASIC RECIPE FOR ICE-CREAM CUSTARD (2)

4 egg yolks
110g (4 oz) caster sugar
450ml (¾ pint) milk
150ml (¼ pint) cream

1 Beat the eggs with the sugar.
2 Heat the milk and cream, then stir into the eggs, pouring in a gentle, continuous flow.
3 Now cook the mixture over water in the top of a double boiler, stirring constantly until the mixture is a nice creamy custard.
4 Allow to cool.

For Vanilla Ice-Cream

Add ¾ teaspoon vanilla extract – or substitute vanilla sugar for caster sugar (*see* Techniques). Fruit pulp can obviously be added to this recipe.

Serves 6; with pulp fruit added will serve 8

To Freeze: You can either use an ice-cream tub (hand or electrically operated), or simply freeze in the freezing compartment of a refrigerator. If you freeze it in a refrigerator, the mixture with or without fruit should occasionally be beaten to prevent ice from forming and to obtain a creamy consistency. Each time the mixture is whisked, it must be returned at once to the freezing compartment.

Home-made ice-cream should be consumed on the day it is made.

Any fruit used in any of the ice-cream recipes must not be over-ripe. It is essential to follow the basic freezing instructions for any of the following recipes.

BANANA ICE-CREAM

To basic recipe 1: add 4–5 well-mashed ripe bananas and freeze as per instructions.

To basic recipe 2: add 3 mashed ripe bananas.

COCONUT ICE-CREAM

Basic recipe 1: use 1 litre (1¾ pints) double cream instead but add 425ml (¾ pint) of thick coconut cream made from two freshly grated coconuts (*see* Techniques).

Basic recipe 2: substitute 600ml (1 pint) coconut milk made from 2 freshly grated coconuts for the milk (*see* Techniques).

In both coconut recipes a drop or two of vanilla extract can be added.

GUAVA ICE-CREAM

To basic recipe 1: add 600ml (1 pint) puréed guava, stewed with about 75g–110g (3–4 oz) caster sugar.

To basic recipe 2: add 450ml (3/4 pint) puréed guava, stewed with 50g (2 oz) caster sugar.

MANGO ICE-CREAM

To basic recipe 1: add 600ml (1 pint) mango pulp sweetened with 75g–110g (3–4 oz) caster sugar.

To basic recipe 2: add 450ml (3/4 pint) mango pulp sweetened with 50g (2 ozs) caster sugar.

PINEAPPLE ICE-CREAM

To basic recipe 1: add 600ml (1 pint) puréed fresh pineapple stewed with 75g–110g (3–4 oz) caster sugar.

To basic recipe 2: add 450ml (3/4 pint) puréed fresh pineapple stewed with 50g (2 oz) caster sugar.

RUM ICE-CREAM

To basic recipe 1: add 7 tablespoons dark rum when the custard is cool.

To basic recipe 2: add 4 tablespoons dark rum when the custard is cool.

RUM AND RAISIN ICE-CREAM

Basic recipe 1: put 225g (8 oz) of raisins to soak overnight with 8 tablespoons of dark rum. Mash lightly with a fork and add to the cool custard and freeze.

Basic recipe 2: overnight soak 150g (5 oz) raisins with 4 tablespoons of dark rum. Mash lightly with a fork and add to the cool custard and freeze.

PEANUT ICE-CREAM

To basic recipe 1: add 225g (8 oz) of crushed roasted unsalted peanuts.

To basic recipe 2: add 150g (5 oz) of crushed roasted unsalted peanuts. A little vanilla extract may be added to both.

SORBETS

French speaking Islands

Sorbets are popular not only on the French Islands, but throughout most of the world as well. The following is a basic recipe using any fruit pulp or juice you prefer: limes, lemons, mangoes, pawpaws, passion fruit, oranges, soursop, guavas, etc.

450g (1 lb) caster sugar
600ml (1 pint) water

1. Make a syrup from the sugar and water (it must be fairly thick) and allow to cool.
2. When cool, measure the quantity of syrup and add to it an equal amount of fruit pulp and juice.
3. Blend well with a wooden spoon or fork. A liquidizer is not suitable as it froths up too much.
4. Pour into suitable bowls, to fit your freezer or ice compartment. (If you are using mangoes, guavas, soursop or any fruits that are fibrous or contain seeds, first pass the mixture through a fine sieve before freezing.)
5. After about 1½ hours in the freezer, remove and beat or whisk to get rid of any ice crystals that have formed. At this stage a blender can be used at a low speed.
6. Return to ice compartment for a further 1½ hours and then beat again. But this time you will have to make use of a wooden spoon or fork once more.
7. Return to the freezer and allow to set for about 1½–2 hours. Sorbets should not be allowed to set to too hard a consistency. The sorbet can be made the day before it is needed, but should be removed from the freezer or ice compartment about an hour before it is needed and left to soften in the general section of the refrigerator.
8. Serve in individual bowls or glasses. Citrus sorbets may be served in their own shells having first frozen the shells well. Garnish the shells with citrus leaves or petals.

Serves 6–12

CHILLED GRAPEFRUITS

Most Islands

Grapefruits (cut into half – one or two halves per person, according to size of fruit)
1 teaspoon rum for each piece of fruit
1–3 drops angostura bitters for each piece of fruit
Little grated nutmeg
Brown cane sugar
Cherries to decorate
Citrus leaves to decorate

1 With a sharp pointed knife remove the top of the grapefruit.
2 Now cut vertically, preferably with a double-edged serrated grapefruit knife, to release the pithy centre.
3 Cut between the pith and the peel to free as much of the flesh as possible, without removing it and without breaking the shell of the fruit.
4 Now pour in rum and angostura, sprinkle nutmeg and sugar into the cavity, removing any excess juice if necessary.
5 Chill for at least 1 hour before serving.
6 Decorate each fruit with a cherry and some citrus leaves.

FROZEN JOYS

Author's recipe

2 medium size ripe but firm mangoes
6 halves of canned guava
3 mandarins
12 macerated Continental or American cherries
Fruit salad syrup
Rum or brandy (optional)
700–850g (1¼–1½ pints) ice-cream

For garnish

1 ripe mango, peeled and nicely sliced
2 mandarins, peeled and segmented
A few slices of guava
Some cherries

1 Peel, stone and neatly dice the mangoes (do not chop), remove any seeds from the guava halves, peel and segment

the mandarins (removing the fleshy layer of skin over the segments) and slice the macerated cherries.

2 Place the various fruits into individual bowls. Pour over each a little fruit salad syrup and a dash of rum or brandy.
3 Place the bowls in the freezer or ice-compartment of a refrigerator, and allow to reach just below freezing-point.
4 Spread a quantity of the ice-cream in a mould large enough to hold all the ingredients. Arrange the cherries on the ice-cream, then cover the cherries with more ice-cream. Repeat the process with the other fruits; with the mandarin last. Finish with a layer of ice-cream.
5 Place the mould in a freezer and leave for two hours or longer.
6 Remove from freezer and turn mould onto a decorative serving platter. To help remove the mould wrap with a hot towel. Leave to stand at room temperature for about 8 minutes.
7 Garnish with the various fruits and serve. Serve in slices.

Serves 6–8

MANGO FOOL

English speaking Islands

6–8 ripe mangoes (choose mangoes that are not too fibrous)
Juice ½ a lime (to prevent mango purée from losing its colour)
110g (4 oz) caster sugar
450ml (¾ pint) whipped double cream

1 Peel and stone the mangoes and purée with the lime juice.
2 Pass through a fine sieve, using a wooden spoon to extract as much of the juice as possible, if there are any fibres.
3 Blend together the mango purée and sugar.
4 Taste to check if more sugar is needed.
5 Chill in the ice-compartment or a freezer for about half an hour. But do not allow to ice up.
6 Meanwhile whip the cream; chill as well.
7 Gently fold the two mixtures together and serve.

Serves 6–8

CARIBBEAN FRUIT SALAD

Throughout the Islands

2 ripe but firm bananas, peeled and cut into small rounds
2 ripe but firm mangoes, peeled, seeded and cut into cubes
2–3 slices of pineapple, peeled and cubed
1 pink grapefruit, peeled and segmented with seeds discarded
1 white grapefruit, peeled and segmented with seeds discarded
Juice 4 passion fruits (*see* Techniques)
1 tablespoon light brown cane sugar
2 tablespoons light rum
Freshly grated nutmeg
Juice 1 lemon

1. Peel and prepare the soft fruits over a sieve placed over a bowl so as to collect all juices.
2. Combine together any juice collected, the passion fruit juice, sugar to taste, rum, nutmeg and lemon juice.
3. Arrange the fruits in a bowl and pour the liquid over them.
4. Allow to stand in the refrigerator for about an hour.
5. Garnish with citrus blossoms, leaves, and a passion flower. Serve with whipped cream or home-made ice-cream.

Serves 6–8

MANGO MOUSSE

Barbados

2–2.25kg (4–5 lb) ripe mangoes (a *stringy* mango is not ideal)
Juice 1–2 limes according to size
1 packet gelatine
65g (2½ oz) caster sugar
2 egg whites
Pinch of salt
150ml (5 fl oz) double cream (a small carton)

1. Peel the mangoes and cut away the flesh from the stone.
2. Purée the flesh, then stir in the lime juice immediately.
3. Dissolve the gelatine in a little warm water (2 tablespoons at the most), and set it aside to cool.
4. Stir the sugar into the mango mixture.
5. Now mix in the gelatine.

6 Beat the egg whites with the salt until stiff and able to stand in peaks.
7 Whip the cream until it is as stiff as the egg whites.
8 Fold the two together, then gently fold into the purée.
9 Put into a large serving bowl or into individual dishes and refrigerate until set (about 2–3 hours).

Serves 6–8

GINGER MOUSSE

English speaking Islands

170g (6 oz) ginger in syrup, or crystallized ginger
3 tablespoons cold water
1 tablespoon gelatine (1 packet)
600ml (1 pint) evaporated milk, or half evaporated milk and half double cream
5 eggs, separated
110g (4 oz) caster sugar
6 tablespoons, light to medium Island rum
Very little salt

1 Dissolve the gelatine in the water on a very low heat.
2 Remove from heat but keep warm to prevent the gelatine from setting.
3 Heat the evaporated milk in a saucepan.
4 Remove from the heat.
5 Beat the egg yolks with an electric beater or a whisk.
6 Add the sugar a little at a time and continue beating until it has turned yellow and is able to form a ribbon.
7 Now start pouring the heated milk into the whisked yolks, beating constantly until well blended.
8 Pour back into the saucepan.
9 Place on a low heat, stirring until the mixture turns into a rich creamy custard. Do not allow to boil or burn.
10 Add the gelatine and ginger to the custard.
11 Add the rum; blend in well.
12 Remove from heat and set aside to cool.
13 Beat the egg whites with the salt until stiff and able to stand in peaks.
14 Mix about a third of the egg whites into the custard.
15 Carefully fold in the balance.

16 Pour into a bowl with the aid of a rubber spatula or spoon.
17 Put into the coldest part of the refrigerator until set or you may set in individual serving bowls if you wish.

Serves 6

TAMARIND BALLS

Eastern Caribbean

165g (6 oz) tamarind pulp (you may need about 900–1.25kg (2–2½ lbs) whole tamarinds)
450g (1 lb) white sugar (for mix)
1 teaspoon lime juice
Pinch white pepper
110g (4 oz) sugar for coating

1. Shell the tamarinds, pull away the inner fibres and scrape off the pulp from the seeds.
2. Do not allow any bits of the brittle shell to remain with the pulp.
3. Mix together all ingredients, except the 110g (4 oz) sugar, until well blended.
4. Roll into balls about the size of a small lime.
5. Coat with sugar and store in a tightly closed jar or tin, lined with greaseproof paper.

PEANUT PRÂLINES

Most Islands

This sweet is very popular in the Caribbean and is similar to the Prâline Créole of New Orleans.

450g (1 lb) shelled peanuts
450g (1 lb) brown sugar (best cane sugar like demerara)
3 tablespoons water

1. In a saucepan mix the sugar with the water, place on the heat and slowly bring to the boil.
2. Reduce to a moderate heat and cook until it forms a syrup.
3. Add the peanuts and cook for another 5–8 minutes or until the mixture begins to bubble.
4. Stir constantly to avoid any burning. Always be careful when working with sugar syrups as the temperature is very high

and like oil can cause severe burns, even from the smallest drop.

5 Butter a wooden or marble slab or a large shallow dish and mould a tablespoonful of the mixture at a time into round or oblong shapes. It is very important that this is carried out as quickly as possible, immediately the mixture is removed from the heat.

6 Allow to dry and lift with a spatula or knife.

7 The prâlines can be eaten at once or stored in a tight greaseproof lined tin or jar.

CASHEWNUT PRÂLINES

As peanuts, but the cashews must be coarsely chopped or broken.

COCONUT PRÂLINES

This is more painstaking and takes longer but is as delicious as the nut prâlines, if not more so – and is certainly more popular in the Islands.

450g (1 lb) coconut, carefully cut into pieces, each about the size of a peanut
150ml (¼ pint) water
450g (1 lb) brown cane sugar
1 cinnamon stick
Peel of 1 lime, chopped (optional)

1 In a large pot bring the water to the boil together with about a third of the sugar, and the cinnamon stick.
2 Add the coconut and cook on a medium heat until the coconut is almost tender.
3 Now add the lime peel and the rest of the sugar and cook, uncovered, until a heavy syrup.
4 The coconut should be cooked right through by now.
5 Stir constantly to prevent burning.
6 Adjust the heat as the syrup thickens.
7 Turn out by the spoonful on to a floured board or marble.
8 Allow to dry and lift with a spatula or knife.

TABLETTES

CANDIED COCONUT (1)

French speaking Islands

225g (8 oz) freshly grated coconut, brown skin of flesh scraped or peeled off before grating, using a small sharp knife
4 egg whites
225g (8 oz) caster sugar (or same quantity of vanilla sugar – then omit the vanilla essence)
Drop or two of natural vanilla essence.

1 Preheat the oven to 160°C (325°F/Gas 3).
2 In a large bowl lightly beat the egg whites, add the coconut, sugar and vanilla essence and blend until well mixed.
3 Grease a warm baking sheet with butter.
4 Place individual tablespoonsful on the baking sheet and bake for about 30 minutes.
5 Remove from the oven and allow to cool before lifting.
6 Store as peanut prâlines (p.231).

If you wish you may add any food colouring, provided it is safe. Natural ingredients are best.

TABLETTES

CANDIED COCONUTS (2)

French and English speaking Islands

340g (¾ lb) freshly grated coconut (substitute desiccated)
150ml (¼ pint) water
450g (1 lb) light brown sugar
1 cinnamon stick
Caramel colouring (about 2 tablespoons)

1 Boil together the water, sugar and cinnamon stick until very thick and syrupy then stir in the coconut and caramel colouring.
2 Cook for about 30 minutes, on a low to medium heat, stirring constantly.
3 Remove from heat and allow to cool.
4 Before it becomes hard shape into small balls or any shape you wish.

CONFITS DE PATATE FLAMBÉE

CANDIED SWEET POTATOES

French and Patois speaking Islands

3–4 sweet potatoes, each about 10–12½cm (4–5 inches) long, peeled
1 lime or lemon for scrubbing the potatoes
170g (6 oz) brown cane sugar
4 tablespoons water
1 teaspoon lime juice
½ teaspoon powdered cinnamon
1 teaspoon grated lemon rind
2–3 tablespoons rum
¼ teaspoon grated nutmeg

1. Peel and wash the potatoes in cold water, scrubbing with citrus.
2. Set to boil with enough water to cover. Cook until almost tender but still quite firm.
3. Drain and allow to cool.
4. Meanwhile combine the sugar, water, lime juice, cinnamon, lemon rind and boil into a thick syrup – then lower the heat.
5. Slice the potatoes in rounds 1cm (⅜ inch) thick. Gently immerse them in the syrup and cook, over a very low heat, for about 10–12 minutes. Do not allow to burn.
6. Carefully turn out into a serving platter.
7. Heat the rum in a small saucepan, quickly pour it over the candied potatoes, set alight to flambé, sprinkle with grated nutmeg and serve.

BANANE CREOLE

4–6 ripe but firm bananas
1½ tablespoons unsalted butter
1½ tablespoons brown cane sugar
Peel of 1 orange, thinly peeled and cut into fine strips
Juice 3 oranges
Juice 1 lemon
½ teaspoon cinnamon
2 tablespoons rum
1 tablespoon Crême de Banane liqueur (optional but very good)

1 In a frying pan large enough to hold the bananas make a syrup with the butter and cane sugar.
2 Add the orange peel and cook for about 5 minutes on a low heat.
3 Add the orange and lemon juice and reduce, uncovered, by a third.
4 Now add the peeled bananas and the cinnamon.
5 Simmer very gently until the bananas are soft and the liquid has reduced further.
6 Pour in the rum and Crême de Banane.
7 Leave on low heat for 2 minutes.
8 Serve at once.

Serves 4–6

I have served this dish at 'Le Caraïbe' restaurant with creamed cheese on the top – quickly grilled for about 3–4 minutes. It is well worth trying.

FRIED BANANAS

Popular on most of the Islands

Bananas (allow 1–2 bananas per person according to size or appetite)
Batter
4–5 tablespoons rum
2 teaspoons lemon juice
2 tablespoons brown sugar
Oil for frying

First make the batter:

110g (4 oz) plain flour
Pinch salt
1 egg yolk
1 tablespoon melted butter
1 tablespoon milk
7 ml (2½ fl oz) warm water
1 egg white

1 Mix the flour, salt, egg yolk, melted butter and milk – mix well.
2 Gradually pour in the warm water, beating continuously until smooth.

3 Set aside in a cool place for about 1 hour.
4 Whisk the egg white until stiff and add to the mixture at the end of the hour.
5 Immediately you have set aside the batter, peel the bananas, cut each into quarters, once lengthways then across.
6 Place in a flat, shallow dish, pour the rum and the lemon juice over the fruit and sprinkle with the sugar.
7 Allow to stand for 1 hour.
8 Turn the bananas a few times in the liquid.
9 Remove the bananas and add any liquid left to the batter and mix.
10 Dip the bananas in the batter and fry in almost boiling oil until brown.
11 Serve sprinkled with brown cane sugar.

Serves 6

FRUIT SALAD SYRUP

110g (4 oz) caster sugar
1 stick cinnamon
Juice ½ orange
2 tablespoons water
Juice ½ lemon
2 drops natural vanilla essence
1 tablespoon white rum
½ teaspoon grated nutmeg

1 In a small saucepan mix together the sugar, cinnamon, orange juice and water, then bring to the boil, stirring constantly.
2 Lower the heat and continue to boil until the liquid becomes syrupy, but not too thick.
3 Remove from the heat and allow to cool.
4 When cold add the lemon juice, vanilla essence, rum and nutmeg and mix well.
5 Pour over the fruit salad and allow to stand for an hour or so before serving.

STUFFED PINEAPPLE DESSERT

1 large pineapple
1½ tablespoons sugar
1 tablespoon Curaçāo
1 tablespoon light but mature rum
1 ripe mango, peeled, stoned and cut into wedges
Juice 2–3 passion fruits
Juice ½ lemon
½ small ripe pawpaw, peeled, seeded and cubed
1 orange, cut into wedges
6–8 red cherries
1 ripe banana, peeled and cut into 1cm (½ inch) pieces

1 Cut the pineapple lengthways in half.
2 Carefully remove the flesh with a small sharp knife.
3 Discard the core and cut the flesh into small spear-shaped pieces.
4 Mix together the sugar, Curaçāo, rum, passion fruit juice, lemon juice and any juice you may have collected from the various fruits you have peeled and cut. Blend well.
5 Taste for sweetness, add more sugar if you wish.
6 Fill the pineapple halves with the remaining fruit and pour the liqueur mixture over them.
7 Place on an attractive dish or two dishes and serve.

I have served this best as a communal 'help-yourself' dessert in the centre of the table.

Serves 6–8

PINEAPPLE FRITTERS

8–12 pineapple slices
Oil
Batter (*see* Breads)
Caster sugar

1 Heat enough oil in a deep pan to cover the pineapple slices.
2 Dip the pineapple in the batter and fry each piece until brown.
3 Drain on a cloth.
4 Serve hot, sprinkled with caster sugar.

Serves 4–6

SWEET POTATO FRITTERS

1 Peel 2 or 3 potatoes and parboil them.
2 Allow to cool and slice into rounds.
3 Proceed as with Pineapple Fritters. They are delicious with a little grated nutmeg as well as the sugar.

ORANGE OR GRAPEFRUIT FRITTERS

1 Peel 4 oranges or 2 large grapefruits and remove the pith.
2 Cut into rounds, remove pips and the central pithy stem.
3 Dip into batter and proceed as for pineapple fritters.

BANANA FRITTERS (1)

All Islands

4 ripe bananas
1 egg
25g (1 oz) caster sugar
50g (2 oz) plain flour
1 level teaspoon baking powder
Oil

1 Peel and mash the bananas, add the egg and then the sugar, beating continuously.
2 Sift the flour and baking powder, stir into the banana mixture and blend well.
3 Heat the oil in a shallow frying pan.
4 Fry the mixture a tablespoonful at a time.
5 Serve sprinkled with sugar and freshly ground cinnamon, if you wish, or flambé them in warm rum.

Serves 4–6

BANANA FRITTERS (2)

8 small ripe bananas (the smallest firm ones you can find)
2 tablespoons caster sugar
1 teaspoon powdered cinnamon
4 tablespoons rum
A little lime or lemon juice (strictly to prevent the fruit from darkening)
Batter (*see* Breads)

1 Peel the bananas and place them in a bowl with the above ingredients (not the batter).
2 Allow to stand at room temperature for about 2 hours, occasionally turning the bananas in the liquid.
3 In a large frying pan deep enough to hold at least 4 bananas with enough oil to seethe over them, heat oil until quite hot, but not smoking. Thoroughly coat each banana in the batter and fry until golden brown. Do not attempt to fry too many at a time.
4 Drain on kitchen paper.
5 Serve sprinkled with caster sugar.
6 Serve with whipped cream if you wish.

Serves 4–8

These fritters can be served hot or cold, but are I think best hot.

PUMPKIN FRITTERS

St Kitts

225g (½ lb) pumpkin, peeled, seeded and grated
50g (2 oz) caster sugar
50g (2 oz) margarine
2 small eggs, beaten
½ teaspoon nutmeg
¼ teaspoon powdered cinnamon
110g (4 oz) flour
1 teaspoon baking powder
Salt
Milk
Oil

1 Cream together the sugar and the margarine.
2 Beat in the eggs.
3 Add the grated pumpkin, nutmeg and cinnamon, mixing well.
4 Sift together the flour, baking powder and salt.
5 Add to the mixture, blending well.
6 Make into a thick batter with the milk.
7 Heat the oil in a heavy frying pan.
8 Fry the fritters (each one equivalent to about two tablespoons of the mixture) until golden brown on both sides.
9 Serve sprinkled with sugar.

Serves 4–6

LIME SOUFFLÉ

Rind of 4–5 limes, finely grated
35g (1½ oz) butter
3½ tablespoons cornflour
75ml (3 fl oz) evaporated milk
175g (6 oz) caster sugar
55ml (2 fl oz) lime juice
4 egg yolks
5 egg whites
¼ teaspoon salt

1. On a low heat melt the butter in a saucepan, add the cornflour and cook until well mixed. Do not allow to burn.
2. Add the milk a little at a time, stirring constantly.
3. Add the sugar and continue to cook for 5 minutes.
4. Mix in the lime juice and rind.
5. Remove from heat, allow to cool, then beat in the egg yolks one at a time.
6. Whisk the egg whites with the salt until stiff and able to stand in peaks.
7. Mix about a third of the beaten egg whites into the mixture, then fold in the balance of the whites.
8. Pour into a buttered soufflé mould.
9. Bake in a pre-heated oven 190°C (375°F/Gas 5) until done (about 35 minutes).
10. Serve at once.

Serves 4–6

ORANGE SOUFFLÉ

Juice 1 orange
Grated rind of 1 orange
4 eggs, separated
110g (4 ozs) caster sugar

1. Pre-heat oven to 160°C (325°F/Gas 3).
2. Beat the egg yolks until stiff.
3. Add half the sugar, the orange juice and rind and continue to beat until well blended.
4. Whip the egg whites to a stiff peak, gently beat in the rest of the sugar.

5 Fold into the yolk mixture.
6 Turn into a dish or soufflé mould and bake for about 20–30 minutes.
7 Serve immediately.

Serves 4–6

GUAVA CHEESE

Most Islands

This is a very popular sweet on the Islands and well worth trying. Children will love it.

20 very ripe guavas
Light brown cane sugar
Caster sugar (for dip)

1 Wash the guavas in cold water. Do not peel.
2 Purée the guavas, then pass through a sieve.
3 Measure the quantity of the purée.
4 Now measure an equal amount of brown sugar.
5 Put both ingredients into a heavy pot and slowly bring to the boil, stirring constantly.
6 Lower heat, to avoid burning, and cook, stirring from time to time, until the mixture is thick and does not stick to the sides of the pot.
7 Test in a saucer of cold water – the mixture must become firm when dropped into the water.
8 Pour into a lightly greased large but shallow tin about 1–2cm (½–¾ inch) deep. Allow to set.
9 When set, cut into small squares and dip each square in caster sugar.

STEWED GUAVAS

All Islands

450g (1 lb) fresh guavas, washed and cut into pieces
250–300ml (9–10 fl oz) water
6cm (2½ inch) piece of green lime peel
5cm (2 inch) piece of cinnamon stick
Pinch of grated nutmeg
170g (6 oz) light brown cane sugar

1. Bring the water to the boil in a heavy pot, with the lime peel, cinnamon and nutmeg.
2. Add the sugar. Lower the heat and simmer, uncovered, for about 6 minutes.
3. Add the guavas and cook until tender, stirring from time to time.
4. Remove from heat and allow to cool.
5. When cool, discard the lime peel and cinnamon stick and pass through a sieve.

Use in ice cream, Guava Fool (recipe as for Mango Fool, p.228) or as a sweet by itself. Can also be served with a mild cheese or cream.

Breads, Cakes and Puddings

Caribbeans are very fond of their doughy breads like bakes and floats. You will not pass a street corner, a market place or even a rum shop and not find a vendor with a tray of assorted breads, 'rough' cakes, slices of home-made puddings, accras, and delicious pieces of marinated fried fish such as tuna, dolphin fish, small snappers, sprats and big jacks. The most popular of the breads are Mastiff and Penny bread. Not that you can still buy a loaf of bread for a penny, no matter how small the loaf. But bread remains a staple, and there are times when it is all the less well-off can afford to eat, be it with the odd avocado they have picked from the tree in their back yard, a dry coconut from someone else's yard or beach, a ripe banana or whatever they can find to supplement it.

And the cakes? Well, for those who can afford it, a Christmas cake is a must, and so is a cake for christenings and confirmations. Cakes are made from almost everything the Islands can produce – coconuts, bananas, oranges, cornmeal and much more. As are many delicious puddings served hot or cold, whole or in slices, made from the same variety of fruits, nuts, and vegetables, such as sweet potatoes and pumpkins. These are not necessarily served as part of a main meal.

It would require a whole book to cover the many breads, cakes and puddings from the Islands, whether Spanish, Dutch, French, Portuguese or English speaking. But I hope you enjoy making and eating the few that I have provided; and may your guests be as delighted as I hope you will be.

BAKES (1)

Eastern Caribbean

Another recipe from a friend, Sandra Knight, now living in England.

450g (1 lb) self-raising flour
2 teaspoons salt (or to taste)
50g (2 oz) lard or margarine
50g (2 oz) sugar
Water (preferably iced)
Oil for frying

1. Sift the flour and salt together into a bowl.
2. Rub in the fat until the mixture is crumbly.
3. Add the sugar and mix in well.
4. Pour in enough cold water to make into a dough.
5. Turn out and knead lightly on a floured board or marble slab.
6. Put into a container, cover, and refrigerate for about 30 minutes.
7. Pinch off pieces of dough the size of a lemon, roll into balls, then flatten into rounds about ½ cm (¼ inch) in thickness.
8. Heat the oil in a large heavy frying pan, then fry the bakes, a few at a time, until golden brown on both sides.
9. Serve as bread with accras or any other dish of your choice.

I have known people with so little in the larder that bakes were all they could make to keep them going. Instead of lard or margarine, coconut oil was used. Sometimes a gravy was served made of water, salt, herbs, spices, and whatever vegetables they were able to grow in their yards. I have even known of bakes being made from green bananas, grated, left to dry in the sun, then pounded into flour.

BAKES (2)

Trinidad

225g (½ lb) plain flour
1 teaspoon salt
40g (1½ oz) lard
1½ teaspoons baking powder
1½ teaspoons sugar

Water
Oil for frying

1 Sift flour, salt and baking powder and proceed as first recipe.

Bakes can also be baked on a hot greased griddle or on greased baking sheets in the oven as you would bread.

FLOATS

Trinidad

A fried yeast bread, also served with accras, or as a bread with a breakfast dish of your choice.

Lukewarm water
2 heaped teaspoons dried yeast
1 teaspoon sugar
400g (14 oz) plain flour
1 teaspoon salt
110g (4 oz) lard, chilled and cut into very small pieces
Oil for frying

1 Pour a little of the warm water into a bowl and mix in the yeast and sugar.
2 Allow to stand for a few minutes in a warm draught-free place until the mixture bubbles and doubles in quantity.
3 Sift the flour and salt in a bowl and rub in the pieces of chilled lard until the mixture crumbles.
4 Pour in the yeast mixture with enough (but not too much) warm water and make into a dough.
5 Turn the dough out on to a lightly floured board and knead for about 12–15 minutes, until the dough is smooth and bounces back when pressed. Do not allow the dough to stick to the board. Use a little flour during the kneading process.
6 Cover with a clean cloth and allow to rest in a warm place until the dough doubles in size.
7 Lightly flour your hands and roll the dough into at least 18–20 balls. Place, a little apart from each other, on a sheet of greaseproof paper in a warm place and allow to rise to twice the size.
8 Heat enough oil to cover in a large, heavy frying pan.
9 On a floured surface, roll out 3–4 balls at a time into flat rounds and fry until brown on both sides (3–4 minutes).

10 Place on kitchen paper, but keep warm until all the floats have been fried.
11 Serve as bread with accras or with any appropriate dish of your choice.

DUMPLINGS (1)

FLOUR AND CORNMEAL

225g (½ lb) flour
110g (4 oz) cornmeal
1 teaspoon baking powder
1 teaspoon powdered dried thyme
½ teaspoon ground allspice
Salt to taste
Black pepper
2 tablespoons butter
1 egg, beaten
Milk or milk and water

1 Mix together the flour, cornmeal, baking powder, thyme, allspice, salt and pepper.
2 Rub in the butter then mix in the egg.
3 Taste for salt.
4 Make into a soft dough with the liquid: flour your hands and roll into several small balls, or roll into a long rope and cut off sections with kitchen scissors.
5 Put into stews or soups for the last 15–20 minutes of cooking time.

DUMPLINGS (2)

PLAIN FLOUR

225g (½ lb) plain flour
1 teaspoon baking powder (optional)
Salt to taste
Black pepper
Water

1 Sift the flour with all the dry ingredients.
2 Pour the water into a well made in the flour mixture and stir.
3 Mix into a stiff dough on a floured surface until you can handle it properly.

4 Roll into balls as in previous recipe.
5 Put into stews or soups for the last 15 minutes of cooking time.

DHAL PURI, ROTI

Trinidad

Roti is of Indian origin and very similar to parathas, though like all else that has been introduced into the Caribbean area has gone through the usual changes. The flat bread folded and filled with beef, chicken, goat, shellfish or vegetable curries is deliciously wonderful as a snack, a main meal or for large parties. It can be eaten opened on a plate, with a knife and fork, or held between the thumb and first two fingers of the right hand to scoop up the curried meats, fish or vegetables. There are many Trinidadian people living in England (they are called 'Southey Indians') who will appreciate your understanding of such customs. The following recipe was given to me at a party by a Trinidadian friend, Errol Romilly, who is also one of the top wire benders and costume designers for the Carnival in Notting Hill, bringing his own band each year.

450g (1 lb) self raising flour
1 teaspoon salt
1 teaspoon baking powder
25g (1 oz) lard
25g (1 oz) margarine
Water
Vegetable oil

For the Dhal Puri

225g (8 oz) yellow split peas
Salt to taste
2 teaspoons geera (ground cumin)

1 Sift into a large bowl the flour, salt and baking powder, and then rub in the fats. Knead into a firm dough with some water. As for all breads do not allow the dough to become too stiff or sticky.
2 Cover with a clean cloth, leave in a warm place for about 45 minutes.

3 Knead again for about 5 minutes then divide into 10–15 equal balls. Cover these and leave for another 30 minutes.
4 Make a hollow well in each ball and fill with equal amounts of the Dhal Puri. Close the hollows properly with the fingers.
5 Lightly flour a working surface.
6 Spread out each ball carefully then roll it out to around 25–30cm (10–12 inches) in diameter, as thinly as possible, without tearing.
7 Heat a griddle or a very shallow flat-bottomed frying pan on a medium to high heat. A little water dropped on the surface should splutter.
8 Using a soft cloth or a brush (though there are brushes available for such culinary purposes, a brush may shrivel or burn, so a small piece of cloth folded and tied on the end of the handle of a wooden spoon is often used for this purpose in Trinidadian homes) spread a very thin layer of oil on the griddle or frying pan, place a roti in it and cook for one minute.
9 Spread a thin layer of oil on the upper side of the roti then turn. Always try to use a wooden spatula as metal ones tend to tear the dough. Cook on the second side for a minute or two but no longer.
10 Again spread a thin layer of oil on the roti, turn, and cook for a few seconds (½–1 minute) more.
11 Remove from heat. As each roti comes off, wrap in a clean cloth until they are all cooked. The roti can be placed one on the other under the same cloth, and can be kept like that until needed, although not for hours.
12 The roti can be heated up very quickly on the same griddle, frying pan, or in a moderately heated oven. But they must be kept covered in the oven, otherwise they will be too crusty and dried up. If the roti are being filled with a hot mixture they should not need to be warmed up.

TO MAKE DHAL PURI

1 Parboil the split peas by dropping them into boiling water until they are just slightly cooked.
2 Drain thoroughly in a sieve or colander until there isn't any liquid left. The parboiled dhal must be dry; but do not allow to cool too much.

3 Purée the peas in a blender or mortar and pestle.
4 Add salt and geera, to taste.
5 You are now ready to fill the roti dough.

PLAIN ROTI

To make plain roti simply omit the dhal and proceed with all other instructions. There are several recipes for roti but this is one of the tastiest and easiest to make that I have come across.

CORNMEAL BREAD

Most Islands

This is one of the first breads that I can remember baking as a child in a home-made oven, built from an empty oil drum lined with a cement mixture with iron rods inserted. An opening was cut from the drum and rehinged with wire. The oven was heated by charcoal or wood. You see, we do not only make steel-band pan from oil drums.

110g (4 oz) plain flour
170g (6 oz) fine cornmeal
2 teaspoons baking powder
1–1½ teaspoons salt
50g (2 oz) caster sugar
110g (4 oz) butter
1 egg, well beaten
½ teaspoon freshly grated nutmeg
110g (4 oz) freshly grated coconut
300ml (½ pint) thick coconut cream

1 Preheat the oven to 180°C (350°F/Gas 4).
2 Sift together the flour, cornmeal, baking powder and salt.
3 Cream the sugar and butter, and blend in the beaten egg well.
4 Mix in the sifted ingredients a little at a time, then the nutmeg and grated coconut.
5 Blend in the coconut cream. Mix well.
6 Pour into a greased 23cm (9 inch) loaf tin.
7 Bake for about 30–40 minutes.
8 The breads are done when a thin instrument is inserted into the centre and comes out dry.
9 Can be served hot or cold spread with butter.

CASSAVA BREAD

MANIOC

Most Islands

Like 'boucan' meat, this is another contribution handed down by the Carib Indians. It is still very popular on the islands, especially Dominica which has the only extant Carib reserve. The following recipe is more elaborate and lends itself to modern taste and changes in culinary preparation. However, among many of the poorer classes it is still prepared very closely to the original; the grated cassava, the juice having been extracted, is dried in the sun, then made into a flat bread and baked over an open wood fire or charcoal (*see* Cassareep under Techniques on how to extract the juice).

110g (4 oz) lard or margarine, or 50g (2 oz) of each
50g (2 oz) sugar (optional)
1 egg, well beaten (not originally used)
340g (¾ lb) grated cassava root
170g (6 oz) finely grated fresh coconut
170g (6 oz) plain flour (not originally used)
1 teaspoon baking powder (not originally used)
Salt to taste (possibly not used)
A little water or milk (if needed)

1. Pre-heat the oven to 220°C (425°F/Gas 7).
2. Cream together the fat and sugar.
3. Thoroughly beat in the egg, cassava and grated coconut.
4. Sift together the flour, baking powder and salt.
5. Add a little at a time, beating in, to the cassava mix.
6. Turn out onto a lightly floured board and knead into a stiff dough (using a little milk or water only if needed).
7. Knead as you would bread.
8. Divide into three.
9. Roll into balls, then roll out each ball into rounds not more than ½cm (¼ inch) thick.
10. Bake for about 25 minutes; until brown.

MASTIFF BREAD

Eastern Caribbean

This is one of the breads I grew up with. It is made on quite a few of the islands with some changes in the ingredients. But I can only give the one I like best, from Dominica.

900ml (1½ pints) warm water
2 teaspoons brown cane sugar
25g (1 oz) yeast
1.5kg (3 lb) strong white flour
3 teaspoons salt
75g (3 oz) lard or margarine

1. Mix 450ml (¾ pint) of the warm water in a bowl with the sugar and yeast.
2. Mix well and set aside for about 20 minutes until it bubbles (when making bread it is always best to work in a warm area, where there are no cold draughts).
3. Add the flour and salt to the yeast mixture and rub in the lard or margarine.
4. Gradually adding a little of the remaining warm water knead into a dough.
5. Turn out on to a lightly floured board and continue to knead until the dough is firm and elastic but not too stiff or sticky.
6. Return to the bowl, cover and set aside in a warm place (without any draughts) until it rises to double its size.
7. Knead for a second time on a lightly floured board.
8. Shape into two loaves.
9. Place on a fairly large greased baking sheet and allow about 5–7 cm (2–3 inches) space between the loaves.
10. Cover with a clean cloth and let rise for a second time in a warm place.
11. Bake in a pre-heated oven 230°C (450°F/Gas 8) for about 35–40 minutes or until a light golden brown.
12. Test each loaf by tapping the underside: if the bread has a hollow ring, then it is done.

COCONUT BREAD

225g (8 oz) plain flour
1 teaspoon salt
2 teaspoons baking powder
110g (4 oz) caster sugar
110g (4 oz) butter or lard, melted
1 egg
150ml (¼ pint) coconut milk
½ teaspoon natural essence of almonds
170g (6 oz) freshly grated coconut, or equivalent of desiccated

1. Preheat the oven to 180°C (350°F/Gas 4).
2. Sift together the flour, salt and baking powder.
3. Add the sugar and mix in well with your fingers or a wooden fork.
4. Mix in the melted butter or lard.
5. Beat the egg with half the milk and the essence and blend in well.
6. Add the rest of the milk and the grated coconut and blend thoroughly.
7. Turn out on to a floured board or marble, and knead for a minute or two.
8. Shape into a loaf, put into a greased loaf pan and bake for about 1–1½ hours.

GINGERBREAD

Jamaica

225g (½ lb) plain flour
2 teaspoons baking powder
½ teaspoon baking soda
1 teaspoon allspice, freshly ground
½ teaspoon freshly grated nutmeg
½ teaspoon salt
225g (½ lb) butter
110g (4 oz) soft brown sugar
125ml (4 fl oz) molasses
125ml (4 fl oz) evaporated milk
2 eggs, well beaten
40g (1½ oz) ginger, freshly grated

1 Sift together all the dry ingredients except the sugar and ginger.
2 Melt the butter in a saucepan on a low heat, and mix in the sugar, molasses and milk.
3 Remove from heat, allow to cool and blend in the beaten eggs.
4 Pre-heat the oven to 180°C (350°F/Gas 4).
5 Combine the sifted ingredients with the molasses mixture, and thoroughly blend in the grated ginger.
6 Pour into a well-greased 23cm (9 inch) loaf tin and bake for about 50 minutes. A sharp instrument inserted into the loaf should come out almost dry.

ORANGE LOAF

English speaking Islands

225g (½ lb) plain flour
¾ teaspoon baking powder
¼ teaspoon bicarbonate of soda
½ teaspoon salt
110g (4 oz) caster sugar
1 egg
300ml (½ pint) freshly squeezed orange juice
1 tablespoon orange liqueur (substitute brandy)
50g (2 oz) melted butter
Grated rind of 1 orange (use one of the oranges to be juiced)

1 Pre-heat the oven to 190°C (375°F/Gas 5).
2 Sift together the flour, baking powder, soda and the salt.
3 Mix in the sugar using a fork.
4 Beat the egg and blend in the orange juice (whipping continuously), liqueur, melted better and the orange rind.
5 Stir in the sifted flour a little at a time and mix thoroughly.
6 Pour into a greased cake tin and bake for 30–40 minutes. A sharp thin instrument inserted into the centre of the cake should come out fairly dry when the baking is done.
7 Turn out of the tin when cool.

Orange loaf is traditionally served with marmalade.

BANANA LOAF

225g (8 oz) plain flour
Pinch salt
1½ teaspoons baking powder
½ teaspoon bicarbonate of soda
110g (4 oz) butter
170g (6 oz) caster sugar
2 eggs
550g (1 lb 4 oz) ripe bananas (weight with skin on)
55g (2 oz) walnuts, chopped

1. Pre-heat the oven to 180°C (350°F/Gas 4).
2. Sift together the flour, salt, baking powder and bicarbonate of soda.
3. Cream the butter and sugar then beat in the eggs one at a time.
4. Peel and thoroughly mash the bananas, add to the mixture and stir well.
5. Now add the sifted flour a little at a time and blend well.
6. Mix in the walnuts.
7. Pour into a well-greased loaf tin.
8. Bake for 1½ hours.
9. Serve hot or cold.

CHRISTMAS CAKE

Dominica

This is my mother's recipe. I remember the days, even in the capital, when almost everyone carried their Christmas cake to the local bakery – where the ovens were wood-fired – and for a small fee had their cakes baked for them. Every child, stopping to have a smell of each other's cake, would take bets on whose mother's cake was the best. Those days are gone, in all but a very few small villages.

450g (1 lb) raisins
450g (1 lb) sultanas
450g (1 lb) currants
225g (½ lb) mixed peel
225g (½ lb) stoned prunes
1 bottle port

450g (1 lb) plain flour
1½ teaspoons salt
2 teaspoons baking powder
1 teaspoon baking soda
1 teaspoon nutmeg, freshly grated
½ teaspoon cloves, freshly ground
½ teaspoon cinnamon, freshly ground
450g (1 lb) light brown sugar
450g (1 lb) unsalted butter
10–12 eggs according to size
Caramel colouring (*see* Techniques)
2–3 teaspoons natural essence of vanilla
2–3 teaspoons natural essence of almond
½ bottle rum

1 Put all the fruits into a large glass or earthenware jar or bowl, to soak in the port for 2–4 weeks. It must be covered and left in a cool place. Stir at least twice a week.

2 Preparing for the baking of the cake: sift together the flour, salt, baking powder and soda. Add the nutmeg, cloves and cinnamon.

3 Cream together the sugar and butter (this may take a very long time).

4 Add the eggs, one at a time, to the creamy mixture, beating each in thoroughly.

5 Now mix in the soaked fruit with the liquid that has accumulated.

6 Pour in enough caramel colouring to give a nice, rich brown. But be careful not to put in too much as it may result in a bitter-tasting cake.

7 Add the essences and blend in well.

8 Now add, a little at a time, the sifted flour and mix very well.

9 Pour into greaseproof paper lined cake tins (you may need 3 tins – never fill the tins above more than two thirds).

10 Bake in pre-heated oven 130°C–140°C (250°F–275°F/Gas ½–1) for about 2½ hours, or until a slim instrument comes out dry when inserted in the centre of the cakes.

11 Remove from the oven.

12 Leave the cakes in the tins for anything between 2–4 days.

13 On the second and third day pour rum over each cake.

14 Remove and place on stands, suitably decorated.

ORANGE CAKE

75g–100g (3–4 oz) caster sugar
110g (4 oz) unsalted butter
3 eggs (separated)
Juice and rind of 2 oranges
165g (6 oz) plain flour (sifted with the baking powder)
1 teaspoon baking powder
1 dessertspoon rum (optional)
1 dessertspoon orange liqueur

1 Pre-heat the oven to 190°C (375°F/Gas 5).
2 In a bowl, beat the sugar and butter until it is creamy and forms a ribbon.
3 Add the egg yolks one at a time, continuously beating.
4 Whisk in the orange juice.
5 Gradually and carefully, add the flour and baking powder.
6 Continue to mix well.
7 Add the rum, orange rind and liqueur.
8 Fold in the beaten egg whites.
9 Mix well, but not excessively.
10 Pour into a well-greased baking tin and bake for 50–60 minutes.

RICH SHORTCRUST PIE SHELL

170g (6 oz) plain flour
Pinch salt
25g (1 oz) caster sugar
25g (1 oz) lard
55g (2 oz) unsalted butter
Yolk of 1 small egg
2–3 tablespoons iced water
(A pinch of grated nutmeg or powdered cinnamon can be sifted with the flour)

1 Put the flour, salt and sugar into a large chilled mixing bowl.
2 Cut the lard and butter into small pieces and scatter over the flour.
3 Make a well in the centre and drop in the egg yolk. Mix with the finger tips.
4 Add 2 tablespoons of iced water and mix to form a dough. If

the mixture is still slightly crumbly add 2 or 3 teaspoons more.

5 Form into a ball, sprinkle all over with a little flour, and wrap in waxed paper, strong cellophane or greaseproof paper and refrigerate for 45–60 minutes.
6 Grease a 23cm (9 inch) pie tin or dish.
7 Remove the dough from the refrigerator. Unwrap – place on a lightly floured board or marble slab. Sprinkle with a little flour and roll out to about 2.5cm (1 inch) thick. Fold, and roll out again. Repeat this process 3 to 4 times.
8 Roll out finally to about 30–32.5cm (12–13 inches) in diameter.
9 Carefully lift and place the dough over the pie dish. This requires a certain skill. Gently press the pastry into place. Cut any excess dough – but leave about 1–1.5cm (½–¾ inch) hanging over the rim.
10 Refrigerate again for 45–60 minutes.
11 Pre-heat the oven to 190°C (375°F/Gas 5).
12 Having removed the unbaked shell from the refrigerator, carefully mould a sheet of greaseproof paper over the shell and fill it with dried beans. (Baking foil can be used instead of the greaseproof paper and beans.)
13 Place into the oven and bake for about 12 to 14 minutes.
14 Remove the beans and greaseproof paper. (Save the beans to use again.) Continue to bake for a further 8 to 10 minutes. Do not overbake. Watch for excessive browning, especially round the rim, since you may be cooking the shell further with its contents.
15 Remove from the oven and allow to cool before filling.

RICH SHORT PASTRY

FOR FLANS AND FRUIT PIES

165g (6 oz) plain flour
Egg yolk
40g (1½ oz) caster sugar
50g (2 oz) butter

1 Sift the flour on to a wooden board or marble slab.
2 Create a hollow in the centre and put in the egg yolk and sugar.

3 Cut the butter into small pieces and scatter over the flour.
4 Mix thoroughly with your fingers.
5 Roll into a ball – then roll out and fold again to roll out once more. Repeat this several times.
6 Arrange in a pie dish and bake as directed in recipe (*see* Techniques *also*).
7 To flavour the pastry, sift flour with, for example, 1 teaspoon powdered cinnamon or allspice.

SHORT PASTRY

250g (8 oz) plain flour
½ teaspoon salt
110g (4 oz) lard, butter or margarine
Iced water

1 Sift the flour and salt into a bowl.
2 Cut the fat into pieces and work into the flour with a knife or fork until it makes a finely crumbled mixture.
3 Add a little water at a time, still using the fork or knife to work thoroughly, until it is well mixed, but not sticky.
4 Turn out on to a floured surface and roll to desired shape. This should be sufficient for one pie top and bottom or two shells. One of the secrets of making good and successful pastry is to avoid handling the dough with your warm hands, so work in a cool part of the kitchen.
5 Afterwards, pastry is best left in the fridge for about 1 hour, before rolling out.

COCONUT TURNOVERS

Eastern Caribbean

These are usually sold in small shops, or by vendors from their trays or wicker baskets on street corners and in market places.

For the filling:
1 freshly grated coconut (*see* Techniques)
Sugar, equal in weight to the amount of grated coconut (white or light brown sugar)
110ml (4 fl oz) water
1 teaspoon natural almond or vanilla essence

1 teaspoon grated lemon peel
Pinch powdered cinnamon

For the casing:
50g (2 oz) caster sugar
170g (6 oz) unsalted butter
2 eggs
450g (1 lb) plain flour
1 teaspoon salt
25g (1 oz) yeast, preferably fresh
300ml (½ pint) lukewarm milk
50g (2 oz) melted butter

1. In a heavy saucepan, over a medium heat, mix the sugar and water and bring to the boil.
2. Mix in the coconut thoroughly.
3. Lower the heat and cook to a thick consistency, stirring often. (This is very similar to a coconut jam or sweet made on the Islands and could be served as such with hot bread.)
4. Remove from heat and stir in the essence, lemon peel and cinnamon, then set aside to cool.
5. Meanwhile, in a bowl, cream the sugar and unsalted butter, then beat in the eggs one at a time, blending well.
6. Thoroughly mix in the flour and salt.
7. Mix the yeast with about two tablespoons of tepid water, add to it the lukewarm milk and mix in with the dough mixture.
8. Now knead, until smooth.
9. Place in a bowl, cover and set aside to rise in a warm place; 30–40 minutes.
10. Divide into about twenty equal pieces.
11. Shape each piece quickly into a ball.
12. Roll out as thinly as possible on a floured surface. Avoid using too much flour on the board or marble. Each piece should be rolled out in a circular shape.
13. Place an equal amount of coconut filling on each, fold to form a semi-circle, pinch the edges to close them, using the thumb and first finger or a fork.
14. Brush with the melted butter (or you may prefer to use a beaten egg).
15. Arrange on one or two greased baking sheets, and bake in pre-heated oven 200°C (400°F/Gas 6) until golden brown.

16 For the last few minutes of baking sprinkle a little caster sugar over each turnover.

Very ripe plantain or banana are good examples of the kind of fruits that can equally well be used as fillings for turnovers. Plantains or bananas should be quartered by being cut lengthwise and then crosswise (*see* Techniques).

BATTER (1)

FOR PANCAKES AND FRITTERS

110g (4 oz) plain flour
Pinch salt
A little powdered cinnamon
1 egg, beaten
150ml (¼ pint) milk

1 Sift the flour and salt.
2 Add the cinnamon, egg and milk, stirred into a well in the flour, then mix thoroughly, using a wire whisk.
3 Place on the lower shelf of a refrigerator for about 30 minutes.
4 Now the batter is ready for use.

Makes 6–8 pancakes

BATTER (2)

FOR FISH AND MEATS

110g (4 oz) plain flour
Salt
Black pepper, freshly ground
2 eggs, beaten
75ml (⅛ pint) water mixed with an equal amount of milk
A little garlic powder

1 Sift the flour, salt and pepper.
2 Now add the beaten eggs and the milk and water mixture to a well in the middle of the flour, mixing thoroughly with a wire whisk.
3 Sprinkle the garlic powder over the mixture as the whisking becomes more vigorous.
4 Leave to settle in your refrigerator for 30 minutes.
5 Now the batter is ready for use.

BANANA PANCAKES

This is a very simple and easy dish to make, using up bananas that are just slightly too ripe. My daughter was the guinea pig for the testing of this dish. She loved it.

2 bananas
1 tablespoon caster sugar
1 egg
3 tablespoons self-raising flour
Pinch powdered cinnamon
Butter for frying (unsalted)

1. Peel and mash the bananas in a bowl, add the sugar and blend well with a fork.
2. Beat in the egg, then lastly beat in the flour and cinnamon and mix thoroughly.
3. Heat the butter in a frying pan, on a medium to low heat, to prevent burning.
4. Spoon in the mixture in equal amounts to make 4 or 6 cakes.
5. Fry gently on both sides until golden brown.
6. Serve hot, with very little sugar sprinkled on each if you wish. If your frying pan is not too small make two or three at a time.

Serves 4–6

CITRUS PIE

1 baked pie shell
300g (11 oz) caster sugar
3 tablespoons cornflour
2 teaspoons plain flour
450ml (¾ pint) warm water
1 tablespoon butter
3 egg yolks, well beaten
225ml (8 fl oz) lime or lemon juice
Grated rind of 2 limes or lemons
2 egg whites

1. In a saucepan or double boiler, mix together 225g (½ lb) of the sugar, the cornflour and plain flour. Then gradually pour in the water stirring constantly to blend well.

2 Cook on a low heat, stirring, until the mixture thickens. Then add the butter.
3 Remove from the heat, allow to cool slightly and stir in the egg yolks. Mix well.
4 Return to heat and add the citrus juice and rind of 1 lime or lemon; stirring constantly, cook until the mixture thickens.
5 Cool and pour into the pie shell.
6 Meanwhile mix the remaining citrus rind with the remaining 75g (3 oz) of sugar.
7 Whip the egg whites until able to stand in a peak, and add the rind and sugar mixture.
8 Spread over the pie and bake in a preheated oven 200°C (400°F/Gas 6) for about 8–10 minutes or until nice and lightly brown.
9 Allow to cool completely before serving.

COCONUT PUDDING

1 finely grated coconut, or substitute 1 packet desiccated
5 eggs, separated
225g (8 oz) caster sugar
1½ teaspoons lemon juice
140g (5 oz) fresh breadcrumbs
600ml (1 pint) milk
1 teaspoon lemon rind, grated

1 Whisk the yolks until light and creamy, then stir in 150g (5 oz) of the sugar, lemon juice, coconut and breadcrumbs.
2 Gradually add the milk and continue stirring.
3 Pour into a greased pie tin and bake in a pre-heated oven 170°C (375°F/Gas 3) for about 20 minutes.
4 Meanwhile, towards the end of the baking time, make a topping by beating 4 egg whites, together with the grated lemon rind and the remaining 75g (3 oz) caster sugar.
5 Spread over the coconut pudding and brown in the hot oven.

Serves 6

SWEET POTATO AND COCONUT PUDDING

900g (2 lb) sweet potatoes
1 freshly grated coconut
Rind and juice of 2 limes or lemons
2 egg yolks
340g (¾ lb) caster sugar
½ teaspoon freshly ground cinnamon
2 drops vanilla extract

1 Peel and boil the sweet potatoes with the rind of the lime or lemon. Drain and cool.
2 Mash thoroughly and blend well with the egg yolks and sugar.
3 Add the other ingredients.
4 Mix thoroughly.
5 Turn into a well greased baking pan and bake in a pre-heated oven 180°C (350°F/Gas 4) for about 1¼ hours.

Serves 8

POTATO CAKE

Dominica

675g (1½ lb) sweet potatoes
110g (4 oz) brown sugar
1 tablespoon butter, melted
3 medium sized eggs
3 tablespoons single cream, or milk
Rind of a lime, grated
1 tablespoon lime juice
¾ teaspoon grated nutmeg
2 teaspoons baking powder
½ teaspoon baking soda
Pinch salt
1 tablespoon dark rum

1 Peel and cut the potatoes into convenient cooking pieces.
2 Cook until tender enough to pierce with a fork. Drain thoroughly.
3 Mash the potato with sugar and butter.
4 Now beat in the eggs one at a time.
5 Add the cream, grated lime rind and juice, then mix well.

6 Add the nutmeg, baking powder, baking soda, salt and rum, and blend thoroughly.
7 Pour into a greased baking tin and bake in a pre-heated oven 160°C (325°F/Gas 3) for about 1½ hours.

Rum, Rum Punches and Other Drinks

Rum plays an important part in the Caribbean way of life. It is an every day, every occasion drink, from birth to death, be it christening, confirmation, marriage or wake, Christmas or carnival 'jump up' time. In fact, no festivity or ceremony is considered a worthy event without rum, and no Island is without its favourite – on some there are many. You will not enter through any door and not be offered a rum, with a cool glass of water, grapefruit or orange juice, or 'jelly' coconut water to 'wash it down weef'.

Rum is distilled from molasses, which itself is a by-product of the sugar cane. Yeast is added to the molasses, and left to ferment. This produces what is known as the 'wash'. The 'wash' is then distilled to create rum.

Natural rum spirit or unmatured rum can be as high as 200%

proof. I have drunk illegally brewed 'mountain dew' which was pretty close to that. The effect was like that of being kicked in the stomach by a horse that had just been shod, with the shoes still hot.

When it first comes out of the still rum is a colourless spirit. The darker rums are derived by adding colourings, themselves made from burnt sugar and molasses. On the whole, Caribbean people prefer the lighter rums of the Islands, the dark navy 'issue' rums being too heavy and syrupy.

Rum has from earliest times suffered a reputation as being the drink of the devil himself; known as 'kill devil', it has been blamed for many an unwanted disturbance, even among the most gentle and docile people. The word rum is supposed to have derived in the seventeenth century from 'rumbullion', a Devonshire term for rumpus. But no matter what its ill reputation, rum remains one of the great drinks, and today the best rums, like the famous St James, still come from the French island of Martinique. Many Martinican rums can be purchased in Europe. Haiti, Cuba, Trinidad, Jamaica and Guadeloupe also produce some wonderful rums. And there are some excellent rums from the islands of Dominica and Barbados. But regardless of where the rum is from in the Caribbean, it remains a drink to relax and watch the sunset with wherever you are. And if perchance you happen to be in the tropics, then listen with a glass in your hands, with someone close to you, to the night sounds of cicadas and tree frogs.

At the end of this section you will find a selection of typical soft drinks from the Islands.

The following is a list of recipes of a few of the many rum punches.

A word of advice. Regardless of what any producer or supplier may tell you, the cheapest rums sometimes make the best rum punches.

There is a good selection of Island rums now on sale in England; and the numbers increase each year. Among the more available are the Mount Gays, Cockspur, Appleton, Dry Cane and Lemon Hart. One or two of the better stores like Harrods carry a selection of Martinican rums.

Next time you are in France try to bring some rum back with you – St James is one of the best.

The classic formula for a rum punch is:

One of sour
Two of sweet
Three of strong
Four of weak

BARBADOS RUM PUNCH

1 of lime juice
2 of syrup
3 of rum
2 of water
Dash Angostura bitters
Crushed ice
Grated nutmeg

1 Put the lime juice, syrup, rum, water, Angostura and ice into a cocktail shaker.
2 Shake vigorously.
3 Serve with a little grated nutmeg.

SIMPLE SYRUP (1)

450g (1 lb) granulated sugar
425ml (¾ pint) water

1 Mix the sugar and water in a saucepan.
2 Put on a high heat, quickly bring to the boil.
3 Reduce the heat immediately, before the syrup boils over.

4 Simmer uncovered for about 6 minutes.
5 Allow to cool, then bottle and store at room temperature.

SIMPLE SYRUP (2)

450g (1 lb) very light brown cane sugar
570ml (1 pint) water
2.5cm (1 inch) cinnamon stick
Peel of 1 lime

1. Combine the sugar and water in a saucepan.
2. Bring to the boil.
3. Reduce heat immediately before the liquid boils over.
4. Add the cinnamon stick and lime peel.
5. Simmer, uncovered, for 10 minutes.
6. Allow to cool, then bottle.
7. Store at room temperature.

PLANTER'S PUNCH

Barbados

100ml (3½ fl oz) rum, Mount Gay, Cockspur or similar
2 tablespoons lime juice
2 tablespoons simple syrup
1 wineglass crushed ice
3 tablespoons orange juice
Dash Angostura bitters

1. Put all the ingredients into a cocktail shaker.
2. Shake vigorously and pour into a tumbler.
3. Serve garnished with a slice of lime and a cherry on a cocktail stick if you wish.

Serves 1

PLANTER'S FRUIT PUNCH

Most Islands

3 tablespoons rum (matured)
2 tablespoons water
2 tablespoons simple syrup
1 tablespoon fresh lime juice
Tropical fruit, cut into chunks – banana, pineapple, orange, mango, etc.

Grated nutmeg
Dash of Angostura bitters
Crushed ice

Mix all the ingredients in a tall glass with the grated nutmeg floating on top and serve.

Serves 1

PETIT PONCHE

Martinique and Guadeloupe

This punch from the islands of Martinique and Guadeloupe is very much a matter of taste – how sweet or strong you like your Petit Ponche. Each time I have had Petit Ponche on either of the two islands, I have had a bottle of local white rum, sugar syrup, lime peel, ice and water put on the bar or the table in front of me. One is charged according to how much rum is left in the bottle. There is little capacity for cheating: the people serving are very good at judging and need to be scrupulously fair.

I give a basic recipe – but in the end it is all left to you and your taste. I was brought up on rum from the age of six months, for a toothache or gripe or a bad stomach. No better way to get a howling, vexed little monster to sleep!

3 tablespoons rum
2 teaspoons syrup
Piece of lime peel
Ice cubes (optional)
Water to your taste (optional)

1 Pour the rum and syrup into a small glass.
2 Twist the peel to release the oil, and drop it into the glass. Add ice cubes and water if desired (it is best without).

Serves 1

BANANA DAIQUIRI

Cuba

150ml (5 fl oz) light rum
1 small banana, peeled and chopped
3 tablespoons banana liqueur
1½ wineglasses crushed ice

1 Place all the ingredients into an electric blender and whisk at high speed until smooth.
2 Serve in any attractive glass.
3 Garnish with a slice of banana and a slice of lime on a cocktail stick.

Serves 2

PINEAPPLE DAIQUIRI

Cuba

150ml (5 fl oz) pineapple
100ml (3½ fl oz) light Island rum
Juice ½ lime
25ml (1 fl oz) orange liqueur
Ice
Caster sugar to taste

1 Place all the ingredients except the ice and sugar into a blender.
2 Blend quickly, and add a little sugar to taste.
3 Blend very quickly again, and pour into glasses over the ice.

Serves 1–2

PINEAPPLE DAIQUIRI

Antigua

150ml (5 fl oz) fresh pineapple juice
100ml (3½ fl oz) rum
25ml (1 fl oz) Cointreau
1 tablespoon lime juice
2 teaspoons caster sugar
Ice cubes

1 Place the pineapple juice, rum, Cointreau, lime juice and the sugar into a blender and blend at high speed.
2 Pour over the ice cubes in a glass.

Serves 1

RUM SOUR

Most Islands

3 tablespoons light dark rum
2 tablespoons lime juice
1 teaspoon syrup
1 tablespoon orange juice
Crushed ice

1. Put all ingredients into a cocktail shaker.
2. Shake vigorously.
3. Strain into a glass and serve.

Serves 1

CURAÇÃO COCKTAIL

Curação

100ml (3½ fl oz) Curação
55ml (2 fl oz) dark rum
1 teaspoon syrup
1 tablespoon lime juice
Crushed ice
About 7.5cm (3 inches) lime peel

1. Put the Curação, rum, syrup and lime juice into a cocktail shaker.
2. Shake vigorously.
3. Pour over crushed ice in a glass.
4. Twist the lime peel directly over the cocktail, drop it in and serve.

Serves 1–2

YELLOW BIRD

Trinidad

25ml (1 fl oz) Cointreau
25ml (1 fl oz) Trinidadian rum
1 teaspoon syrup
2 teaspoons lime juice
Juice 1 large orange or 2 small ones
Drop Angostura bitters
Crushed ice

1 Place into a cocktail shaker and shake well.
2 Serve garnished with a slice of orange on each glass.

COCONUT PUNCH (1)

150ml (5 fl oz) light rum
100ml (3½ fl oz) coconut milk
2 teaspoons caster sugar
¼ teaspoon Angostura bitters
Grated nutmeg
Grated cinnamon
Crushed ice

1 Combine all the ingredients except the ice in an electric blender.
2 Blend at high speed.
3 Pour over the crushed ice in 2 tumblers.

COCONUT PUNCH (2)

This is one of the favourites on the island of Dominica.

225ml (8 fl oz) light rum
150ml (5 fl oz) thick coconut milk
75ml (3 fl oz) sweet condensed milk
Grated nutmeg
Grated cinnamon
Vanilla extract
Ice cubes

1 Combine all the ingredients, except the ice, in an electric blender.
2 Blend at high speed.
3 Pour over the ice cubes in small tumblers.
4 Stir once and serve, sprinkled with nutmeg.

Serves 4

COCONUT MILK PUNCH

French and Patois speaking Islands

1 bottle white rum
1.1 litres (2 pints) coconut milk
1 teaspoon natural vanilla essence

1–2 teaspoons Angostura bitters
Grated nutmeg
1 tin sweetened condensed milk

1 Put all the contents into a large jug and whisk until well blended.
2 Decant into bottles and place in the lowest part of the refrigerator until needed. Coconut milk tends to thicken the colder it gets, so you may have to allow the bottles to stand at room temperature before serving.
3 Each bottle must be shaken vigorously before being used, or poured into a cocktail shaker.
4 Serve with ice cubes. A little grated nutmeg may be sprinkled on top.

Sufficient for a party

PASSION FRUIT PUNCH

Most Islands

3 tablespoons passion fruit juice (*see* Techniques)
1 tablespoon lime juice
2–3 tablespoons syrup
4 tablespoons white rum
Dash Angostura bitters
Crushed ice
Grated nutmeg

1 Place the passion fruit juice, lime juice, syrup, rum and Angostura into a cocktail shaker.
2 Shake vigorously.
3 Pour over the crushed ice in a glass.
4 Serve with the grated nutmeg on top.

Serves 1

PAWPAW PUNCH

Most Islands

1 wineglass chopped ripe pawpaw, fresh or tinned
150ml (5 fl oz) light rum
2 teaspoons syrup
1 tablespoon lime or lemon juice
1 tablespoon Curaçao

Crushed ice
2 cherries

1. Place the pawpaw, rum, syrup, citrus juice and Curaçāo in an electric blender.
2. Blend at high speed.
3. Stop and add the ice.
4. Blend again.
5. Pour into cocktail glasses.
6. Garnish each glass with a slice of pawpaw, a slice of lime and a cherry on a cocktail stick.

Serves 2

CREOLE FRUIT PUNCH

NON-ALCOHOLIC

French and Patois speaking Islands

Juice 4 oranges
Juice 3 grapefruits
Juice 2 limes
Juice 2 lemons
Juice extracted from 2 tablespoons Maraschino cherries
2 teaspoons Angostura bitters
6 slices of orange
6 slices of lemon
2 passion fruits, washed and cut into halves
Sugar syrup to taste, well stirred in
Crushed ice.

1. Mix the first five ingredients and then carefully add the remaining six.
2. Serve in large tumblers with straws and garnish with slices of any of the fruits used.

DOMINICAN RUM PUNCH

Dominica

Juice 1½ limes
3 of syrup
6 of rum
3 of water
Drop vanilla extract

Dash Angostura bitters
Ice cubes
Lime peel
Grated nutmeg

1. Place all the ingredients except the ice, lime peel and nutmeg into a shaker.
2. Shake vigorously.
3. Pour into a tumbler with the ice and lime peel.
4. Serve with grated nutmeg floating on top.

Serves 2

BLUE MOUNTAIN COCKTAIL

Jamaica

55ml (2 fl oz) light Jamaican rum (Appleton)
25ml (1 fl oz) Tia Maria
25ml (1 fl oz) vodka
3 tablespoons orange juice
1½ tablespoons lime juice
5 ice cubes

1. Put all the ingredients into a cocktail shaker.
2. Shake and pour unstrained into a tumbler.

Serves 1

PARTY PUNCH BOWL

Dominica

This is an expensive drink, though rum is very much cheaper in the Caribbean. So it is best kept in reserve for a large breakfast party or similar. Excellent on a cold winter's day.

850ml (1½ pints) water or soda water
Peel of 1 orange
Peel of 1 lime
6–8 cloves
1 cinnamon stick
1 bottle white rum
1 bottle brown rum
1 bottle port
1 bottle of red table wine

Juice 4 oranges
Juice 4 limes
Crushed ice, if required
Sugar to taste
1 orange, unpeeled but thinly sliced
1–2 limes, unpeeled but thinly sliced

1. Pour about 150ml (¼ pint) of the water into a pan and bring to the boil with the orange peel, lime peel, cloves and cinnamon stick.
2. Simmer for a few minutes to extract the flavours.
3. Remove from heat.
4. Allow to cool and strain, discard the spices and reserve the liquid.
5. Pour the liquid into a punch bowl large enough to hold all the ingredients.
6. Mix everything except the citrus slices.
7. Sweeten to taste.
8. Drop in the sliced citrus.
9. Decorate the bowl with citrus leaves if you wish.

Sufficient for a party

KILLJOY

Barbados

3 tablespoons rum
2 tablespoons gin
A squeeze of lime juice
1 tablespoon brandy
Sugar to taste
Ice

Put all the ingredients into a glass, stir and kill.

Serves 1

DANSE JOMBIE

Haiti

100ml (3½ fl oz) light Jamaican rum
55ml (2 fl oz) Curação
100ml (3½ fl oz) dark Haitian rum
25ml (1 fl oz) brandy

3 tablespoons orange juice
3 tablespoons grapefruit juice
Juice 1 large lime
1 tablespoon granulated sugar
Crushed ice

1 Place all except ice into a shaker and shake vigorously.
2 Serve over crushed ice.

Serves 4–6

LIME SQUASH

Juice 3–4 limes
4 tumblers soda water or water
1 teaspoon Angostura bitters
Sugar syrup to taste (*see* p.268)
Grated nutmeg
Crushed ice
4 slices lime peel

1 In a large jug or electric blender combine all the ingredients, except the lime peel and ice.
2 Half fill each tumbler with crushed ice.
3 Taste the squash for sweetness.
4 Pour the squash over the crushed ice and serve with a slice of lime peel in each glass. There should be enough for a second helping.

To make a lemon squash simply substitute lemon for lime. Or you can make a squash with a mixture of both.

Serves 4

SORREL

This is a very popular Christmas drink on all the Islands.

450g (1 lb) sorrel petals
1 generous cinnamon stick
Dried peel of one orange (*see* p.25)
8–10 whole cloves
Small piece of crushed ginger
4.5 litres (1 gallon) boiling water

900g–1kg (2–2½ lbs) granulated sugar (or according to taste)
1–2 wine glasses rum

1 Quickly rinse the sorrel petals under cold running water.
2 Put into a large bowl or jar together with the cinnamon stick, dried orange peel, cloves and crushed ginger.
3 Pour the boiling water over.
4 Allow to cool, cover, then leave in the refrigerator for 2–3 days.
5 Strain and use a wooden spoon to press the petals.
6 Pass through a fine cloth or strainer again.
7 Sweeten and add the rum (most Caribbean people like their sorrel very sweet).
8 Bottle carefully. (You will need approximately 7–8 wine, rum or whisky bottles.)
9 The Sorrel can be served now – but it is best left for another 2–3 days.
10 Serve chilled or with ice. Again more rum can be added when drinking. The drink should be a clear beautiful red in colour.

Sufficient for a party

GINGER BEER

Most Islands

110g (4 oz) fresh ginger (according to your taste)
4.5 litres (1 gallon) water
700g–900g (1½–2 lb) granulated sugar
Juice 1 lime
Peel 1 lime
A few grains white rice

1 Wash and scrape the ginger then crush or pound it.
2 Place in a large bowl or stoneware ginger jar.
3 Boil the water.
4 Add the sugar, lime juice and peel to the ginger.
5 Pour the boiling water over.
6 Add the rice.
7 Cover and allow to stand for a week. Stir at least 4 times during that period.
8 Strain, at the end of the week, and bottle.

9 Refrigerate or store in a cool place, whereupon the drink should keep for a week or longer.
10 Serve with ice. A little rum may be added to each glass.

Sufficient for a party

PINEAPPLE AND ORANGE DRINK

2 thick slices pineapple, cubed
Juice 4 oranges
Rind of 1 orange
Sugar to taste
Angostura bitters (optional)
Small piece of mace, ground
½ teaspoon ground cinnamon
2 tablespoons rum (if you are serving children, you may wish to leave this out)
Ice cubes

1 Liquidize all the ingredients, except the ice cubes.
2 Pour the mixture over the ice cubes and serve. A scoop of vanilla ice-cream put into each glass makes this a wonderful treat.

Serves 2–3

PINA COLADA

Puerto Rico

225ml (8 fl oz) pineapple juice (made from pineapple pieces pressed through a sieve then strained through a fine cheese-cloth)
110ml (4 fl oz) rich coconut cream (*see* Techniques)
110ml (4 fl oz) medium light rum
2 teaspoons syrup
Ice cubes

1 Put all the ingredients except the ice in an electric blender at high speed and mix until creamy and smooth.
2 Pour into 2 tumblers half filled with ice cubes and serve.
3 Garnish with a slice of coconut, pineapple and a cherry on cocktail sticks.

Serves 2

SOURSOP AND PAWPAW

Dominica

150ml (5 fl oz) soursop juice
225g (½ lb) ripe pawpaw, peeled, seeded and chopped
2 tablespoons condensed milk
½ teaspoon Angostura
Grated nutmeg
Crushed ice

1. Combine all the ingredients except the ice in a blender at high speed.
2. Taste for sweetness.
3. Pour into glasses filled with the crushed ice.

Serves 2

GUAVA CUP

225g (½ lb) guavas, seeded and purééd
Sugar syrup or sugar to taste
Juice ½ lemon
Little grated nutmeg
700ml (1¼ pints) water
Crushed ice

1. Blend all the ingredients except the ice in a liquidizer or mix well in a jug.
2. Strain and chill.
3. Serve in cups or tumblers with crushed ice.
4. Garnish each with a slice of guava.

Serves 4

Appendix: Importers, Wholesalers and Retailers of Caribbean and Other Tropical Produce

BRIXTON MARKET, London SW9 (around the area off Coldharbour Lane and Atlantic Road).

Wide selection of almost all produce, fresh, dried and tinned.

BALHAM MARKET, Harberson Road, London SW12 (off Balham High Road).

Good selection. Fresh, dried and tinned.

SHEPHERDS BUSH MARKET, London W12 (between Goldhawk Road and Uxbridge Road. Tube stations Goldhawk Road and Shepherds Bush – Metropolitan Line).

Wide selection. Fresh, dried and tinned.

PORTOBELLO ROAD MARKET, London W10–W11.

Good. But not as varied a selection.

TOMMY SPENCER (retailer), 61 Lancaster Road, London W11 (off Portobello Road).

Good selection of fruits and ground provisions. Tinned, bottled and dried produce. Also whole saltfish, smoked herrings, salted pigs' tails, frozen pigeon peas and frozen cassava.

MATAHARI IMPEX, 11–12 Hogart Place, Earl's Court, London SW5. Tel. 01–370 1041.

102 Westbourne Grove, London W2. Tel. 01–229 4280.

328 Balham High Road, London SW17 (almost opposite Balham Market). Tel. 01–767 3107.

Fresh banana leaves, Annatto seeds and liquid, fresh and saltwater crayfish, other shellfish (frozen). And an unimaginably varied selection of fresh fruit and provisions, tinned, bottled and dried produce. Service helpful and friendly.

ENCO PRODUCTS (London) Ltd, 71–75 Fortess Road, London NW5.

Mainly importers and wholesalers of sauces, creamed coconut, tinned, bottled and dried products.

B. TERFLOTH & CO (UK) Ltd, Richmond, Surrey.

Importers and wholesalers of tinned and bottled produce.

BRANDS TO LOOK FOR

Enco
Encona
Dunn's River
Grace (produce of Jamaica and Dominican Republic). *Their tinned ackee is good.*
Windmill (produce of Barbados). *Excellent pepper sauce and Mauby syrup.*
Scotts

As already mentioned there are many Asian and West Indian shops in cities and towns where there are a number of Asian, Caribbean and other nationalities in which quite a selection of tropical produce is available. It is also worth trying some of the better supermarkets and the more adventurous greengrocers.

FISH

The fish listed on page 75 are imported fresh on ice from the Seychelles and the Indian Ocean by:

C. J. NEWNES & PARTNERS, 73 Billingsgate Market, West India Dock Road, Poplar, London E14 8ST. Tel. 01–515 0793/0798.

I found them extremely helpful. Many of the better fishmongers, small and large, carry a selection of their fish. Newnes can inform you of retail outlets.

Frozen flying fish, tuna and snappers and a few others are available from many of the markets, Brixton and Balham among others. Inquire of your fishmonger – I am certain that he or she may be of help.

A word of caution: fish such as the members of the tuna family do not have a pleasant taste if frozen without first being gutted. When defrosted the blood often seeps into the flesh and the flesh is then tainted. I have known people wash the fish with lime and even soap to no effect whatsoever.

Index

International cookery books available in Panther Books

Elizabeth Cass		
Spanish Cooking	£1.25	☐
Arto der Haroutunian		
Complete Arab Cookery	£1.50	☐
Modern Jewish Cookery	£2.50	☐
Robin Howe		
Greek Cooking	£1.95	☐
German Cooking	£1.95	☐
Italian Cooking	£1.95	☐
Kenneth Lo		
Cooking and Eating the Chinese Way	£1.95	☐
The Wok Cookbook	£1.50	☐
More Wok Cookery	£1.95	☐
F Marian McNeil		
The Scots Kitchen	£1.95	☐
The Scots Cellar	£1.95	☐
David Scott		
The Japanese Cookbook	£1.95	☐
E P Veerasawmy		
Indian Cookery	£1.50	☐

To order direct from the publisher just tick the titles you want and fill in the order form.

HB581

Cookery handbooks now available in Panther Books

L D Michaels		
The Complete Book of Pressure Cooking	£1.95	☐
Cecilia Norman		
Pancakes & Pizzas	95p	☐
Microwave Cookery Course	£1.95	☐
The Pie and Pastry Cookbook	£2.50	☐
Barbecue Cookery	£1.50	☐
Franny Singer		
The Slow Crock Cookbook	£1.95	☐
Janet Walker		
Vegetarian Cookery	£1.50	☐
Pamela Westland		
Bean Feast	£1.95	☐
The Complete Grill Cookbook	£1.50	☐
High-Fibre Vegetarian Cookery	£1.95	☐
Marika Hanbury Tenison		
Deep-Freeze Cookery	£1.95	☐
Cooking with Vegetables	£1.95	☐
Sheila Howarth		
Grow, Freeze and Cook	£1.50	☐
Jennifer Stone		
The Alcoholic Cookbook	£1.25	☐
Beryl Wood		
Let's Preserve It	£1.50	☐
Barbara Griggs		
Baby's Cookbook	£1.95	☐
Wendy Craig		
Busy Mum's Cookbook	£1.95	☐
Carolyn Heal and Michael Allsop		
Cooking with Spices	£2.95	☐

To order direct from the publisher just tick the titles you want and fill in the order form.

HB681

Cooking for good health books now available in Panther Books

Ursula Gruniger
Cooking with Fruit 50p ☐

Sheila Howarth
Grow, Freeze and Cook £1.50 ☐

Kenneth Lo
Cooking and Eating the Chinese Way £1.95 ☐
The Wok Cookbook £1.50 ☐

L D Michaels
The Complete Book of Pressure Cooking £1.95 ☐

Franny Singer
The Slow Crock Cookbook £1.95 ☐

Janet Walker
Vegetarian Cookery £1.50 ☐

Beryl Wood
Let's Preserve It £1.50 ☐

Gretel Beer and Paula Davies
The Diabetic Gourmet £1.95 ☐

David Scott
The Japanese Cookbook £1.95 ☐

Marika Hanbury Tenison
Cooking with Vegetables £1.95 ☐

Pamela Westland
Bean Feast £1.95 ☐
High-Fibre Vegetarian Cookery £1.95 ☐
The Complete Grill Cookbook £1.50 ☐

David Canter, Kay Canter and Daphne Swann
The Cranks Recipe Book £3.95 ☐

To order direct from the publisher just tick the titles you want and fill in the order form.

HB381

All these books are available at your local bookshop or newsagent, or can be ordered direct from the publisher..

To order direct from the publisher just tick the titles you want and fill in the form below.

Name ____________________

Address ____________________

____

Send to:
Panther Cash Sales
PO Box 11, Falmouth, Cornwall TR10 9EN.

Please enclose remittance to the value of the cover price plus:

UK 45p for the first book, 20p for the second book plus 14p per copy for each additional book ordered to a maximum charge of £1.63.

BFPO and Eire 45p for the first book, 20p for the second book plus 14p per copy for the next 7 books, thereafter 8p per book.

Overseas 75p for the first book and 21p for each additional book.

Panther Books reserve the right to show new retail prices on covers, which may differ from those previously advertised in the text or elsewhere.